# Desegregation

## of the Methodist Church Polity;

*Reform Movements That Ended Racial Segregation*

*by*

W. Astor Kirk, Ph.D.

PITTSBURGH, PENNSYLVANIA 15222

ISBN # 0-8059-9725-3
Printed in the United States of America

*First Printing*

For additional information or to order additional books,
please write:
RoseDog Publishing
701 Smithfield Street
Pittsburgh, Pennsylvania 15222
U.S.A.
1-800-834-1803
Or visit our web site and on-line bookstore at
www.rosedogbookstore.com

This Book Is Dedicated To:

Bishop James S. Thomas (Retired)
Dr. Grover C. Bagby (Retired)
The Memory of Dr. James P. Brawley
The Memory of Miss Thelma Stevens

# CONTENTS

Chapter 4 focuses on changes in inter-"racial" relations in the larger society of which The Methodist Church was a part, and the implications that such changes had for the continued existence of involuntary "racial" segregation in The Methodist Church.



This chapter discusses how the 1960 Quadrennial Meeting of the Church's legislative body failed to take bold legislative action to address the "Central Jurisdiction problem" and how that failure resulted in aggressive, organized action by leaders of the Central Jurisdiction.



In 1960 the Central Jurisdiction Organization established a committee of five individuals to develop strategies and plans for the abolition of the organization as a "racially" segregated entity within The Methodist Church polity. The author was secretary of the committee. This chapter discusses the "foundational" work of the Committee of Five.



Chapter 7 discusses the Committee of Five's work aimed at getting the Church's legislative body to make basic changes in the body of Church law dealing with "race" relations throughout the denomination.

# APPENDICES

# PREFACE

From the summer of 1960 through the fall of 1967, I was directly and deeply involved in a major reform movement to purge The Methodist Church polity of organizational structures based on *race* alone.

The targeted organizational structure was a special governance institution—the Central Jurisdiction Organization. This institution was not only defined in racial terms; its definition was also incorporated in the constitution of The Methodist Church.

From 1960 to 1965 I served as secretary of a committee established by the Central Jurisdiction Organization to plan its own "death with dignity." I chaired the committee from 1965 to 1967.

For more than a decade many individuals and groups, both within and outside the United Methodist Church, have urged me to write a book about the processes of eliminating the Central Jurisdiction Organization from the polity of the Church.

*Some urgently pressured, cajoled, and petitioned me to do so!*

Until almost two years ago I remained steadfastly impervious to all these pleas. There were three main reasons for my resistance.

**First,** I thought a book written by me on the subject of Church desegregation would probably be too autobiographical in content and style. Besides, there are other dimensions of my "social activism" that I believe are more deserving of autobiographical exposition—e.g., my "civil rights activities" in desegregating the University of Texas Graduate School, and the libraries and swimming pools in Austin, Texas.

**Second,** and most important, I did not believe it would be possible for me to "invent" generally acceptable or *politically correct* terminology and language usage that would enable meaningful communication with people in the world of their *today's* experiences. And I had been amazed and surprised to discover that the traditional jargon used to discuss the polity of the United Methodist Church "turns off" most people who are not professional Methodists.

**Third,** I was keenly aware of the fact that book publishers are driven by "bottom line" considerations. The kind of book that many individuals and groups had suggested would give minimal scholarly treatment to a significant desegregation movement, which occurred over thirty years ago, within a mainline Protestant denomination. It would be difficult to assess the market potential of the book

Approximately a year and a half ago the Religion, Race and Culture mission group at Foundry United Methodist Church in Washington, DC invited me to discuss "institutional racism" in religious organizations. When the meeting ended, the group quashed all my objections to, as they put it, "freezing in written form" an explanation of how the Central Jurisdiction Organization of The Methodist/United Methodist Church was dismantled. They said it would be a disservice to the Church if I failed to provide a written account of this bit of United Methodist history.

That was the moment when I conceived an idea for **Desegregation of The Methodist Church Polity: *Reform Movements That Ended Racial Segregation*.**

I chose the title and subtitle of the book after much reflection. I want readers to realize up front that the book is about desegregation of *governance* institutions, systems and processes within the denomination.

In the western world the term "polity" has historically been used to refer to both secular and ecclesiastical organizations. Thus in *Webster's New Collegiate Dictionary* (1981 edition), the fourth definition of the term *polity* is "the form of government of a religious denomination." Hence this book is about desegregating the *form of government* of The Methodist Church. I have written it mainly for two types of audiences: a primary one and a secondary one.

My primary audience consists of (1) readers who are not members of the United Methodist Church, but who nevertheless have a genuine interest in the role that United Methodists play nationally and internationally; (2) the millions of members of local United Methodist congregations who have come to the United Methodist Church from other denominations; and (3) the several millions of local church members who have grown up as United Methodists since the late 1960s.

As I have traveled throughout the country during the past decade, I have been surprised to discover that only a very few people comprising my primary audience know that The Methodist Church/United Methodist Church was once *formally* segregated. Many who have heard of the Central Jurisdiction Organization assumed it to be a "Black denomination," like the African Methodist Episcopal Church or the African Methodist Episcopal Zion Church.

I have tried to fulfill the wishes of the Race, Religion and Culture mission group at Foundry United Methodist Church: To write a book that individuals and groups comprising my primary audience may find both informative and useful.

A wide range of individuals and groups comprise this book's secondary audience. They include

- Teachers at seminaries and schools of religion
- Seminary students
- Professors of departments of religion in colleges and universities
- Graduate students studying for masters and doctorate degrees in the sociology of religion
- Faculties and students of African-American and ethnic minority studies programs in undergraduate colleges
- "Social justice" organizations within Protestant, Catholic, Jewish and Muslim faiths
- Media writers and commentators who's beat is the world of religious organizations.

There is a **Book of Discipline of The United Methodist Church *(Discipline)***. It contains a listing and description of the *governing* institutions and bodies of the denomination. The *Discipline* refers to these bodies as "conferences" (i.e., "General Conference," "Jurisdictional Conference," "Annual Conference," "District Conference," and "Church Conference").

The term "conference" has a dual meaning. It may refer to both a *corporate entity* and a formal *meeting* for the performance of some transaction.

In order to clarify my reference to corporate entities, I add the word "organization" after the term "conference." For example, in the book I use the terms "General Conference Organization," "jurisdiction conference organization" and "annual conference organization."

The church desegregation movement that the book deals with pre-dates the use of "African-American" terminology. In the historical period involved, "black/white" terminology was in vogue. The book uses those terms. For professional and personal reasons, however, I have refrained from using the terms "black" and "white" as adjectives. I use them as nouns only.

It has been my experience that when the terms "black" and "white" are used as *nouns*, that usage evokes quite different cognitive responses and emotional feelings than when the words are used as *adjectives*.

**Cognitively and emotionally for most people in the United States of America today, there is a subtle but real difference in meaning between a "black" church and a church whose entire membership may consist of "Blacks" only.**

I believe the distinction is not simply a matter of semantics. It also involves *behavior-influencing perceptions*.

In the book I intentionally capitalize the term "Black" and the word "White" while using them as nouns. At times my phraseology may appear a little awkward. But I am willing to pay that price in order to convey with greater clarity the phenomena being discussed.

If I could have avoided doing so, I would not have used the term "race" in the book. Like the late Methodist and distinguished sociologist Dr. C. Eric Lincoln, I believe "Race is a state of Mind. It has no objective reality" (Lincoln, 1996, p. 41). Following the practice of Patterson (1997, p. x), when I used the word in any of its forms, I placed it in quotation marks.

The book is both descriptive and interpretive in nature. I describe (or report) the major actors and events involved in the "eliminate the Central Jurisdiction Organization" reform movement. But, also, I often express my views regarding the motivations of actors, and the impact and significance of major events. I try to articulate my values up front so that the reader will know exactly "where I am coming from."

It has been my desire to avoid burdening general readers of the book with a lot of references. However, I felt a need to assure academic colleagues, researchers, and historians that my main analyses and arguments do not ignore relevant generalizations found in major social science, theological and ethical studies. Therefore, I have included in the text and in the **Chapter Notes** (at the end of each chapter) quotations and other reference notations whenever I thought they were needed to put my principal commentary in a broader context.

Initially I intended to include primary documentary materials in the text of the chapters where they are first referenced. The idea was to let selected primary documents tell the story of how the Church was desegregated and who the major actors were.

The first draft of the book indicated that such approach would impose too much of a burden on those readers for whom those documentary materials are of minor importance. Consequently, nine of the documents involved are included in the book as **Appendixes**. References to others are included in some of the Chapter Notes.

The first two chapters of the book are mainly historical in content and emphasis. Some readers may already know how the "racially" segregated Central Jurisdiction Organization came to be, and how it performed, as a special governance entity within the polity of The Methodist Church. Those individuals may begin their reading at Chapter 3 of the book. It discusses the beginning of internal vocal opposition to the Great Compromise of 1939, which created a "racially" segregated governance organization in the polity of The Methodist Church.

In Chapter 4, I briefly highlight and examine some major social-change events, with reference to inter-ethnic relationships, that were occurring in the larger society of which The Methodist Church was a part. The primary purpose is to focus attention on "anti-segregation" movements in society that had a negative impact on the legitimacy of the apartheid system existing within the polity of The Methodist Church. Consequently, the chapter is appropriately entitled "The Methodist Church in the Public Eye."

Chapter 5 provides a brief analysis and discussion of dynamic forces that led Blacks in the "racially" segregated Central Jurisdiction Organization of The Methodist Church to take charge of their own religious destiny. The legislative body of the Church greatly disappointed Blacks by refusing to take bold and decisive action to break the shackles of *involuntary* "racial" separatism, which had been in existence for two decades.

When the 1960 quadrennial meeting of the Church's legislative body decided it would "undertake no basic change" in the body of church law supporting separation of Methodists on the basis of "race," Blacks resolved to create and direct their own reform movement. The immediate goal of the movement would be to eliminate the Central Jurisdiction Organization.

Blacks vowed to dissolve the Central Jurisdiction Organization within a framework of policies and procedures designed to promote "an inclusive Methodist fellowship at all levels of the Church's life."

In many respects, Chapters 6 through 11 are the core chapters of the book. They review and analyze the strategies that Blacks in The Methodist Church developed to take charge of their own destiny, with respect to eliminating *involuntary* "racial" separatism within the Church's polity. These chapters also explain and discuss how the social-change strategies were coordinated and directed by the Committee of Five, which the Central Jurisdiction Organization established in July 1960.

The book's Chapters 6-11 also document the profound impact that the Committee of Five had on inter-ethnic thinking and actions of The Methodist Church throughout the decade of the 1960s. And as Chapter 11 shows, in particular, the impact of the Committee of Five extended to ensuring that "inclusiveness" principles were incorporated in the constitution of the new United Methodist Church.

My primary purpose in Chapter 12, the last chapter of the book, is to encourage serious thinking about and reflection on some fundamental and critical issues. For example:

1. Why hasn't the elimination of the Central Jurisdiction Organization resulted in significantly different patterns of membership and attendance in local United Methodist Churches?

2. Why are most United Methodist Blacks not members of and do not regularly attend local churches in which non-Blacks constitute a numerical majority?

3. Why are most United Methodist Whites not members of and do not regularly attend local churches in which non-Whites constitute a numerical majority?

4. What lessons are there to be learned from the unexpectedly significant and positive outcomes of episcopal election processes since the dissolution of the Central Jurisdiction Organization?

When each reader finishes reading this book, that individual will form his or her own overall conclusions about the issues the book raises and discusses. After reviewing what I have written, I now have five Mega-Conclusions that I want to share with the reader in the book's Preface.

**First.** The Great Compromise of 1939 that facilitated creation of The Methodist Church was, in one respect, like the *Three-Fifth Compromise* that facilitated establishment of the constitution of the United States of America. In both cases there was a critical "stumbling-block" issue. It involved the status and role of Blacks. Also in both cases, although their dignity and equality as human beings created in the image of God were at stake, Blacks were powerless. They could not shape or significantly influence the basic terms of the compromise agreement.

**Second.** In the 1940s and 1950s major social-change movements drastically altered historic patterns of inter-ethnic relationships throughout American secular society. The changes helped to reveal glaring contradictions between The Methodist Church's "Christian" pronouncements on "race" and the clearly "un-Christian racial practices" in many institutional areas of the Church.

**Third.** As Dr. James P. Brawley stated so poignantly, Blacks in The Methodist Church " could not with prudence be a part of the struggle for desegregation in the community life outside of the Church, and at the same time not favor or urge the same reform within the Church." This unwillingness to make any distinction between involuntary "racial" segregation outside of the Church and that within the Church gave momentum to the movement to eliminate the Central Jurisdiction Organization from the polity of The Methodist Church.

**Fourth**. Through systematic research, polemical tracts, seminar presentations, and formal lectures I persuaded many younger clerical and lay leaders of The Methodist Church that the Church was a major *social institution*. Thus it was more than simply an instrument for mediating the gospel, and a channel through which men and women might come to know, worship and serve God. I argued persuasively that The Methodist Church was an enormously powerful social institution in modern society as—

> **An employer of labor, a provider of social services, an educational entrepreneur, a sponsor of recreational, entertainment, and cultural enterprises...a landlord as well as a tenant. It consumes natural resources, collects, expends, and invests money, and enjoys the many benefits which derive from our civil society**

> **Racism in The Methodist Church, therefore, is of no small consequence. It affects lives, bruises the spirits, punctures the hearts, and warps the minds of people—those who discriminate as well as those who are discriminated against. Honest candor must compel all to admit that it denies equality of opportunity for jobs, education, spiritual growth, and service to God.**
>
> **Racism in The Methodist Church, including the Central Jurisdiction problem, is not alone a result of prejudice. It is also a product of institutions and institutional patterns and practices. The institutional dimensions can be dealt with effectively if the power structures of The Methodist Church unequivocally commit themselves to the kind of positive and creative decision-making exemplified...in government and many other secular organizations of society.** (Kirk, 1963, pp. 6-7)

**Fifth.** A "new breed" of well educated, socially sophisticated, and very articulate Blacks in The Methodist Church created conditions favorable to reform. Their "anti-segregation" pressures resulted in a state of affairs where the *disvalue* of involuntary "racial" separatism for The Methodist Church as a whole far outweighed its *value* to special interest groups. When that happened the "power elites" within the denomination abandoned the anachronistic notion of *voluntarism*, which had undergirded involuntary "racial" separatism since the Great Compromise of 1939. The abandonment of spiritually and intellectually anemic concepts of voluntarism was quite evident in the actions of the Church's legislative body in 1972.

# ACKNOWLEDGMENTS

I owe a huge debt of gratitude to a lot of people who are deceased but whose spirits are very much alive. They very generously shared with me their thoughts, ideas and opinions, when I was involved as a leading participant in many of the events discussed in the book

The book is dedicated to four persons—two deceased and two living—who had a major and enormously beneficial impact on my work with the Committee of Five from 1960 to 1967. Without the wise counsel and steady guidance of Bishop James S. Thomas, Dr. Grover C. Bagby, the late Dr. James P. Brawley, and the late Miss Thelma Stevens some of the key events discussed in the book would not have occurred.

I thank the hundreds of United Methodists throughout the Church who were persistent in urging and encouraging me to write the book. Included among them are the members of Foundry's Religion, Race and Culture mission group. I hope the book will fulfill the desires of all these individuals for first-hand information about the historic desegregation movement within their Church.

Special thanks go to Chuck Hilty, my fellow parishioner at Foundry United Methodist Church, for his editorial work on several chapters of the book. Also, I say a special "thank you" to my son William A. Kirk, Esq., who read Chapter 10 and offered some invaluable suggestions

Finally, the writing of this book would not have been possible without the constant and unselfish support and encouragement of my wife Vivian M. Kirk. She always believed I should write a book about the work of the Committee of Five and she never stopped telling me so. Also, she patiently copy-edited the entire manuscript. For believing in me and for going beyond the call of duty in support of the project, I can never thank her too much.

**W. Astor Kirk**
**Suitland, MD**
**August 24, 2004**

# ABOUT THE AUTHOR

W. Astor Kirk has B. A. and M. A. degrees from Howard University and a Ph.D. from the University of Texas. He has also done postgraduate studies at the London School of Economics and Political Science in London, England.

From July 1961 to March 1966 W. Astor Kirk was a staff associate at the denominational Board of Christian Social Concerns, serving as director of the Board's governmental affairs programs.

He served as a Regional Director of the U. S. Office of Economic Opportunity (later renamed Community Services Administration). He is an adjunct Associate Professor of Organization Theory in the Graduate School of Management and Technology at the University of Maryland; and he has taught at Rutgers University (Camden Campus), Boston University (School of Theology), Howard University, and Huston-Tillotson College.

Head of **Organization Management Services Corporation (OMSC)**, an organization development consulting firm, W. Astor Kirk's consulting assignments include serving as interim chief executive officer of (1) the General Board of Church and Society of the United Methodist Church; (2) the Family Crisis Center of Prince George's County, Maryland; (3) the Hotline & Suicide Prevention Center of Prince George's County; (4) Masthope Mountain Resorts, Inc., a private for-profit resort development firm in the Pennsylvania Pocono's; and (5 Maryland Corporation for Enterprise Development. He is the immediate past Chairman of the Board of Directors of the Prince George's Workforce Services Corporation (formerly Private Industry Council).

He is the author of ***NONPROFIT ORGANIZATION GOVERNANCE*** and has written several monographs and articles.

In addition to this book he has just completed another book-length manuscript entitled **GOVERNING BOARD MEMBERS*: Roles in Non-governmental Public-Serving Organization.***

# CHAPTER 1
# A Brief History

In the United States the polity of the United Methodist Church includes five geographical jurisdictions—**Northeastern, Southeastern, North Central, South Central,** and **Western Jurisdiction Organizations.**

The current structure did not always exist. Prior to 1968, in the United States, The Methodist Church (now the United Methodist Church) included a governance structure that was defined in terms of **"race"**. It was the *Central Jurisdiction Organization*. The constitution of The Methodist Church defined the Central Jurisdiction Organization as consisting of "the Negro Annual Conferences, the Negro Mission Conferences and Missions in the United States of America."

**The Central Jurisdiction Organization was superimposed on and overlaid the entire territory of the five geographical jurisdictions.**

This book's primary focus is on major "civil rights" reform movements, both within and outside the Church, which led to the elimination of the Central Jurisdiction Organization from the United Methodist polity.

## STATUS AND ROLE OF BLACKS

At an early stage in the history of the Methodist Movement in the United States, the status and role of Blacks emerged as an important issue. Then most Blacks were slaves. They had no status in the social order of the day. Nor did they have any legal rights in the civil polity of the late eighteenth century. Equal membership rights and duties for Blacks in the American Methodist Movement would have been an anomaly.

Prior to the establishment in America of the Methodist Episcopal Church, Blacks were related to the Methodist societies in England.

In November 1758, John Wesley baptized his first converts who were Blacks. John Wesley claimed that these were the first Christians of African ancestry he had known. According to Culver (1953, p. 42), Wesley wrote in his diary "... shall not our Lord, in due time, have these Heathens also for his inheritance?"

The Historical Statement in the 1980 edition of the *Book of Discipline* captivatingly describes the dynamics of the situation during the first two decades following the founding of the Methodist Episcopal Church.[1]

## Participation of Blacks In Methodist Societies

It will suffice to categorically say here that from the very beginning of the Methodist Movement in this country Blacks were a vital part of it:

- **They internalized the simple but powerful messages of Methodist preachers. They joined the Methodist societies in Maryland, in New York City, in Long Island, in Philadelphia, and later in dozens of other places where the gospel according to the Methodists was proclaimed.**

- **We know from the historical studies of Graham (1979), Cameron (1961), Richardson (1976), and Walls (1974) that (a) in 1789 the New York City John Street Church had 290 Whites and 70 Blacks in its membership, (b) in 1787 St. George's Church in Philadelphia had a membership of 270 Whites and 17 Blacks, and (c) the membership of the Calvert Circuit in the state of Maryland consisted of 505 Whites and 342 Blacks.**

- **Graham (1979), relying on data from Barclay (1923), reported that by 1786, ten years after the founding of the American polity, and only fourteen years since the founding of the first Methodist Society, and only four years after the formal establishment of the Methodist Episcopal Church, the new denomination had 1,890 Blacks in its membership.**

Thus, it is quite clear that Blacks (most of whom had been brought to this country in chains as slaves) were among those who listened and responded to the gospel message of Methodist preachers, in the early decades of American Methodism. For them, as Richardson (1976) points out, "becoming a Christian represented a complex of aims and hopes in which [their] soul's salvation was only one." Methodism grew at a relatively rapid rate among these Blacks. In some cases, within local Methodist societies, the number of Blacks equaled or exceeded the Whites.

One plausible explanation for the rapid spread of Methodism among the slaves is the fact that in the early stages of the Methodist Movement slaves were allowed to preach. Some were licensed as local preachers and later as traveling preachers. A converted slave with a gifted tongue and a talent for "exhorting" could be licensed as a "lay preacher" or "exhorter." There emerged an elite group of such "black preachers." They included Harry Hoosier, who traveled with Bishop Francis Asbury; Henry Evans, a free-born Black of Virginia, who is credited with establishing Methodism among both Blacks and Whites in Fayetteville, North Carolina; and John Stewart, who carried out a ministry among the Wyandotte Indians of Ohio, thereby becoming the founder of the home missions enterprise in the Methodist Episcopal Church.[2]

## "The Great Anomaly"

I will discuss in later chapters of this book the 1960-64 work of what is commonly referred to as the Committee of Five of the Central Jurisdiction Organization. Chaired by then Dr. James S. Thomas (later Bishop James S. Thomas, now retired), the committee included Dr. John H. Graham, Reverend John J. Hicks, Attorney Richard C. Erwin and myself. In our deliberations Chairman Thomas would quite often allude to what he described as *"The Great Anomaly."*

As Dr. Thomas viewed it in the early 1960s, the Great Anomaly was the fact that the New Testament standard for The Methodist Church polity mandated *radical inclusiveness* as the norm for church membership and Christian ministry. Yet "racial" exclusiveness, discrimination and segregation were the rules that governed so much of the activities, practices, services and other ministries of The Methodist Church at all levels.

The Great Anomaly was part of the warp and woof of the institutionalization of American Methodism from its very beginning. There was something anomalous, as the slaves must have suspected, with a Christianity that motivated its adherents to affirm justice and righteousness and oneness in Christ. Yet it did not dissuade these same adherents from oppressing sons and daughters of God who were Black, by forcing them to remain slaves, and by seating Blacks in separate areas at worship services.

The Great Anomaly caused an institutional schism within the Methodist Episcopal Church at the quadrennial meeting of the General Conference Organization in 1844. The church that had been born in 1784 in Baltimore, Maryland became two separate denominations: the Methodist Episcopal Church, South (hereafter referred to as *"Southern ME Church"*) and the Methodist Episcopal Church, North (hereafter referred to as *Northern ME Church"*). The two separate denominations remained divided for almost a century.

The breakup of American Methodism into southern and northern branches did not resolve the critical issue, in either branch, of the status and role of their members who happened to be Blacks. In the northern branch, for example, opposition to slavery did not translate into resisting differential treatment of Methodist converts on the basis of "race" and color. The Northern ME Church came no closer than the Southern ME Church to institutionalizing a fundamental tenet of the New Testament Church: *Distinctions of the secular order such as "race", caste and color have no place in any community of Christian believers.*

The circumstances that led to the founding of the Colored Methodist Episcopal, the African Methodist Episcopal, and the African Methodist Episcopal Zion *denominations* provide ample evidence of the failure of the Southern ME Church and the Northern ME Church to operationalize the New Testament standard of *"oneness in Jesus the Christ."*

Unification of the Northern and Southern branches of Methodism occurred in 1939. The price that had to be paid in order to achieve unification included an agreement to provide *constitutional protection* for the Great Anomaly. The disingenuous constitutional device chosen was a "Church within a Church." This time the definitive institutionalizing mechanism was "race" rather than geography. We turn now to the creation of the Central Jurisdiction Organization.

## Road To The Central Jurisdiction Organization

By the end of the Reconstruction period following the Civil War, there was evidence that an increasing number of church leaders were interested in "unification" discussions. In 1876 commissioners from the Southern ME Church and the Northern ME Church met at Cape May, New Jersey. They agreed that the two ecclesiastical bodies were legitimate branches of the same denomination. Affirmation of this principle was very important. It removed the stigma of "secession" from the Southern ME Church. Other inter-organization meetings and conferences followed. However, it was not until 1908 that a specific "unification" proposal was advanced.

From that moment on the *status and role of Blacks* in any "reunited" Methodist Episcopal Church became a critical issue.

As noted earlier, within American Methodism disagreement, controversy and conflict over the status and role of Methodist converts who happened to be Black led to the following events:

- **Founding in 1787 of the African Methodist Episcopal Church, a denomination consisting of local Methodist societies whose members were Black.**

- **Establishment in 1820 of the African Methodist Episcopal Zion Church with Methodist converts who were Black.**

- **Creation in 1870 of the post-slavery Colored Methodist Episcopal Church (now known as *Christian Methodist Episcopal Church*)**

- **Division in 1844 of the American Methodist movement into a northern branch and a southern branch.**

The conventional view of historians, social scientists, ethicists and theologians is that at the time of Methodist Unification in 1939, the core element of the "status and role of Blacks issue" was segregation on the basis of "race".

As a later chapter of this book will discuss in more detail, I have a different belief. **From my perspective, the essence of the "status and role of Blacks issue"—then and to the extent it may exist now—is whether any *community of Christian believers* violates New Testament standards, if that community appropriates and applies secular categories of "race", color, gender and caste in any aspects of its existence as an organization.**

My basic argument is simple and straightforward. With respect to any *authentic* Christian believer—i.e., any Son and Daughter of Christ—there is a realm of being that transcends "race", color, gender and caste. When two or more Sons and Daughters of Christ establish patterns of interaction with one another *as Christians*, (i.e., when they create institutions, organizations or other structures) they may not appropriate and apply secular categories of "race", color, gender and caste without emaciating the *distinctly Christian elements* of the established collective.

In his book *Negro Segregation in The Methodist Church*, Culver (1953) strongly affirms the proposition that the "status and role of Blacks issue" was the most important and difficult problem that the Joint Commission on Unification had to deal with. This is the core perspective of Bishop Earl Cranston of the Northern ME Church.

According to Culver, Bishop Cranston said, "It was thought that if we could come to an agreement *as to the status of the Negro* the other matters will adjust themselves to correspond to that understanding." (Emphasis added.)

In 1939, within the Northern ME Church there were "mixed" annual conference organizations; there were also annual conference organizations that included only local congregations of Blacks. In the Southern ME Church all of the former annual conference organizations consisting of local congregations of Blacks had become part of the Colored Methodist Episcopal denomination.

Since the Colored Methodist Episcopal Church was not involved in the Methodist reunification efforts at that time, its membership did not constitute a dimension of the "status and role of Blacks issue." The "mixed" annual conference organizations and those comprising local congregations with a membership of Blacks were all in the Northern ME Church.

To complicate matters further, most of these conference organizations and their members were located in the southern part of the United States. This circumstance was largely a result of the "Negro work in the South," which the Northern ME Church aggressively promoted following the Civil War. Culver (1953, p. 54n) reports Farish (1938) as estimating that there were in 1896 nearly 254,211 Blacks in the membership of the Northern ME Church, in places in the South where there had been none at the end of the Civil War.

A decision had to be made regarding how these and other Blacks, individually and collectively as components of annual conference organizations, would be related to a *reunited* Methodist Episcopal Church.

- **Response of the Southern ME Church**

Leaders of the Southern ME Church opposed the inclusion in any reunited Methodist denomination of local congregations and annual conference organizations that had Blacks in their membership. They argued that these church entities should become part of the African Methodist Episcopal, the African Methodist Episcopal Zion, and the Colored Methodist Episcopal denominations. Leaders of the southern branch of Methodism believed in rigid "racial" separation within local, state, regional and national religious bodies.

The content and tone of their opposing arguments suggest that the leaders of the Southern ME Church feared a reunited Methodist denomination, with Blacks enjoying the same status and role as Whites, would have a significant destabilizing effect on the "racially" segregated political and social regimes that had emerged in the post-Civil War South.[3] Thus for the leaders of the Southern ME Church it was critical that the issue of the role and status of Blacks in any future reunited Methodist polity be resolved in a way that would not undermine the rigid Jim Crow political and social system. This interest took precedence over any purely ecclesiastical and theological values that might be involved.

- **Response of the Northern ME Church**

Leaders of the Northern ME Church did not approach the "status and role of Blacks issue" with the same degree of consensus and forcefulness as the Southern ME Church leaders manifested. Regarding some critical aspects of the issue, there were disagreements among Northern ME Church joint commissioners. Several of these commissioners were Black and represented the "Negro constituencies" of the Northern ME Church (i.e., conferences, local congregations, and over 250,000 individual members). Most of the joint commissioners agreed that the 250,000 plus Blacks immediately involved should be brought into any future reunited Methodist denomination. But there were different viewpoints regarding the best and most ethical way of achieving the desired goal.[4]

At some point during the 1924-1928 quadrennium the probability became apparent that the Southern ME Church would accept the inclusion of Blacks in a reunited Methodist denomination under one condition: **The Blacks would have to be confined to a separate, "racially"-defined organizational structure of the reunited denomination.** Within eight years of this development the joint commissions completed a Plan of Union and presented it to their parent church bodies.

## Plan of Union

In brief the proposed Plan of Union of the Northern ME Church, the Southern ME Church and the Methodist Protestant Church[5] provided for the following:

1. **A denomination-wide legislative body that would meet every four years and set policy for the whole reunited church. It would have exclusive power over all *"matters distinctively connectional."***

2. **Five geographically defined regional policymaking bodies in the United States of America: the Northeastern, Southeastern, North Central, South Central, and Western.**

3. **A "racially" defined ecclesiastical entity called the Central Jurisdiction, which would overlap the five regional policymaking bodies.**

4. **The five regional bodies and the Central Jurisdiction would elect delegates to the quadrennial meetings of the denominational legislative body. This arrangement would guarantee participation by Blacks in the deliberations of the denominational legislative body.**

5. **Each regional policymaking body and the Central Jurisdiction would elect its own bishops, determine the boundaries of its conference units, and promote the various interests of the reunited denomination in their areas.**

6. **A denominational judicial tribunal to assure that the provisions of the Constitution of the reunited Methodist Church would not be violated.**

In 1936, following a two-hour debate, the General Conference Organization of the Northern ME Church approved the Plan of Union by a vote of 470 to 83. According to Culver (1953, pp. 69-70), "about thirty white delegates and *most of the sixty-two Negro delegates voted against the plan*. About fifty delegates did not vote." (Emphasis in the original.)

In May 1936 the Methodist Protestant General Conference Organization adopted the Plan of Union by a vote of 142 to 39. And in 1938, the General Conference Organization of the Southern ME Church voted 334 to 26 for the Plan of Union.

This approval of the Plan of Union by the denominational legislative bodies of the three "reuniting" groups paved the way for the plan to go to the annual conference organizations of each church for a vote. By the spring of 1939 the required votes had been obtained. At a Uniting Conference meeting in Kansas City, MO **"The Methodist Church"**[6] came into existence as a reunited denomination.

In order to achieve the goal of a reunited denomination the Northern ME Church had to accept an agreement that at best was ethically suspect, and at worst was morally wrong. The agreement involved the inclusion in the **Constitution** of The Methodist Church of a major governance structure that was defined on the basis of "race" rather than in geographical terms, as the other five governance structures were defined.

The "racially" segregated structure in the polity of The Methodist Church was the Central Jurisdiction Organization. From the moment of its establishment in 1939, Blacks who assumed leadership roles vowed to eventually effect its elimination. They planted the seeds of a reform movement that germinated and achieved the desired objective twenty-nine years later.

## Chapter Notes

1. Included here are brief excerpts from the 1980 edition of the *Book of Discipline*

> **Black people embraced the Methodist faith in the United States very early. Two early Methodist societies in America were the John Street Society of New York City and the Log Meeting House in Frederick County, Maryland. Black members are included among the charter members. In the John**

**Street Society, Beatty, a Negro servant of the Heck family, was a charter member. On Sam Creek in Frederick County, Maryland, Anne, a slave of the Schweitzer family, was a charter member. By 1786, there were 1,890 black members in the Methodist Episcopal Church. Methodism won favor with the black people for two main reasons: (1) its evangelistic appeal; (2) the Church's attitude toward slavery. Later its social concern impressed black people.**

**The shortest list of early black Methodists evangelists must include Harry Hoosier, Henry Evans, and John Stewart. Harry Hoosier was a traveling companion of Francis Asbury. He accompanied him to preach to the colored people. In alluding to Harry Hoosier, Thomas Coke said: "I believe he is one of the best preachers in the world." A freeborn Negro of Virginia, Henry Evans possessed genius of organization. He organized the Fourth Street Church in Wilmington, Delaware. He is credited also with organizing the first inclusive church in Fayetteville, North Carolina. The Methodist historian Abe Stevens referred to him as the Father of the Methodist Episcopal Church, White and Black in that city. The first home missionary in the Methodist Episcopal Church was John Stewart. He was a freeborn mulatto from Virginia. He became a missionary to the Wyandotte Indians. The arduous labors of John Stewart led directly to the organization of the Home Missionary Society in the Methodist Episcopal Church.**

2. In a moving, eloquent and quite perceptive paragraph in his informative and thought-provoking book *Black People in the Methodist Church* McClain (1984, p. 32) has poignantly noted that

**"Few have really assessed and appreciated the importance of these black preachers for the conversion of slaves to Christianity, and the spread of Methodism among both blacks and whites. Following the Revolutionary War and into the early decades of the next century, they became the critical link between Christian belief and the experiential world of the slaves. It was these black preachers who saved their souls and sanity with their interpretation of the humanity of God's children and the fatherhood of God. They gave realism and substance to things hoped for and a taste of things not seen. The preacher was a part of the travails of the people, for whatever happened to the people happened to him also. Wherever they were, he was there, too ... kneeling on the cold dirt floor of a**

**slave hut ... picking cotton in the long, hot, dusty and endless rows ... making his way along the long and lonely wilderness trails to get to his church and his people to fulfill his calling and keep his charge. He stood between the inexhaustible storehouse of hope and the depleted lives of his beleaguered and bewildered flock, and shouted a word to keep them going: "Walk together, children! Don't get weary!" And he preached a fiery gospel with a pastor's heart and proclaimed himself a steward of a mystery that offered to the oppressed slaves salvation and hope, and an escape from earthly woes."**

3. The debates of the Joint Commission on Unification of the Methodist Episcopal Church and the Methodist Episcopal Church, South are published in 4 volumes of *Proceedings*. In an extensive review of those *proceedings* for December 1917, Culver (1953, pp. 61-62) quotes a leader of the Southern ME Church as stating:

   **"The South and our grand division of the Methodist Church believe: That the color line must be drawn firmly and unflinchingly, in State, Church, and Society, without any deviation whatsoever; and no matter what the virtues, abilities, or accomplishments of individuals may be, there must be absolute separation of social relations. If the color line is disregarded in relations so intimate as those necessitated by the equal status theory, demanded, as I understand it, by the strongest Negro members of the Methodist Church, North, it will be impossible long to continue the fixed status of separation in affairs governmental, civic and social."**

4. Culver (1953, p. 67) presents the following summary of the stance of the Northern ME Church commissioners:

   **"In the discussions of the Joint Commission on Unification...three rather distinct groupings of opinions [are evident]. (1) A Southern group with some Northern supporters did not want Negroes to remain in the denomination. This group talked of opportunity, independence, and brotherhood through a "nexus" of some sort. Opportune beliefs about "race consciousness" and about the desires of the Negro constituency served to rationalize their position. (2) A Northern group was unwilling to sacrifice any rights and privileges of the Negro minority in order to effect the desired unification. They denounced the concept of "race consciousness" and the**

**practice of discrimination as un-Christian. Even these northern commissioners were swayed by the arguments for separation, which promised opportunity for the Negro, but they turned to colored leaders for advice, being unwilling to legislate without the approval of the minority. (3) The Negro leaders, desiring to retain an organic fellowship in the denomination, were, however, willing to sacrifice and compromise to serve the cause of unification. Believing that both their personal opportunities and their fellowship with whites would be somewhat limited under any plan of union, they saw in the jurisdictional plan a step toward the complete integration they would prefer."**

5. I have not heretofore included any discussion of the Methodist Protestant Church. This denomination was organized in 1830 with 26,000 plus members as a protest against the episcopacy, the presiding eldership, and the exclusion of the laity from the General Conference and the annual conferences in the Methodist Episcopal Church. The Methodist Protestant Church participated in the discussions of union in 1911. It re-entered the unification discussions in 1928 through the denomination's Commission on Interdenominational Relations. Thus the Plan of Union had to be submitted to the Methodist Protestant Church as well as to the Southern ME Church and the Northern ME Church.

6. The corporate or legal name of the reunited denomination is The Methodist Church, with a capital "T." In this book I will use the capitalized "T" when referring to the reunited denomination.

# CHAPTER 2
# The Central Jurisdiction: A Church Within A Church

In Methodism there is one generalization that is widely accepted as historical fact. It is that the 1939 reunification of the Northern ME Church, the Southern ME Church, and the Methodist Protestant Church—creating ***The Methodist Church***—would not have occurred without a compromise involving the "status and role of Blacks." The compromise that was hammered out *concentrated all Blacks in the Northern ME Church in a single organizational unit of* **The Methodist Church**. That single unit was the **Central Jurisdiction Organization.**[1]

As a separate and *"racially" defined*[2] entity of The Methodist Church, the Central Jurisdiction Organization stretched geographically from New England to Florida, from the Great Lakes to the Gulf of Mexico, and from the East Coast to the Rocky Mountains. It had its own legislative body, its own corps of bishops, its own annual conference organizations, and its own local congregations. All of these components of the Central Jurisdiction Organization were composed of Blacks.

The Central Jurisdiction Organization presented the anomaly of instituted and highly visible "racial" separatism that was at once foundational to and located within the polity of a *re-united Methodism.* Creation of this constitutionally protected, "racially" defined governance structure within The Methodist Church polity may have resolved the *pre-unification* issue of the role and status of Blacks. But that arrangement resulted in an ongoing *post-unification* controversy of critical importance, which lasted for three decades. It was the profoundly disturbing moral and ethical issue of *involuntary* "racial" separation in the constitutional fabric of a worldwide, multi-"racial" and multi-cultural denomination.

The "racial" separation was "involuntary," in the sense that the only choice Blacks had at the time was to accept the "segregated" arrangement or withdraw from The Methodist Church.[3] This issue posed complex problems for The Methodist Church outside the United States of America as well as within it.

### Was the Central Jurisdiction Organization *"Racial" Segregation?*

An important dynamic of the controversy over the Central Jurisdiction Organization involved conflicting views regarding whether or not it constituted "racial segregation" per se. The more moderate supporters of the Central Jurisdiction Organization expressed the view that it did not necessarily represent "racial" segregation, as they understood the concept. Their primary argument was that the Central Jurisdiction Organization (1) ensured Blacks representation in the Church's General Conference Organization and in the governing bodies of denomination-wide administrative agencies, boards and commissions; (2) provided opportunities for the exercise of leadership by Blacks, which otherwise might not exist; (3) created sundry settings in which Blacks could demonstrate their abilities; and (4) empowered Blacks with respect to selecting their own bishops, controlling the design of their own annual conference organizations, and choosing their own district superintendents.

This notion that the Central Jurisdiction Organization did not necessarily constitute "racial" segregation was most widely prevalent in the Southeastern and South Central geographical regions of The Methodist Church. But some leaders in the Northeastern, North Central and Western regions also articulated this view from time to time.

A very small minority of leaders in the Central Jurisdiction Organization adhered to the notion that for Blacks, at their then stage of development, it provided more advantages than disadvantages. There is evidence that for some senior ministers the principal advantages of the Central Jurisdiction Organization were perceived opportunities for election to the episcopacy of The Methodist Church.

The Central Jurisdiction Organization's most articulate opponents held a sharply contrasting view and valuation of this "racially" defined ecclesiastical structure within The Methodist Church polity. For that group of Methodists the Central Jurisdiction Organization was blatant "racial" segregation per se. They argued that to employ *"race"* as a criterion to separate Blacks from the general fellowship of Methodist Christians was inherently an act of "racial" segregation. The fact that this separation of the Blacks, who were formerly members of the Northern ME Church, was *involuntary* made the "racial" segregation even more pernicious and "un-Christian" in the eyes of opponents of the Central Jurisdiction Organization.

In 1965, I had the responsibility of preparing a brief in a "racial" segregation case before the Judicial Council of The Methodist Church. In the brief, I defined "racial segregation" as follows:

> **The phrase "racial segregation" is used herein to refer to *racial* distinctions, i.e., the establishment of relationships, the creation of organizational structures, the imposition of obligations, and the provision of opportunities and privileges on the basis of the *racial* backgrounds of individuals involved. Hence, as used here, the term or phrase "racial segregation" does not refer to cultural, language, nationality, or other *ethnic* differentiations. See *Regional Segregation? Before the Judicial Council of The Methodist Church* (March 15, 1965, p.5, n. 4).**

Throughout the ensuing discussions of this book the term or phrase "racial segregation" will have the meaning I gave it in the brief I submitted to the Judicial Council.

**"Voluntary" Versus "Involuntary" "Racial" Segregation in the Church**

There is abundant evidence that "racial" segregation was not absent from the Northern ME Church polity in the period between the Civil War and the establishment of The Methodist Church. What was not clearly evident are the nature and sources of all the factors that caused and shaped the "racial" segregation policy the Northern ME Church brought to the Unification negotiations. That policy contributed significantly to the birth of the Central Jurisdiction Organization.

The Northern ME Church's policy has been characterized as acquiescence in *voluntary* "racial" segregation. There is evidence that shortly after "the Great Separation in 1845" Blacks in local Northern ME churches expressed a preference for separate conferences. According to Culver (1953, p. 52), "The colored ministers felt that a separate conference would meet the arguments of their competitors in the Negro denominations and would be a demonstration of the interest of their own [Northern ME] church in the development of Negro work."

It was not until 1864 that the General Conference Organization of the Northern ME Church authorized the establishment of separate annual conference organizations for local congregations of Blacks. In that year it adopted a resolution affirming **"That justice to those who have been enslaved requires that, in all the privileges of citizenship, as well as in all other rights of a common manhood, there shall be no distinction founded on color."** Quoted in Culver (1953, p. 53). Emphasis added

In the late 1880s some church leaders, mainly in the Southern ME Church, but also with support from a small group of Northern ME Church followers, developed a *theory* of "racial" segregation. A basic presupposition of the theory was the posited existence of "race instinct." Culver (1953, p. 58) quotes Atticus G. Haygood, who eventually became a bishop of the Southern ME Church, as stating **"This instinctive disposition to form church affiliations on the color basis may be wise or unwise. But it is in them [Blacks]—deep in them. The tendency is strengthening all the time. This instinct will never rest till it realizes itself in complete separation."** Emphasis added.

The Reverend L. M. Hagood, who happened to be Black, and also a member of the Northern ME Church, strongly rejected the "race instinct" theory of "racial" segregation. In his book *The Colored Man in the Methodist Episcopal Church* (1890, pp. 199; 215) he asked:

> **"Is it 'race instinct' that tends to segregate the colored man? We answer, No. His desire to segregate is only a self-defense measure. The Colored man in this country is *desperately* in earnest in his effort to remove every vestige of prejudice against him arising from his previous condition of servitude... [S]o far as a majority of our white membership in the South is concerned we, as a Church, have not succeeded in dislodging a *single one* of the old prejudices against 'race and color.'" (Emphasis in the original.)**

During the two decades immediately preceding Methodist Unification in 1939, Blacks in the Northern ME Church had begun to view their segregated status as "voluntary"—a refinement, perhaps, of Reverend Hagood's "self-defense measure" concept. Were the "voluntary" versus "involuntary" characterizations of the "racial" segregation existent in the Northern ME Church at the time of Methodist Unification distinctions without a difference? That issue is beyond the scope of this book.

Our concern here is with the "racial" segregation represented by the Central Jurisdiction Organization. That "racial" segregation can hardly be labeled "voluntary." It was an expression of a *constitutional principle* of The Methodist Church polity. The Central Jurisdiction Organization was incorporated in the constitution of the denomination. It could not be changed through legislative decisions alone. Elimination of that "racial" segregation required a modification of the constitution of The Methodist Church. Changing the constitutional law of The Methodist Church involved a long, arduous and contentious process.

## The Central Jurisdiction Organization As An Institution

The Central Jurisdiction Organization existed as a "racially" defined ecclesiastical entity within The Methodist Church from 1939 to 1969. During that thirty-year period it acquired institutional characteristics, other than those associated with "race", which contributed to its uniqueness. Several of those characteristics are highlighted here.

### Authority, Power and Clientele

While the Central Jurisdiction Organization presented the problem of a separate "racial" ecclesiastical body, it did have the same authority, powers, rights and duties as the five geographical jurisdiction organizations. Thus it had a legislative body that could (1) elect delegates to the Church's General Conference Organization, (2) elect bishops for presidential and residential service within the Central Jurisdiction Organization, (3) choose representatives to serve on the governing bodies of denominational agencies, boards and commissions and (4) design its own structure of annual conference organizations.

With respect to the election of bishops, in the twenty-seven years from 1940 to 1967, inclusive, the Central Jurisdiction Organization elected the following fourteen bishops.

| | |
|---|---|
| **William A. C. Hughes** | **1940** |
| **Lorenzo H. King** | **1940** |
| **Edward W. Kelly** | **1944** |
| **Willis J. King** | **1944** |
| **Robert N. Brooks** | **1944** |
| **J.W.E. Bowen** | **1948** |
| **Edgar A. Love** | **1952** |
| **Matthews W. Clair, Jr.** | **1952** |
| **Prince A. Taylor** | **1956** |
| **Charles F. Golden** | **1960** |
| **Noah W. Moore, Jr.** | **1960** |
| **Marquis L. Harris** | **1960** |
| **James S. Thomas** | **1964** |
| **L. Scott Allen** | **1967** |

But the Central Jurisdiction Organization was unlike the geographical jurisdiction organizations in terms of (1) the delineation of its boundaries and (2) the composition of its clientele (membership) base. The boundaries of the other jurisdiction organizations were delineated *geographically*, while the boundaries of the Central Jurisdiction Organization were defined in terms of *"race"*. Hence Central Jurisdiction Organization boundaries overlapped or extended into each of the five geographical bodies.

With regard to the matter of clientele, Blacks comprised the membership of the local congregations in the Central Jurisdiction Organization, while the membership of local congregations in the geographical jurisdiction organizations consisted primarily, if not exclusively, of Whites. There were several local congregations of Blacks that were part of the Northeastern and Western Jurisdiction Organizations.

According to Frederick A. Shippey's 1960 report to the General Conference Organization, the aggregate membership of all Central Jurisdiction Organization local congregations totaled just over 361,000.[4]

## Educational Connections

Of the more than thirty-six institutions of higher education established historically for the education of Blacks during the post-Civil War period, thirteen were related to and supported by The Methodist Church. The thirteen institutions listed below are all located in states that were part of the Central Jurisdiction Organization.

| | |
|---|---|
| **Arkansas** | Philander Smith College **(Little Rock)** |
| **Florida** | Bethune-Cookman College **(Daytona Beach)** |
| **Georgia** | Clark College **(Atlanta)** |
| | Gammon Theological Seminary **(Atlanta)** |
| | Paine College **(Augusta)** |
| **Louisiana** | Dillard University **(New Orleans)** |
| **N. Carolina** | Bennett College **(Greensboro)** |
| **Mississippi** | Rust College **(Holly Springs)** |
| **S. Carolina** | Claflin College **(Orangeburg)** |
| **Tennessee** | Morristown Industrial College **(Morristown)** |
| | Meharry Medical College **(Nashville)** |
| **Texas** | Huston-Tillotson College **(Austin)** |
| | Wiley College **(Marshall)** |

There were mutually reciprocal relationships between these institutions of higher education and the Central Jurisdiction Organization's members, churches and annual conference organizations.

## Denominational Duties and Responsibilities

Under the constitution of The Methodist Church the Central Jurisdiction Organization had the same denominational duties and responsibilities as each of the five geographical jurisdiction organizations. For example, not only did the Central Jurisdiction Organization have the authority to elect bishops but it also had the duty to cooperate in carrying out denominational plans for episcopal support. Similarly, it had the obligation "to promote the evangelistic, educational, missionary, and benevolent interests of the church, and to provide for interests and institutions within [its] boundaries." As noted earlier, the Central Jurisdiction Organization stretched North-South from New England to Florida and East-West from the Atlantic coast to the Rocky Mountains. Because of the immense geographical territory involved, the Central Jurisdiction Organization determined that the more practicable management approach was to develop its boards and other institutional structures on the basis of Episcopal Areas and annual conference organizations.[5]

The *Central Christian Advocate* journal was one of the most influential enterprises in the promotion of the programs and administrative work of the Central Jurisdiction Organization. For many years prior to unification in 1939 this journal was published under the name *Southwestern Christian Advocate*. At the time of union the name was changed to *Central Christian Advocate*. Thereafter, the journal continued its fine tradition of service not only to the Central Jurisdiction Organization but also to The Methodist Church as a whole.

Finally, the "missionary and benevolent interests of the church" were promoted through charitable enterprises maintained by annual conference organizations of the Central Jurisdiction Organization. These enterprises included homes for the aged, friendship homes, community centers, and orphanages. A unique enterprise was the Gulfside Assembly, located at Waveland, Mississippi. It was established under the leadership of Bishop Robert E. Jones sixteen years prior to unification, and rendered noble service to members of the Central Jurisdiction Organization.

## The Past That Became Prologue

The historical record shows that, in the Northern ME Church, a majority of the annual conference organizations for Blacks were against *constitutionally* incorporating a "racially" defined ecclesiastical structure—the Central Jurisdiction Organization—in The Methodist Church polity. Although most members of these annual conference organizations strongly opposed this aspect of the Plan of Union, they were willing to *compromise* in order to achieve Unification. Moreover, they regarded the Central Jurisdiction Organization as an *interim* arrangement, "necessary in a growing together of relatively unacquainted groups, which would be changed in the course of the years" (*The History of American Methodism, III*, p.494).

The first two decades after the creation of the Central Jurisdiction Organization comprised the twenty-year period preceding the dynamic civil rights movement of the 1960s. During this period increasing numbers of Blacks in The Methodist Church "looked upon the social institutions in the wider society as the norms for church life" (Thomas, 1992, p. 39).

Predominant trends in "race relations" in the secular order—nationally and internationally—did not support the clearly *involuntary* "racial" segregation in The Methodist Church polity. Throughout the denomination, even in the Southeastern and South Central geographical jurisdictions, more and more Methodists became troubled by the moral contradiction manifested in a *constitutionally mandated* "racially" defined structure of The Methodist Church polity—a denomination that enthusiastically verbalized principles of inclusiveness of all peoples, irrespective of "race" or nationality.

By 1960, both within the Central Jurisdiction Organization and throughout the denomination, a strong and fairly widespread conviction had developed that in a multi-"racial" fellowship like The Methodist Church, a way must be found to eliminate all structures based exclusively on "race" and color. Thus the critical issue became not *should* the Central Jurisdiction Organization be abolished but rather *how* to remove it from the *constitutional fabric* of The Methodist Church

In many ways—organized and unorganized, formal and informal—the first two decades following the creation in 1939 of the Central Jurisdiction Organization germinated seeds sown earlier, perhaps unwittingly, for its later elimination. These two decades constituted a past that would become prologue.

In their Episcopal Address to the delegates attending the 1960 quadrennial meeting of the General Conference Organization, the Church's bishops stated:

> **...[W]e are apt to forget, in the midst of our concern for a more adequate solution of the race problem in our Church, that the reality that creates this problem is actually one of the most important assets in it. We already *are* an inclusive church. We intend to remain one. We have come to the time when we must confidently declare to ourselves and to the world that the interracial character of The Methodist Church is one of our greatest sources of strength and opportunity. It may—and it does!—create problems, but in itself it is a great blessing for which we thank God, and an advantage which we must develop to its fullest in this new age.**

During the two quadrennia from 1960 to 1968, The Methodist Church struggled agonizingly to find a way to confidently prove to itself and to the world that its "interracial character" could, in practice as well as in theory, be the Church's "greatest source of strength and opportunity."

**In order to do so in its *tomorrow*, The Methodist Church had to slough off the part of its *yesterday* history that involved a morally questionable 1939 Unification Compromise—the one that established the "racially" segregated Central Jurisdiction Organization and gave it constitutional legitimacy.**

## Chapter Notes

1. Following are some statements that give a relevant historical perspective on the issue of the "status and role of Blacks" at the time.

   **"We suggest that the colored membership of the Methodist Episcopal Church, the Methodist Protestant Church and such acquisitions of Colored Methodists as may enter into agreement with them, may be constituted and recognized as one of the Quadrennial or Jurisdictional Conferences of the proposed organization."** Statement of the Joint Commission on Unification at its May 1911 meeting in Chattanooga, TN. Quoted in ***The History of American Methodism, III*, p. 420.**

   **"The only way in which a union of the Northern and Southern Churches can be brought about will be by the immediate or gradual elimination of the Negro membership and in good faith attempt on the part of both churches, North and South, to cause all Negro Methodists to unite in one great body, which would receive the encouragement of the White Church."** Statement of H.H. White, at a 1916 Joint Commission meeting. Quoted by Culver (1953, p. 62

   **"The problem [confronting the Joint Commission] centered in the fact that the Southern Church had no Negro membership. The Negro Methodists of the South had either joined the Colored Methodist Episcopal Church, sponsored by the Southern Church but *separate* from it; linked themselves with other entirely different denominations, such as the African Methodist Episcopal Church; or joined the Northern Church, where they had, for the most part, their own churches and conferences, but where also they had full standing in the General Conference and thus in the legislative councils of the church. Many of the Southern brethren did not want the Negroes represented in any numbers in the General Conference. If they had a Regional Conference of their own...they would then be represented in the General Conference and also have**

power to elect bishops—bishops who might conceivably be called upon to preside over a predominantly white General Conference.

On the basis of the preliminary discussions, three solutions were being offered: a) They would be left out of the reorganized church—350,000 Negroes bereft of their membership and told to unite with some other colored body or Methodist denomination.

b) They would be an integral part of the reorganized church but not a part of its legislative branch, the General Conference. This suggestion was made by one of the most outstanding of the Northern commissioners, Dr. Edgar Blake, secretary of the Sunday School Board of the Northern church and later bishop, at a Social Union banquet in Boston, February 15, 1917. The reaction was immediate and widespread. While here and there the idea was given favorable consideration, for the most part it drew forth violent statements of denunciation, especially from Negro leaders. "We would not want the blessing of a church that would accept such an attitude, much less a church that would demand it."

c) They would be given "full virile rights, man for man and individual for individual, in the Church to which they belong."

This matter was not decided at [the] Traverse City [meeting].... On adjournment most of the commissioners seemed to be in a reasonably optimistic frame of mind. A few were discouraged. Bishop Mouzon summarized this feeling when he said: "Now, there is one serious difficulty before us, and that is the status of the colored membership in the reorganized Church.... I do not know what the solution of that question is going to be. God knows." *The History of American Methodism, III,* pp. 427-428

2. The Methodist Church's Constitution (Division Two, Paragraph 26) defined the Central Jurisdiction as follows: *"The Negro Annual Conferences, the Negro Mission Conferences and Missions in the United States of America."*

3. When approval of the Plan of Union appeared inevitable, a group of Blacks with leadership roles in the Northern ME Church met in Chicago a year before the Uniting Conference. Convinced that the involuntarily *segregated* Central jurisdiction was "morally untenable," they met to consider whether they should recommend that their conferences withdraw from the Northern ME Church and (a) establish a distinctive church for Blacks or (b) seek union with either the Colored Methodist Episcopal Church, the African Methodist Episcopal Zion Church, or the African Methodist Episcopal Church.

4. In *The History of American Methodism, III* (1964, p. 491), the editors state:

   **"There were nineteen Annual Conferences in the Negro membership at the time of unification and a total membership of just over 300,000. In 1960 the Annual Conferences numbered seventeen, due to mergers of smaller conferences, with a total membership, according to the 1960 General Minutes, of 367,340. There are five areas in the United States and one in Liberia for which the Central Jurisdiction, by action of the General Conference, has provided Episcopal leadership since 1944."**

5. **"The Central Jurisdiction in its operation presents certain inequities which would not exist under integration. Since the Negro ecclesiastical structure must duplicate that of white Methodists over most of the country, the Central Jurisdiction leaders must necessarily travel farther than whites in the supervision of the relatively scattered Negro constituency. For example, the St. Louis [Episcopal] Area of the Central Jurisdiction overlaps all seven of the episcopal areas of the North Central Jurisdiction and at least part of the eight other areas in three different [regional] jurisdictions. The four annual conferences of this St Louis area overlap all or part of thirty-six white annual conferences. The Negro district superintendents must spend a much greater proportion of their time in travel to reach the same number of churches as their white counterparts. For instance, the twenty churches of the Chicago district of the Lexington Conference extend from St. Paul, Minnesota to Detroit, Michigan, and are located in the geographical area served by five white bishops. The Baltimore [Episcopal] Area of the Central Jurisdiction covers the geographical area included in seventeen annual conferences of the Northeastern and Southeastern [regional] Jurisdictions, which are served by six white bishops. Delegates to Negro annual conferences must travel greater distances than do whites. District meetings are less feasible for Negroes, and there are correspondingly more 'sub-district' meetings in the Central Jurisdiction than in the white [regional] jurisdictions. The small groups involved, however, are less able to command the services of outstanding leaders and representatives of denominational boards than are the white district groups."** Culver, 1953, pp. 93-94.

# CHAPTER 3
## *Post-Unification Opposition* To the Central Jurisdiction

There is much evidence to suggest that in the 1940-1960 period genuine theological and religious reflections, dialogues and writings played a significant role in crystallizing post-unification opposition, *within* The Methodist Church, to the "racial" separatism represented by the Central Jurisdiction Organization.

And there is also much evidence to support another important conclusion. Profound mind-changing and institution-reforming events were rapidly occurring in the larger secular society in which The Methodist Church was so deeply embedded. They played a crucial role in shaping the active and sophisticated "desegregation movement" that developed within the denomination during the two tumultuous decades from 1940 to 1960.

### I. Decades of Denominational Agitation: 1940-1960

As a special governance structure within The Methodist Church polity, the history of operations of the Central Jurisdiction Organization began in 1940. At that time, no one knew for sure what the life span of that "racially" segregated entity would be. But beyond a significant group of former members of the Southern ME Church, few Methodists really believed that *constitutionally prescribed* "racial" separation within the new denomination would endure forever.

Those individuals and groups who had vigorously opposed constitutionally mandated "racial" segregation as a norm of The Methodist Church polity were unwilling to give the Central Jurisdiction Organization *eternal life*. Thus, notwithstanding the Great Unification of 1939 that ended the Great Separation of 1845, the stage was set for a further period of denominational agitation—yes, again, over the institutional status and role of Blacks within The Methodist Church.

## A. Quadrenniums 1940-1952—Monitoring Vital Signs

During the 1940-1944 quadrennium of The Methodist Church, denominational leaders, at all levels of operations within the Church, had to adjust to two new institutional realities. Both could affect the moral character and quality of the Church's mission and ministries. The first was *regionalism*—in the form of five geographical jurisdiction organizations. The second was *"racial" separatism*—in the form of a jurisdiction organization delineated in terms of "race" and overlapping the five geographical jurisdiction organizations. Each form of the new institutional realities had its own particular set of complex positive and negative dynamics.

### 1. Regionalism.

Early in the history of The Methodist Church anecdotal evidence of regional concerns began to appear. In some circles, there was dissatisfaction because the word "Episcopal" did not appear in the name of the re-united denomination. It was not easy for thousands of local congregations to become accustomed to "Woman's Society of Christian Service" instead of "Ladies Aid and Missionary Societies." To some church members, the ritual of the Holy Communion did not sound quite right when the words "Holy Spirit" were used instead of "Holy Ghost."

The fact became quite clear during the 1940-1944 quadrennium that regionalism, as a foundational principle of The Methodist Church polity, could and would definitely serve as a safeguard for sectional interests. It would also give support to sectional or regional divisions within the denomination.

A strong symbolic and also substantive "regionalism event" occurred at the first meeting (1940) of the new General Conference Organization. Regionalism dictated that in The Methodist Church bishops would be consecrated by the geographical jurisdiction organizations that elected them, rather than by a denominational-level body.

Thus bishops could, therefore, be perceived as bishops of *geographical jurisdiction organizations*, just as easily as they might be viewed as bishops of *The Methodist Church*.

One inescapable conclusion to be drawn from this and other similar events was apparent. **Regional forces would influence the shaping of denominational legislative policies aimed at coping with the *disvalue* to The Methodist Church as a whole of the "racially" defined Central Jurisdiction Organization.**

It would be possible for opponents of any such legislative proposals to argue that the changes sought constituted an assault on the constitutional principle of regionalism. They could thereby avoid the stigma of being labeled "*pro*-segregationists."[1]

The 1940 meeting of The Methodist Church's legislative body took one specific action that was oriented toward the Central Jurisdiction Organization. The General Conference Organization directed the new General Board of Publications to finance the publication of a *Central Christian Advocate* for the Central Jurisdiction Organization. The editor of this journal was to be elected by the General Board of Publications. However, the editor was to be chosen *from the Central Jurisdiction Organization*, thus ensuring that a Black would be chosen for the position. The *Central Christian Advocate* would later become a powerful voice in support of efforts to eliminate "racial" segregation in The Methodist Church.

### 2. "Racial" Separatism

Organized opposition to the existence of the Central Jurisdiction Organization was sporadic during the 1940-1944 quadrennium. However, perhaps one of the most dramatic precursors of future events occurred in 1941, at the first meeting of the National Conference of the Methodist Youth Fellowship. The conference adopted a resolution committing the Methodist Youth Fellowship to "Work to eliminate the principle of segregation in The Methodist Church jurisdictional organization." Three years later this Methodist youth group recommended, "The Central Jurisdiction administrative setup be removed from the organized structure of The Methodist Church."[2]

In Chapter 2 we noted that most—actually, seventeen of nineteen—of the Northern ME Church's annual conference organizations composed exclusively of Blacks voted against establishing the Central Jurisdiction Organization as part of The Methodist Church polity. The reason for their negative votes was their strong opposition to being separated in an ecclesiastical organization based solely on "race." Principally for the same reason they rejected the option of attempting to merge with one of the three denominations that Blacks established and totally controlled—namely, the African Methodist Episcopal Church, the African Methodist Episcopal Zion Church, and the Colored Methodist Church. However, once the Plan of Union was adopted over their opposition, they chose to operationalize the Central Jurisdiction Organization.

In electing to organize the Central Jurisdiction Organization, leaders of Blacks in The Methodist Church never accepted this "racially" separated governance structure as a permanent institution.

At the 1944 quadrennial meeting of the Central Jurisdiction Organization, for example, the Episcopal Address of the College of Bishops noted that the 1940 quadrennium was begun "under a new arrangement in the new church, which had in it many forebodings and much uncertainty. It was an administrative arrangement against which a majority of us had voted."

Then the Episcopal Address expressed the hope that **"in the near future our Methodism may become sufficiently Christian in character and maturity to find a more excellent way."** Emphasis added.

In the second and third quadrenniums (1944-1952) of The Methodist Church more organized opposition to the existence of Central Jurisdiction Organization occurred throughout the denomination. In July of 1946 the Methodist Information agency reported on the Bishops' Conference with Returned Veterans. The conference participants, consisting of World War II veterans, adopted a resolution stating: "We recommend that a program of education be initiated to bring about the integration of all churches of the Central Jurisdiction into the geographic jurisdiction of The Methodist Church in which they are located."

During the two quadrenniums from 1944 to 1952, The Methodist Church's legislative body received a significant number of "anti-Central Jurisdiction Organization" petitions—commonly referred to as "memorials"—from annual conference organizations throughout The Methodist Church. In one-way or another, they all petitioned for legislative action to "eliminate," "dissolve," "abolish," or otherwise do away with the "racially" separated organization.

Early in 1951, the bishops and district superintendents of the Central Jurisdiction Organization sponsored a conference for urban pastors. Held in Houston, Texas, over 150 urban pastors attended the conference. During the final hour of the conference the issue of "racial" segregation dominated the discussion. The conferees were determined to send a strong message to Whites in leadership positions in The Methodist Church. Their message: *Blacks were not "satisfied with the jurisdictional arrangement and with a segregated church society."* They drafted, and unanimously adopted, a resolution petitioning the 1952 session of the Church's legislative body to abolish the Central Jurisdiction Organization—by integrating its annual conference organizations into the geographical jurisdiction organizations.

***(a) Attempts At Promoting Congregational Development Among Blacks Outside The Central Jurisdiction Organization.*** We noted in the previous chapter that The Methodist Church's constitution defined the Central Jurisdiction Organization as comprised of: "The Negro Annual Conferences, the Negro Mission Conferences and Missions in the United States of America."

Attempts of the Northeastern Jurisdiction Organization and the Central Jurisdiction Organization to solve a problem involving "Negro work" in New York City collided with this constitutional provision.

In the Plan of Union only the "Negro work…already established" in the boroughs of the Bronx and Manhattan in New York City was assigned to the Northeastern Jurisdiction Organization. The remaining "Negro Missions" were included in the Central Jurisdiction organization. They later became the Delaware Annual Conference Organization, a component of the Central Jurisdiction Organization.

The growing population of Blacks in New York City during the 1940s created opportunities to establish more local churches to serve them. In 1944 the New York City Society of The Methodist Church petitioned the Church's legislative body for an enabling act that would permit an expansion of "Negro work" under the auspices of annual conference entities of the Northeastern Jurisdiction Organization. The Church's legislative body adopted legislation authorizing the expansion the New York City Society requested.

When the Northeastern Jurisdiction Organization attempted to exercise the permission granted, its action was challenged. The Judicial Council of The Methodist Church (hereafter **"Judicial Council"**) ruled that the legislative body's Enabling Act was "confusing and inadequate," and that the Northeastern Jurisdiction Organization "was without legal authority to take the action on which the appeal is based" (*Decision No. 32*, December 5, 1944).

At its 1948 quadrennial session, The Methodist Church's legislative body approved a petition requesting certain discretionary authority for designated annual conference organizations of the Northeastern Jurisdiction Organization and of the Central Jurisdiction Organization. Permission was granted "to organize and promote Negro work, which work, when organized, shall be within the geographical boundaries of the [annual conference organization] in which it is organized."

In light of the 1944 ruling in Decision No. 32, this action of the legislative body was referred to the Judicial Council for a determination of its constitutionality. The Secretary of the General Conference Organization provided the Judicial Council with certificates from a majority of the annual conference entities of the Northeastern Jurisdiction Organization and of the Central Jurisdiction Organization showing that they approved the proposed changes. Therefore, the Judicial Council ruled, "Since the procedure provided in the Constitution for the making of [boundary] changes...has been fully complied with, it is the decision of the Judicial Council that the...action of the General Conference changing the boundaries of the Central Jurisdictional Conference of The Methodist Church is constitutional" (*Decision No. 55*, May 6, 1948).

This decision helped efforts to mitigate the negative consequences of the existence of the Central Jurisdiction Organization. It permitted annual conference organizations of the Northeastern Jurisdiction Organization to undertake new "Negro mission work." The other four geographical jurisdiction organizations were not covered by the decision. Other annual conference organizations desiring to establish such work still had to secure the approvals required by the constitution of The Methodist Church.

***(b) Transfer of Local Churches from the Central Jurisdiction Organization into Geographical Jurisdiction Organizations.*** Some opponents of the Central Jurisdiction Organization believed that one way to achieve its elimination was to allow its local churches that wished to do so to transfer into annual conference organizations that were components of the five geographical jurisdiction organizations. Motivated by such belief, they secured petitions from twenty-four annual conference entities in the Northeastern Jurisdiction Organization and in the Central Jurisdiction Organization seeking enabling legislation. These petitions were submitted to the 1952 session of the Church's legislative body. That body's Committee on Conferences presented a Report that recommended

> **the passage of necessary enabling legislation, so that any local church or churches of the Central Jurisdiction may become a part of any other Jurisdiction in which the church or churches concerned may be located, providing such membership is mutually desired by the said church or churches of the Central Jurisdiction concerned, the particular Annual Conference of each Jurisdiction concerned and a majority of the Annual Conferences of each Jurisdiction concerned.**

The Church's legislative body adopted the Report, including the recommendation quoted here. It then referred the matter to the Judicial Council for a *Declaratory Decision* regarding the authority of the legislative body to implement the recommendation by enacting enabling legislation.[3] In *Decision No. 85* (May 1, 1952), the Judicial Council ruled that in principle the "local-church-transfer" approach to removing the Central Jurisdiction Organization from The Methodist Church was not incompatible with the Church's constitution. Because of the critical importance of Judicial Council Decision No. 85, it is quoted in detail in **Appendix 1.** .

For Methodist Church leaders in major urban areas of the Northeastern and North Central sections of the United States, Judicial Council Decision No. 85 had disturbing implications. Both Blacks and Whites in many of these areas had interests in coordinated and integrated planning and supervision of urban ministries of local congregations of The Methodist Church. Judicial Council Decision No. 85 indicated that any pursuit of a "local-church-transfer strategy" involving churches in the Central Jurisdiction Organization would be very difficult. It would involve securing the approval of governance groups not directly affected or involved.

Judicial Council Decision No. 85 also disclosed the managerial rigidities, apart from the doubtful morality, of weaving into the constitutional fabric of The Methodist Church organizational definitions solely in terms of "race". That decision clearly established, as a constitutional principle, that transfer of a local church from the Central Jurisdiction Organization into a geographical jurisdiction organization **"would be, from a 'racial' standpoint, the changing**

**of the boundaries" of the jurisdiction organizations involved.** (Emphasis added.) To effect such a transfer required approvals of multiple organizations, including the Church's legislative body.

At its 1952 quadrennial session, subsequent to the Judicial Council's *advisory opinion* in Decision No.85, The Methodist Church's legislative body addressed the issue of transferring local churches from the Central Jurisdiction Organization into geographical jurisdiction organizations. It enacted legislation establishing the following official procedure for accomplishing such transfers:

A local church could be transferred from the Central Jurisdiction Organization to a geographical jurisdiction organization within whose bounds it is located upon completion of the following actions regardless of the order in which they are taken:

1. Approval by the membership of the local church involved.

2. Approval by the annual conference organization of the Central Jurisdiction Organization and the annual conference organization of the geographical jurisdiction organization involved.

3. Approval by a majority of the annual conference organizations (a) in the Central Jurisdiction Organization and (b) in the geographical jurisdiction organization involved.

4. Approval by the legislative bodies of (a) the Central Jurisdiction Organization and (b) the geographical jurisdiction organization involved.

5. Approval by the General Conference Organization in the form of an enabling act.

6. Certification to the Council of Bishops that all required actions have been taken, and a declaration by the Council of Bishops that the transfer has been duly effected.

Also at its 1952 legislative session, the Church's legislative body used this new legislation to pass several enabling acts. The acts authorized the Detroit, Nebraska, North Iowa, and Iowa-Des Moines Annual Conference Organizations of the North Central Jurisdiction Organization to receive into their bodies any Central Jurisdiction Organization local churches within their respective geographic boundaries, "upon full compliance with all the provisions of the *Discipline* of 1952."

The 1940-1952 years comprised a period that I have referred to as "a time of monitoring vital signs of the Central Jurisdiction Organization" and "performing some diagnostic procedures on The Methodist Church's system of regionalism." This twelve-year period yielded some useful insights regarding the health of the Central Jurisdiction Organization as a "racially" defined entity of The Methodist Church.

Excluding the Southeastern Jurisdiction Organization, there was clear evidence of a growing *organized* opposition throughout the denomination to the continued existence of constitutionally mandated "racial" segregation in the polity of The Methodist Church. The manifest form of this segregation was the Central Jurisdiction Organization.

The Central Jurisdiction Organization was seen as a *religious* type of "separate but equal" system. It was generally unacceptable in the broader secular society in which The Methodist Church was embedded. Members of The Methodist Church from conference organizations outside the United States of America (i.e., the **Central Conference Organizations**) viewed this American *religious* "racial separatism" as indistinguishable from the system of *religious* apartheid in South Africa.

During the period under review here, the Judicial Council expounded a definitive and controlling judicial doctrine. It was that any change of a local church's affiliation from an annual conference organization that was part of the Central Jurisdiction Organization to an annual conference organization within a geographical jurisdiction organization would, *"from a racial standpoint,"* constitute a change in the "boundaries" of the Central Jurisdiction Organization itself.

For any such change to conform to the constitution of The Methodist Church, the change had to have the approval of a multiplicity of Church organizations, including the Church's legislative body. The only way to negate that complex, time-consuming and inefficient process, by providing a more liberal procedure, was to amend the constitution of The Methodist Church.

Within the next four years, internal and external pressures for change would become immense and intense. They would compel denomination leaders, Blacks as well as Whites, to embrace the inefficient process and try "with all deliberate speed" to use it.

## B. Quadrenniums 1952-1960—Testing Change-Options

During debates on the Plan of Union, there was speculation in the religious press that a "gentlemen's agreement" had been consummated between certain very powerful leaders of both the Northern ME and Southern ME Churches. Presumably, there was an unwritten—but arguably binding—understanding that the Central Jurisdiction Organization was to be virtually a permanent structural feature of the polity of The Methodist Church.[4]

Whether a "gentlemen's agreement" did or did not exist is not our main concern. We are interested in other matters. Not the least among them is the fact that in the period under review here organized anti-Central Jurisdiction Organization pressures became strong enough to make genuine consideration of constitutional change appear as a feasible option.

There is much evidence that the experience of the first twelve years with "racial" separation, in the form of a "racially" defined organizational unit of the denomination, showed that such separation could have significant if not substantial *disvalue* for The Methodist Church as a whole. The glaring contradictions between the Church's strong affirmations of *Christian universalism* and its blatant practices of *"racial" separatism* had a de-legitimizing impact on the denomination's social justice stance in the emerging global community.

However, responsible Church leaders, Blacks as well as Whites, faced a dilemma. Even after twelve years of existence as a negative symbol and system of "involuntary" "racial" segregation, the Central Jurisdiction Organization, as an institution, still had emotional, cultural, economic and social *value* for a powerful segment of the membership of The Methodist Church.

That segment of the Church's membership existed outside of the Central Jurisdiction Organization. The leadership challenge was to find a way to facilitate progressive movement away from the constitutionally prescribed pattern of "racial" separatism in the polity of The Methodist Church.

At the level of the General Conference Organization, subsequent to Judicial Council Decision No. 85, the Church's "power elites" resorted to *permissive legislation* as a strategy for change. Such a strategy would work where local churches and affected annual conference organizations of the Central Jurisdiction and geographical jurisdiction organizations desired to create new patterns of relationships and fellowship that would not be defined in terms of "race".

As we shall discuss later, at its 1956 quadrennial session the Church's legislative body proposed a constitutional amendment that would incorporate into the fabric of the constitution of The Methodist Church Bishop Brashares' principle of "permissiveness". Culver (1953, p. 116) quotes Bishop Charles W. Brashares as stating, **"We need some permissive legislation [that] does not have to be mandatory for the whole church, but will set the North free from our present disciplinary straightjacket**. If...Negro churches in Georgia or Mississippi should not belong to white conferences, that does not mean that Negro churches in New York, Michigan, or Iowa should not belong to white conferences."

### *1. Organized Opposition Within The Central Jurisdiction Organization*

Earlier in this chapter we noted the "hope" of the organizing bishops of the Central Jurisdiction Organization that in the near future The Methodist Church might "become sufficiently Christian in character and maturity to find a more excellent way." Upon recommendation of the bishops, the 1948 quadrennial session of the Central Jurisdiction Organization's legislative body created a **Commission to Study the Central Jurisdiction**. The mandate of that Commission was

> **To study the Central Jurisdiction with a view to determining its advantages and its disadvantages; its relationships to [the regional organizations]; its overlapping boundaries; problems arising out of its extensive geography; its status as a racial group in The Methodist Church; and any other problems peculiar to the [Central Jurisdiction organization]. This study shall have as its purpose the establishment of an intelligent basis for determining whether or not the Central Jurisdiction [organization] should be continued as it now exists or eliminated, and what modifications, if any should be made, and the steps necessary to make such modifications.**

The Commission made a report at the 1952 quadrennial session of the Central Jurisdiction Organization's legislative body. It did not find adequate solutions to the complex problems created by a "racially" defined intermediate governance structure within the polity of The Methodist Church. However, the Commission presented objective data regarding the dissatisfaction of Blacks with that arrangement. With a desire to continue seeking satisfactory and ethically defensible solutions, the legislative body extended the life of the Commission for another four years.

That Commission made a second report at the 1956 quadrennial meeting of the Central Jurisdiction Organization's legislative body. In the concluding section of this second report, the Commission called attention to some "basic facts." The critical ones included the following:

> **The major and central problem concerning Negroes in The Methodist Church is *segregation.* This problem is *not* inherent in the Central Jurisdiction [alone], but in the purposes, the minds, attitudes, traditions and customs that have given birth to separation and segregation on the lower structural levels of the Church and the larger community in which the Church exists.**
>
> **...[R}emoval of segregation [will not] follow inevitably [from] abolition of the...Central Jurisdiction. There is and most likely will be segregation with or without the Central Jurisdiction until some other conditions are met.**
>
> ***[Negroes are likely to delude themselves if they] think that merely shifting a Negro church from a Negro conference to a white conference removes segregation. This procedure merely shifts seg-***

***regation from one conference to another.*** Report of the Commission to Study the Central Jurisdiction, April 15, 1956. (Emphasis added.)

The Commission next considered some approaches that the Central Jurisdiction Organization might take with respect to "changing the legalizing provisions for segregation in The Methodist Church." Included is a summary of the major recommendations of the Commission.

1. Request the denominational legislature "to oppose strongly and unrelentingly all forms of racial segregation and to authorize a program that would begin immediately to remove segregation on all levels of relationship in The Methodist Church."

2. Petition the general Church "to open the doors of all colleges, universities, hospitals and other institutions to all groups without regard to race or color."

3. Ask the general Church to schedule and hold "inter-racial conferences without segregation."

4. Request that "discrimination in employment in offices, departments and in all agencies of the Church" be eliminated, and a policy be established of "employment on the basis of merit without regard to race or color."

5. Urge the general Church "to face frankly the responsibility of removing legal barriers that affect the whole Church and prohibit free communication and the establishment of inter-racial churches where this is desired and can be worked out with mutual satisfaction."

6. Request the denominational legislature to establish a quadrennial commission to study "segregation and formulate plans and programs to eliminate it and bring about integration."

The 1956 report of the Commission had a profound impact on the thinking of leaders of the Central Jurisdiction Organization. They recognized for the first time the basic difference between their approach and the strategy of the general Church.

- The "permissiveness" strategy of the general Church merely emphasized transferring local congregations from annual conference organizations of the Central Jurisdiction Organization into geographical jurisdiction organizations

- The Commission's report identified *elimination of segregation in The Methodist Church* as the primary goal. It urged the Central Jurisdiction Organization's leadership to pursue a strategy aimed at achieving a "racially" inclusive fellowship in all areas of the Church's life.

### *2. Expanding Permissiveness: Legacy of The General Conference Organization's 1956 Session*

The Methodist Church's legislative body convened in Minneapolis, Minnesota in the spring of 1956 for its quadrennial session. National attention was focused dramatically on the desegregation movement in American society. That movement had gained momentum, as a result of the United States Supreme Court's decisions of 1954 and 1955 in public school segregation cases. Partly influenced by the atmosphere of the times, Methodists from all over the nation sent over 4,000 petitions to the Church's legislative body requesting elimination of the Central Jurisdiction Organization from The Methodist Church polity.

Following intense study and prolonged debates, the legislative body took two very important actions: (1) It drafted a proposed Ninth Amendment to the constitution of The United Methodist Church; (2) it created a broadly representative quadrennial study commission. A brief discussion of each of these actions is presented here.

***(a) Amending the Constitution of The Methodist Church.*** The appropriate standing committee of the legislative body carefully examined the Church's experiences with local church transfers under the ruling of the Judicial Council in Decision No. 85, and the subsequent *permissive legislation* implementing that ruling. It analyzed a large body of data from the Central Jurisdiction Organization and four of the five geographical jurisdiction organizations. The evidence indicated a need to clarify and simplify as much as possible the process for achieving local church transfers.

The standing legislative committee recommended, and the members of the legislative body adopted, a proposed ninth constitutional amendment, which became commonly known as **Amendment IX**. By April 1958 the required affirmative votes of annual conference organizations throughout the Church were obtained. Thereupon, the Council of Bishops declared Amendment IX to be part of the constitution of The Methodist Church.

Amendment IX established machinery for inter-organizational transfers of two types of constituent units of The Methodist Church: a **local church** and an entire **annual conference organization** of the Central Jurisdiction Organization.

Under Amendment IX, a **local church** had the option of transferring from the Central Jurisdiction Organization into a geographical jurisdiction organization in which it was "geographically located." The transfer had to be approved by a two-thirds vote of those present and voting in each of the following meetings:

1. A quarterly conference of the local church;

2. A church conference of the local church;

3. The annual conference organization of the Central Jurisdiction Organization of which the local church was a part; and

4. The annual conference organization of the geographical jurisdiction organization into which the local church desired to transfer.

There was no provision in Amendment IX for the transfer of a pastor of a local church from the Central Jurisdiction Organization into an annual conference organization of a geographical jurisdiction organization. Thus the transfer of a local church did not automatically effect the transfer of the minister(s) involved.

It was entirely possible that the membership of a particular local church affiliated with the Central Jurisdiction Organization might be acceptable to a recipient annual conference organization of a geographical Jurisdiction organization while its minister(s) might be unacceptable. These types of problems will be discussed in Chapter 6 of this book.

The steps involved in the transfer of an entire **annual conference organization** of the Central Jurisdiction Organization under Amendment IX were as follows:

1. A Central Jurisdiction annual conference organization that desired to transfer into a geographical jurisdiction organization was required to formulate a resolution expressing that desire. The resolution had to be adopted by a two-thirds majority of the members present and voting at a session of the annual conference organization. The secretary had to certify results of the vote to the two Colleges of Bishops involved.

2. The remaining Central Jurisdiction annual conference organizations had to vote separately on the transfer resolution. In order for it to be adopted at that stage of the process, the resolution had to receive an affirmative vote of two-thirds of the total voting members, *within the Central Jurisdiction Organization*, present and voting at separate sessions of their respective bodies. Each of the votes taken had to be certified by the secretary to each College of Bishops involved.

3. Each annual conference organization in the prospective recipient geographical jurisdiction organization had to vote to adopt or reject the transfer resolution as certified by the secretary of the Central Jurisdiction annual conference organization that initiated it. In order for the resolution to be approved at that stage of the Amendment IX process, it had to be adopted by a two-thirds majority of the total members, *within the geographical jurisdiction organization*, present and voting at separate sessions of their respective annual conference organizations. The voting results had to be certified to each College of Bishops involved.

4. The vote to approve or disapprove a particular annual conference organization transfer resolution had to be taken "at the first session after the matter is submitted to it."

At its 1956 quadrennial session, the legislative body of The Methodist Church faced a serious problem. The *disvalue to* the denomination of a "racially" segregated intermediate governance structure in its polity was beginning to out weigh that structure's *collective value* to special interest groups throughout The Methodist Church.

The legitimacy of the Church's moral and theological affirmations—of its social justice proclamations—was being seriously questioned, not only in the United States of America but abroad, in the **Central Conference Organizations**.

Unfortunately, Amendment IX was inherently limited—in terms of the scope of the objective it was initially intended to achieve. In 1956, when the legislative body was considering the Amendment IX proposal, one delegate pleaded for a tool that would enable the Church to move away from "every form of racism." That delegate was Thelma Stevens, a Mississippi native and one of the most courageous Whites with whom the author worked four years later. She argued that as proposed, Amendment IX was merely an instrument for moving The Methodist Church away from only "the most visible national expression of racism" in its polity.

The basic objective of the drafters of Amendment IX was to facilitate the transfer of local churches and annual conference organizations of the Central Jurisdiction Organization, *as "racially" segregated entities*, into the five geographical jurisdiction organizations of The Methodist Church. It was assumed that ultimately the Central Jurisdiction Organization itself, *as an intermediate governance structure based solely on "race,"* might be eliminated. And from the perspective of Thelma Stevens, that objective, alone, was entirely too limited.

***(b) Creation of a Quadrennial Study Commission on the "Jurisdictional" System of The Methodist Church***. The volatile issue of a "racially" constituted intermediate governance structure was intertwined with questions concerning the advisability of continuing support for the system of regionalism incorporated in The Methodist Church polity. In the Episcopal Address to the 1956 quadrennial session of the Church's legislative body, the Council of Bishops offered the following recommendation:

> **The Council of Bishops...recommends that a commission large enough to be truly representative of all our people be constituted [at this legislative session] for the purpose of studying the jurisdictional structure of the Church, its philosophy and its effectiveness, and that [the commission] report its findings with recommendations to [our] 1960 session. Through this medium we believe that a way can be charted to advance the Church steadily toward the fulfillment of the Christian imperative for race relations.**

In addition to the Episcopal Address, the delegates to the 1956 quadrennial legislative session had before them many petitions. Moreover, several resolutions were introduced from the floor of the meeting. A wide diversity of points of view existed. Some petitions and resolutions called for an immediate end of the Central Jurisdiction Organization; some commended the "jurisdictional" system and called for its continuation; some called for an end to the "jurisdictional" system.

The resolution that finally reached the floor of the session generally called for an immediate and careful re-examination of the philosophy and operation of the system of five regional organizations, in the light of the Church's sixteen-years experience with it.

The legislative body established **The Commission to Study and Recommend Action Concerning the Jurisdictional System.** This group had seventy members, which is why it was popularly referred to as the "Commission of Seventy." It was composed of

> **...one minister and one lay person from each jurisdiction for each 500,000 church members or major fraction thereof, with a minimum of three ministers and three lay persons from each "jurisdiction," elected by this [Legislative Body] on nomination by the Council of Bishops after consultation between the bishops and the chairmen of the "Annual Conference" delegations within their respective "jurisdictions."... The membership shall also include twelve bishops, two from each "jurisdiction," and twelve additional laymen, two from each "jurisdiction," nominated by the Council of Bishops and elected by this [Legislative Body].**

The Church's legislative body gave the Commission of Seventy a very broad mandate. It stated explicitly that:

**"The responsibilities and authority of this commission shall be as follows:**

**a. To make a thorough study of our jurisdictional system, with special reference to its philosophy, its effectiveness, its weaknesses, and its relationship to the future of The Methodist Church.**

**b. To carry on studies and conduct hearings in all the jurisdictions on "racial" segregation in The Methodist Church and all other problems related to the jurisdictional system.**

**c. To develop courses of action directed toward greater interracial brotherhood and the spirit of Christian love.**

**d. In the performance of its duties, to draw on the resources of other agencies of The Methodist Church to assist in such research.**

**e. To distribute to the local churches such facts and information during the quadrennium as may be deemed helpful to the work of this commission and of value to the church.**

**f. To present its findings and recommendations to the "General Conference" of 1960 in a report which shall be printed and distributed to the delegates thereof at least three months prior to the convening of the conference."**

The Commission of Seventy was organized at the site of the 1956 quadrennial session of the Church's legislative body, before it adjourned. August 6-7, 1956 was set as the date for the Commission's first meeting.

The Commission of Seventy took seriously its assigned task of making a thorough study of the system of regional governance institutions, which comprised a foundation stone of The Methodist Church polity. During the course of the 1956-1960 quadrennium the Commission organized and conducted public hearings within the bounds of each geographical jurisdiction organization.

Varying in length from one to two days, the hearings were held in the following cities: Atlanta, GA; Baltimore, MD; Boston, MA; Charlotte, NC; Chicago, IL; Columbus, OH; Denver, CO; Detroit, MI; Kansas City, MO; Los Angeles, CA; Louisville, KY; Minneapolis, MN; Montgomery, AL; New

Orleans, LA; New York, NY; Oklahoma City, OK; Orangeburg, SC; Philadelphia, PA; Pittsburgh, PA; St. Louis, MO; San Antonio, TX; San Francisco, CA; Seattle, WA and Shreveport, LA.

The Commission submitted a detailed report of its findings and recommendations to the 1960 quadrennial session of the General Conference Organization. See The Commission To Study and Recommend Action Concerning The Jurisdictional System, ***Report to the 1960 General Conference of The Methodist Church***, January 6, 1960 (referred to hereafter as "*Commission of Seventy Report*").

With respect to the five *geographical* jurisdiction organizations in the United States of America, the Commission of Seventy found strong support for them in the Southeastern and South Central Jurisdiction Organizations. The leaders of those geographical jurisdiction organizations believed that regional governance institutions were important agencies for implementing the promotional work of The Methodist Church.

In contrast, the Northeastern, North Central and Western Jurisdiction Organizations were predominantly critical of such regional institutions. The leaders of these three geographical jurisdiction organizations believed that regional governance structures in the United States of America were unnecessary, economically wasteful and in some respect a divisive addition to The Methodist Church polity.

The primary concern of this book is the *non-geographically defined* Central Jurisdiction Organization, which was a manifestation of constitutionally prescribed "racial" segregation within The Methodist Church polity. Regarding the Central Jurisdiction Organization, the Commission of Seventy reported the following findings, inter alia:

> **The Central Jurisdiction is by definition composed of the Negro Annual Conferences, and a desire to have it abolished was discovered in varying degrees in all Jurisdictions. Throughout the Church there is a growing conviction that the pattern of racial segregation existing in our country today is morally wrong and the Central Jurisdiction for many people has become a symbol of segregation. However, among those urging an early elimination of the Central Jurisdiction there was difference of judgment as to how and when this could be accomplished...**
>
> **... After careful study, your Commission is convinced that there are vital problems which must be solved before the Central Jurisdiction can be abolished other than by the *voluntary decision* of the Annual Conferences as now provided in Amendment IX. *Commission of Seventy Report*, pp. 11-12.** (Emphases added.)

A critical recommendation of the Commission of Seventy was that the 1960 quadrennial session of the Church's legislative body **"undertake no basic change in the Central Jurisdiction [Organization]."**

It was the view of the Commission of Seventy that the *principles of voluntarism* incorporated in Amendment IX, which had been in effect for only a year, should be given a chance to operate. With that end in mind, it recommended the establishment of procedures, at the level of annual conference organizations, which the Commission believed would facilitate the process of transferring component entities of the Central Jurisdiction Organization into geographical jurisdiction organizations.

As noted above, the Commission of Seventy did not believe additional legislation was needed to accomplish the eventual elimination of what it acknowledged as "forced segregation" (*Report*, p. 22). Consequently, it recommended that, in 1960, "no basic change" should be made in the Central Jurisdiction Organization (*Report*, p. 12).

That recommendation evoked a high level of consternation, especially among Blacks, throughout the denomination. It grew in intensity during the 1960-1964 quadrennium. We will revisit this issue in a later chapter of the book.

## CONCLUDING SUMMARY

The **Central Jurisdiction Organization** was an unfortunate outcome of a Great Compromise between three separate Methodist denominations. The compromise, consummated in 1939, enabled the denominations to unite and establish The Methodist Church.

That compromise may be one of those instances where, in the recent words of Episcopal Bishop John Shelby Spong (2001, p. 226) "the agenda of the church in history has quite often been antithetical to the agenda of God's realm."

One of the critical controversies that the Great Compromise had to resolve was the "status and role of Blacks issue." That issue was resolved by creating six *intermediate* governance institutions within The Methodist Church polity. Five were defined geographically. One—the Central Jurisdiction Organization—was defined in terms of "race".

From the very beginning there were groups, including both Blacks and Whites, who opposed the creation of the Central Jurisdiction Organization. They viewed it as *involuntary "racial" segregation*, which, they argued, had no place in a fellowship of believers in Christ.

There was a second group of Blacks and Whites who did not prefer the Central Jurisdiction Organization but were willing to accept it as a *temporary expedient*. As the bishops stated, when they organized the Central Jurisdiction Organization after the Plan of Union was adopted, they looked forward to "*the near future* [when] our Methodism may become sufficiently Christian in character and maturity to find a more excellent way." (Emphasis added.)

Jointly, these two groups of opponents of the Central Jurisdiction Organization comprised a vital core of *anti-segregationists* within the fellowship of The Methodist Church. Some Church leaders and individual Church members became *active* anti-segregationists. Others were, for the most part, *passive* anti-segregationists. During the first two decades—1940 to 1960—of The Methodist Church, it was the active anti-segregationists that provided organized opposition, within the denomination, to the continued existence of the Central Jurisdiction Organization. They were united in their determination to remove constitutionally prescribed "racial" segregation from The Methodist Church polity.

In this chapter we have highlighted, documented and discussed the principal intra-denominational decisions and actions taken to *desegregate* The Methodist Church polity. The constitutional, legislative and administrative changes that occurred during the 1940-1960 period resulted from the interplay of various principles and strategies collectively characterized as *voluntarism*. They included formal procedures whereby a particular annual conference organization might *voluntarily* transfer from the Central Jurisdiction Organization into a geographical jurisdiction organization, provided there was *voluntary* agreement on the part of (1) the other Central Jurisdiction annual conference organizations and (2) all the annual conference organizations of the geographical jurisdiction organization involved.

These *voluntary* procedures sought to achieve some measure of structural desegregation. In the 1940-1960 period, there were only "recommendations," but no "legislation," that addressed non-structural "racial" segregation in The Methodist Church. One of the most influential recommendatory documents was the 1956 denominational statement on **The Methodist Church and Race.**[5]

That document was used in creative and imaginative ways by several active anti-segregationist units of denominational boards, commissions and agencies. They included the Women Division's Department of Christian Social Relations (General Board of Missions) and the Division of Human Relations (General Board of Church and Society).

During the period covered in this chapter The Methodist Church was subjected to external as well as internal pressures to eliminate involuntary "racial" segregation from its institutional life. Before going to the 1960-1968 quadrenniums, which produced a union of The Methodist Church and the Evangelical United Brethren Church, we will briefly discusses some of the external pressures the denomination faced. That discussion is the subject of the following chapter.

## Chapter Notes

1. In a later section of this chapter I will discuss the fact that during the 1950s and 1960s the concept of "voluntarism" rather than "regionalism" became the ruse for opposition to legislative proposals aimed at mitigating the negative effects of the Central Jurisdiction Organization. Those who championed the concept of voluntarism neglected to acknowledge that for Blacks the "racial" separation represented by the Central Jurisdiction Organization was an *involuntary* arrangement, which was ensconced in the Church's constitution.

2. *Methodist Youth United: The Report of the First National Conference, 1941* (Nashville, National Conference of the Methodist Youth Fellowship, 1941); and *Our World for Christ: Report of the Second National Convocation* (Nashville, National Conference of the Methodist Youth Fellowship, 1944). Quoted in Culver (1953, p. 102).

3. The Judicial Council has the authority to render *Declaratory Decisions* in certain situations to serve as a guide to the denominational legislative body, the Council of Bishops and other parties in framing legislation relating to the subject involved. In this case, the denominational legislature contemplated enacting legislation dealing with transferring local churches out of the Central Jurisdiction organization.

4. The following statement in Judicial Council Decision No. 85 may have *extra-constitutional* meaning: **"Regardless of...*changes in sentiment and thought* it must be held in mind that *this Constitution was prepared with a view of getting it adopted* by all three of the uniting churches, and such procedural restrictions were inserted as seemed necessary to bring about the desired result—unification"** [emphasis added].

   At the 1952 session of the denominational legislature Chester A. Smith, a delegate from the Northeastern regional organization, proposed a constitutional amendment that would abolish the Central Jurisdiction organization. Speaking on behalf of his proposal he made the following statement: "I realize that we are under a certain gentlemen's agreement with certain members of the Church on this question, to continue the Plan of Union for a certain period of time without amending it, but now I think the situation has changed." Quoted by Culver (1953, p. 113).

   **".... Methodists have discovered, just as the nation has discovered,**

**that in the long run the forces holding our Church together have been stronger than the forces of division and disunity. Hence, *if any single philosophical principle may be admitted by all as undergirding the jurisdictional system, it is that compromise may be an instrument to serve the highest ethical values.*"** The Commission To Study and Recommend Action Concerning the Jurisdictional System (January 6, 1960), *Report to the 1960 General Conference of The Methodist Church*, p. 6. [Emphasis added.}

5. The 1956 denominational statement is as follows:

**THE METHODIST CHURCH AND RACE**

**"... We recommend the following:**

**1. That the institutions of the church, local churches, colleges, universities, theological schools, publishing agencies, hospitals, and homes carefully restudy their policies and practices as they relate to race, making certain that these policies and practices are Christian.**

**2. That Methodists in their homes, in their work, in their churches, and in their communities actively work to eliminate discrimination on the basis of race, color, or national origin. That parents, teachers, and others who work with children and youth help create attitudes which make it easy to live in harmony with those of other races.**

**3. That Methodist churches in changing neighborhoods, rather than seeking new locations, early prepare their people to welcome into their fellowship all races, as they become a part of their community. That our pastors, upon whom rests the responsibility of receiving individuals into church membership discharge that responsibility without regard to race, color, or national origin.**

**4. That bishops, district superintendents, pastors, and lay leaders seek ways for the implementation of better fraternal relations between the Central Jurisdiction and other jurisdictions where they are adjacent, by closer cooperation at Annual and District Conferences, and at local church levels.**

**5. That Methodists at national and international meetings of the Church make provision for equality of accommodations for all races, without discrimination or segregation.**

**6. That the many racial and national groups which make up our Methodist world fellowship be afforded the opportunity without discrimination to enjoy full participation in all the activities of the Church."**

SOURCE: ***The Book of Discipline*** (1956), Paragraph 2026

# CHAPTER 4
# The Methodist Church In The Public Eye

Theologically, ethically and historically the correct presumption is that religious organizations and ecclesiastical orders are or should be powerful forces in the shaping of society's norms regarding *involuntary* "racial" segregation.

In the case of The Methodist Church, there is a basis for reasonable doubt that the presumption held true. The Methodist Church itself, during its twenty-nine year history, maintained a "racially" segregated governance institution—the Central Jurisdiction Organization. That institution was mandated by the constitution of The Methodist Church.

The Methodist Church came into being at a time when a trend toward new, more democratic—indeed, more *Christian*—norms of "inter-racial" relationships" was clearly emerging in the United States of America. **Perceptible over the horizon in 1939 was a somewhat lesser willingness, in large areas of the country, to accept involuntary separation of human beings on the basis of "race" alone.**

The creation of the Central Jurisdiction Organization in 1939, as a "racially" defined institution within The Methodist Church polity, represented an embarrassing counter-trend.

The "racial" segregation symbolized by the Central Jurisdiction Organization was bizarre because it was woven into the constitutional fabric of the new denomination. Endowing involuntary "racial" segregation with constitutional protection meant that in the future its removal would be more difficult. Strong external influences as well as organized internal pressures would likely be required.

Consequently, around the mid-1940s members of the Central Jurisdiction Organization—and their committed *anti-segregationist* friends throughout The Methodist Church—began, as Thomas (1992) described the process, to "look upon the social institutions in the wider society as the norms for church life." Hedgeman (1964) and White (1955) expressed similar viewpoints.

## 1. Early Signs of External Hostility

Throughout the United States during the existence of the Central Jurisdiction Organization, there were Blacks outside The Methodist Church who held important local, state and national leadership positions—in business and professional associations, in fraternities and sororities, in civic clubs, and in civil rights organizations. Most of these Blacks were opposed to all forms of involuntary "racial" segregation. Generally, they harbored hostile feelings toward The Methodist Church because of the Central Jurisdiction Organization.

Occasionally prominent Blacks not associated with The Methodist Church expressed public hostility toward the existence of the Central Jurisdiction Organization. Thus, in 1940 the *Chicago Defender* reported that an Urban League executive had stated publicly that the creation of the Central Jurisdiction Organization marked The Methodist Church as "the most reactionary Protestant group so far as segregation is concerned."

The most influential civil rights publication, *Crisis Magazine*, carried a caustic editorial in one of its issues. Excerpts from it are included below.

> **We hope God has the Methodist in mind and that He will give compassionate attention to their special needs. They separated a hundred years ago over slavery. Now they have got together again with old wounds fairly well healed, and with the persistent black man roped off into a separate conference where he will be happy riding to Glory on a sort of Jim Crow train. We trust that if heaven is truly one great unsegregated family, God will not induct the American Methodists in too great numbers, or too rapidly, into a society that would shock them, perhaps, beyond hope of salvation. *(Crisis Magazine*, June 1939.)**

The first time I read this *Crisis Magazine* editorial was in October 1940. I was a freshman student at Wiley College, an institution established historically for Blacks. My social science teacher, Professor A. P. Watson, had included that editorial in a list of assigned readings. In class, Professor Watson had us to discuss whether we believed heaven would be segregated on the basis of "race" and color. I was then eighteen years old, and had been a Methodist for five years.

Methodist Unification apparently meant very little to Professor Watson; however, as an intellectually gifted professor in "racially" segregated Marshall, Texas, "Jim Crow" (an epithet for *"racial" segregation*) had a lot of meaning for him.

Over the next few years, articles similar to the *Crisis Magazine* editorial appeared in the *Chicago Defender*, the *Pittsburgh Courier*, and the *Houston*

*Informer*. These were among the most influential weekly newspapers that Blacks owned and published.

I remember another Wiley College professor—Dr. J. L. Farmer, father of the famous civil rights leader James Farmer—reading to his class in religion and philosophy a particular article in the *Pittsburgh Courier*. The writer of the article excoriated Albert C. Knudson, dean of Boston University School of Theology, for attempting *theologically* to justify segregation in The Methodist Church.

## II. Norm-Changing Events At The Borders Of The Methodist Church

The principle is well established in contemporary organization theory that when an organization faces paradigm shifts or other fundamental changes in the external environment in which it is embedded the organization will, over time, have to make adjustments in its own internal life. Otherwise, the organization is likely to become irrelevant.

Stimulated partly (1) by dynamics of the New Deal/Fair Deal administrations in the United States of America, (2) by revelations of Hitler's barbarism, (3) by economic and social pressures of war mobilization and the aftermath of war, (4) by the increasingly effective activism of the NAACP and the National Urban League, (5) by the aggressiveness of the United Nations' Commission on Human Rights, and (6) by the social-justice demands of newly independent Third World nations—by the end of the 1940s new patterns of inter-ethnic relationships were emerging at the external borders of The Methodist Church.

In 1960, the Central Jurisdiction Organization still had *value* for some special interest groups within The Methodist Church. But events were rapidly occurring at the borders of the Church that clearly indicated the *disvalue*, for the denomination as a whole, of that "racially" segregated institution. Brief comments on selected events follow.

### A. Myrdal's "An American Dilemma"

In 1944 the Swedish economist/sociologist Gunnar Myrdal published his voluminous two-volume study of relations between Blacks and Whites in the United States, which he termed **An American Dilemma.** According to Myrdal, the dilemma was both moral and political—in the form of an enormous gap between America's proclaimed self-image as a democratic and Christian society and the actual behavior of Americans with respect to "race" relations. It is appropriate to note here that the subtitle of Myrdal's book is "*The Negro Problem and Modern Democracy.*"

Myrdal's book was a milestone in its analysis of the breadth and effect of "racial" segregation in America. Its very size, range, and completeness made its findings seem almost inarguable. Written with the aid of a task force of widely acknowledged scholars and researchers, including Ralph Bunche, Otto Klineberg, Melvin Herskovits, Howard Odum, and Guy Johnson, Myrdal's indictment of the race problem was so comprehensive that it became the principal frame of reference for almost all literature in the field.

The Myrdal book said things "with a dispassionate directness that demanded attention"(Kluger, 1976, p. 313). It was virtually impossible for dominant leaders of The Methodist Church to be impervious to the *dispassionate directness* with which **An American Dilemma** condemned involuntary "racial" segregation in all major institutions in the United States.

## B. Changes in Public Policy

As the term is used in this book, *involuntary "racial" segregation* exists where legal, economic, or social sanctions are employed to effect and enforce separation of individuals on the basis of "race"/color. We view the existence of the Central Jurisdiction Organization in The Methodist Church as an example of such separation.

Wherever one finds involuntary "racial" segregation, its presence is tolerated, if not directly supported, by public policy. Consequently, changes in the substance or orientation of public policy have implications for any regime of involuntary "racial" segregation. Here we comment on several public policy change-events, at the borders of The Methodist Church, which had implications for the continued existence of the Central Jurisdiction Organization.

### *1. War Mobilization Policy*

For over a decade prior to World War II national, state and local leaders of Blacks had been engaged in campaigns to obtain full exercise of rights guaranteed by the Constitution of the United States of America. As the nation prepared for and became actively involved in war, the intensity of these campaigns increased. Added impetus came from the fact that the United States was engaged in a war against the Nazis and Japanese, who were exponents of theories of "racial" superiority.

Blacks and many Whites insisted that the best way to prove American sincerity on the subject of "racial" equality was to eliminate segregation of and discrimination against Blacks. In other words, "racial" segregation at home could not be squared with the fight against intolerance overseas.[1] This aggressive and expanding campaign for a "full measure of freedom" produced some repercussions. Especially in the South a negative reaction set in against the determined attempt to change the status of Blacks.

***(a) Fair Employment Practice Policy***. As the war mobilization effort got under way, Blacks protested their exclusion from new war-related employment opportunities. In 1941, the NAACP, the National Urban League, the National Council of Negro Women, and the Brotherhood of Sleeping Car Porters threatened to bring 250,000 Blacks to Washington, DC to demonstrate against congressional resistance to the establishment of a national policy of fair employment. The threat prompted President Roosevelt to issue Executive Order 8802 creating the Fair Employment Practices Committee (FEPC). The order declared "there shall be no discrimination in the employment of workers in defense industries or government because of race, creed, color, or national origin."

By 1943 there was abundant evidence that in defense industries employers had hired Blacks mostly for menial jobs. Reluctant defense industry employers refused to comply with Executive Order 8802, arguing that if Blacks were hired as janitors, the employers had "integrated" their workforce. In 1943, after learning about how some employers were violating the spirit of the new order, President Roosevelt strengthened the FEPC. He increased its budget and replaced the part-time Washington, DC staff with a professional full-time staff distributed throughout the country.

***(b) Military Service Policy.*** In April 1942, the navy announced that it was opening combat units for Blacks. Prior to that time, Blacks had been accepted for noncombatant services only. The following month the U. S. Marine Corps also announced the formation of combat units consisting of Blacks. Earlier that year the army revealed that it was forming a new infantry division and a second pursuit squadron consisting of Blacks. However, the formation of "racially" separate units incurred the protest of several civil rights groups who wanted Blacks and Whites to serve side by side in the same units.

### 2. *Policy of Truman Presidency*

In terms of potential impact on The Methodist Church, with respect to its "racially segregated" Central Jurisdiction Organization, the public policy of the Truman presidency was unsurpassed.

Upon the death of President Roosevelt in April 1945 Harry Truman became President. Within two years he began to articulate his vision of new norms for America regarding inter-ethnic relations.

***(a) Commission on Civil Rights.*** In December 1946 Truman appointed a distinguished panel to serve as the President's Commission on Civil Rights. The Commission issued its report, ***To Secure These Rights***, in October 1947. That report defined the Nation's civil rights agenda for the next generation.

***(b) NAACP Civil Rights Address.*** Speaking at the Thirty-eighth Annual Conference of the NAACP in June of 1947, Truman provided the delegates a glimpse of the future *"civil rights and human freedom"* policy of his presidency. His address included the following statements:

> **It is my deep conviction that we have reached a turning point in the long history of our efforts to guarantee freedom and equality to all our citizens... And when I say all Americans—I mean all Americans...**
>
> **We can no longer afford the luxury of a leisurely attack upon prejudice and discrimination. There is much that state and local governments can do in providing positive safeguards for civil rights. But we cannot any longer await the growth of a will to action in the slowest state or the most backward community. Our national government must show the way.**

***(c) Congressional Civil Rights Message.*** In February 1948, President Truman did something no previous President had ever done: he sent to Congress a special message on civil rights. In it he recommended legislation that would:

1. Establish a permanent Commission on Civil Rights, a Joint Congressional Committee on Civil Rights, and a Civil Rights Division in the Department of Justice.

2. Strengthen existing civil rights statutes.

3. Provide Federal protection against lynching.

4. Protect more adequately the right to vote.

5. Establish a Fair Employment Practice Commission to prevent discrimination in employment.

6. Prohibit discrimination in interstate transportation facilities.

7. Provide home-rule and suffrage in Presidential elections for the residents of the District of Columbia.

***(d) Eliminating "Racial" Segregation in Military Services.*** In July 1948 President Truman issued Executive Order 9981. The order established a policy of bringing to an end "racial" segregation within the ranks of the United States military forces. Executive Order 9981 addressed four areas:

1. It declared the President's policy of equality of opportunity for all persons in the armed services without regard to "race," color, religion, or national origin.

2. It created a Presidential seven-member Committee on Equality of Treatment in the Armed Services.

3. It authorized the Committee to examine existing rules and determine what changes would be necessary to carry out the policy of integrating the services.

4. It directed all executive departments and agencies of the Federal Government to cooperate with the Committee in its work.

I must note here that Truman's bold decisions and actions during that period were unprecedented examples of real "profiles in courage." They were taken in a year in which Truman had to fight for the Democratic presidential nomination, and wage a four-way race for the presidency. Henry A. Wallace (on the "left") and J. Strom Thurmond (on the "right") had bolted the Democratic Party to form their own candidacies.

### 3. Policy of Johnson Presidency

Early in 1963 President John F. Kennedy sent to Congress a proposal for a new civil rights bill. Later that year, in a television speech, he urged the members of Congress to act without further delay. The President declared boldly:

> **We preach freedom around the world, and we mean it. And we cherish our freedom here at home. But are we to say to the world—and much more importantly to each other—that this is the land of the free, *except for the Negroes*; that we have no second-class citizens, *except Negroes*; that we have no class or cast system, no ghettos, no master race, *except with respect to Negroes*.** (Emphasis added.)

President Kennedy was assassinated in November 1963. Lyndon B. Johnson became the new President. Although as a member of Congress he had a poor record on civil rights issues, President Johnson forcefully took up the cause on behalf of new civil rights legislation. On November 27, 1963, addressing the Congress and the Nation for the first time as President, Johnson called for passage of the civil rights bill as a monument to the fallen Kennedy. He said: "[T]he ideas and ideals which [Kennedy] so nobly represented must and will be translated into effective action." Using his considerable influence with Congress, President Johnson was able to get the "Kennedy" legislative proposals enacted—as the Civil Rights Act of 1964. The Act—

- Prohibited "racial" discrimination in public places, such as theaters, restaurants and hotels.

- Required employers to provide equal employment opportunities.

- Authorized the withdrawal of federal funds for projects where there was evidence of discrimination based on color, "race" or national origin.

- Authorized the U. S. Attorney General to initiate legal action in any area where there was a finding of a pattern of resistance to the law.

For some time prior to 1965 efforts had been under way to end state disenfranchisement of Blacks. The murder of voting-rights activists in Philadelphia, Mississippi, along with other acts of violence and terrorism, gained national attention. And the March 7, 1965 unprovoked attack by state troopers on peaceful marchers en route to the state capitol of Alabama influenced President Johnson to issue a call for a strong voting rights law. In a voting rights policy speech on March 15, 1965, he stated:

> **Every American Citizen must have an equal right to vote. Yet the harsh fact is that in many places in this country, men and women are kept from voting simply because they are Negroes. Every device of which human ingenuity is capable has been used to deny this right... This bill [proposed Voting Rights Act] will strike down restrictions to voting in all elections—federal, state, and local—which have been used to deny Negroes the right to vote.**

With the strong support of the White House and civil rights groups throughout the nation, the Congress was persuaded to pass the Voting Rights Act of 1965. President Johnson signed it into law on August 6, 1965.

### C. Precedent-Setting Supreme Court Decisions

The massive governmentally enforced (hence *involuntary*) "racial" segregation in the United States of America was constitutionally grounded in the Supreme Court's 1896 *Plessy v. Ferguson* decision. That decision declared that state Jim Crow laws did not violate the "equal protection" principles of the U. S. Constitution as long as "racially" separate facilities and services were equal. This was the so-called "separate but equal" legal rule, which governed state-regulated relations between Blacks and Whites in large areas of the nation.

During the period that the "racially" segregated Central Jurisdiction organization of The Methodist Church was in existence, several important decisions of the Supreme Court began to cast doubt on the presumed *correctness* of the separate-but-equal judicial norm. From the perspective of the legitimacy of involuntary "racial" segregation in The Methodist Church, the most important of these post-*Plessy* decisions included the following:

- *Smith v. Allright* (1944). In this decision the Supreme Court struck down the exclusion of Blacks from participation in the "White" primary system of nominating candidates for public office in a number of the southern states.

- *Morgan v. Virginia* (1946). The significance of this decision is that it declared state laws mandating "racial" segregation in transportation could not apply to *interstate* travel.

- *Shelly v. Kraemer* (1948). This decision said that Blacks in this country have a constitutional right to equal access to housing opportunities. Specifically, the Supreme Court ruled that "racially" restrictive covenants in real estate deeds may not be enforced by governments.

- *Sweatt v. Painter* (1950). This case involved Texas' refusal to admit Herman Marian Sweatt to the stated-supported University of Texas Law School. Sweatt refused to apply to the hastily established "racially" segregated law school for Blacks at Texas State University for Negroes, arguing that it was not equal to the University of Texas Law School. The Supreme Court agreed and ordered the University of Texas Law School to admit Sweatt. A very important aspect of the Court's decision pertains to the "intangible" as well as the tangible factors cited in reaching a finding of inequality. For example, the Court said,

  **"...the University of Texas Law School possesses to a far greater degree those qualities which are incapable of objective measurement but which make for greatness in a law school. Such qualities, to name but a few, in_hase reputation of the faculty, experience of the administration, position and influence of alumni, standing in the community, traditions and prestige... The law school to which Texas is willing to admit [Sweatt] excludes from its student body members of the racial groups which number 85% of the population of the State and include most of the lawyers, witnesses, jurors, judges and other officials with whom [Sweatt] will inevitably be dealing when he**

**becomes a member of the Texas bar. With such a substantial and significant segment of society excluded, we cannot conclude that the education offered [Sweatt at Texas State University for Negroes] is substantially equal to that which he would receive if admitted to the University of Texas Law School"**

- *Brown v. Board of Education* (1954). The landmark decision in this case overturned the ruling in the 1896 *Plessy v. Ferguson* case. In other words, the Supreme Court abandoned the so-called "separate but equal" rule, declaring that it should no longer be considered *constitutionally correct.* Governmentally mandated involuntary "racial" segregation is inherently unconstitutional.

### D. Civil Rights Movement

The 1950s and early 1960s produced and sustained an aggressive civil rights movement in the United States of America. The movement was directed by such prestigious organizations as the Student Non-Violent Coordinating Committee, the Southern Christian Leadership Conference, the National Council of Negro Women, the National Urban League, the Leadership Conference on Civil Rights, and the National Association for the Advancement of Colored People.

The leaders of the civil rights movement were prominent Blacks who had experienced the most blatant forms of "racial" segregation and discrimination in America. Their ultimate goal was to achieve a truly *integrated* American society. However, their immediate objective was to eliminate *involuntary* "racial" segregation from the major institutions of this nation. The strategies and tactics of the movement included demonstrations, public policy advocacy, litigation and moral persuasion.

The most dramatic examples of the movement's strategies and tactics, perhaps, were the student sit-in demonstrations, the "freedom rides," the Montgomery bus boycott, the March on Washington in 1963, the litigation that produced a Supreme Court renunciation of the *Plessy v. Ferguson* "separate but equal" doctrine, and the moral appeal of Martin Luther King, Jr. in his famous *Letter from a Birmingham Jail.* The civil rights movement played an invaluable role in causing the fundamental changes in public policy discussed earlier in this chapter.

## CONCLUDING SUMMARY

Over fifty years ago a group of courageous public sector leaders—spearheaded by Eleanor Roosevelt and Presidents Harry Truman, John Kennedy and Lyndon Johnson—set for this nation a great but complex and difficult goal: **To rid itself of a century-old system of *racist* discrimination against and governmentally-sanctioned "racial" segregation of Blacks.**

Through concerted and persistent efforts of these leaders, encouraged, cajoled and supported by a determined and disciplined civil rights movement, by the mid-1960s far-reaching changes in *inter-ethnic* public policy had been achieved throughout the United States. The secular domains of American society were far more democratic and egalitarian than they had ever been since the end of slavery.

To be sure, many critical "human rights" battles remained to be waged, and some intricate institutional barriers to a full measure of freedom for Blacks posed new challenges for the future. Nevertheless, evidences of the new norms and patterns of inter-ethnic relationships were manifest in many secular domains—in sports, in participation in political affairs and public service, in executive level employment in business and industry, in the professions, and in the public policy of several states, to name but a few.

By 1960, profound changes had already taken place, and others were beginning to occur, at what I have alluded to as the "external borders" of The Methodist Church. That denomination maintained within its own polity a glaring symbol and system of involuntary "racial" segregation—the Central Jurisdiction Organization.

Apart from the immorality involved, the Central Jurisdiction Organization represented a governance regime of involuntary "racial" segregation, in an enormously powerful denomination—in stark contradiction to the democratic ideals and egalitarian principles that had fundamentally changed the orientation and direction of public policy in the secular domains of American society.

The chapters that follow will show how the decision of the 1960 quadrennial session of The Methodist Church's legislative body to "undertake no basic change" in the Central Jurisdiction Organization precipitated an organized and well-coordinated *civil rights movement* within The Methodist Church. That movement was effective in putting pressure on the new Commission on Interjurisdictional Relations, which the legislative body created for the 1960-1964 quadrennium.

That group of thirty-six individuals, which became popularly known as the Commission of Thirty-Six, was given the task of coordinating and directing educational and related activities throughout the denomination—as part of **"the continuing program of The Methodist Church to abolish the Central Jurisdiction, promote interracial brotherhood through Christian love, and achieve a more inclusive church."** (See *Book of Discipline*, 1960 Edition, Paragraph 2013.)

In 1960 the failure of the denomination's legislative body to take decisive steps to end the Central Jurisdiction Organization had a profound impact on the attitudes and thinking of the clergy, lay and episcopal leaders of the Central Jurisdiction Organization.

**Those leaders decided that the time had come for Blacks "to take charge" of the movement to purge The Methodist Church of structures, institutions, programs, and processes based on "race!"**

They persuaded the delegates to the 1960 quadrennial meeting of the Central Jurisdiction Organization to establish an ad hoc agency—the **Committee of Five**—to plan and implement *civil rights* strategies to eliminate involuntary "racial" segregation from The Methodist Church.

Chapters 5, 6, 7, 8, 9, 10 and 11 of this book document, analyze, discuss and assess important decisions and actions of that Committee's members and other leaders of the Central Jurisdiction Organization—from July 1960 through the fall of 1968.

The author was privileged to have a unique opportunity to play pivotal roles in the key decisions and actions involved in the "anti-segregation" reform movements within The Methodist Church during that period. Consequently, an autobiographical flavor pervades much of the discussions of the next seven chapters. In these chapters I attempt to explain, from my perspectives and values, the impact of many dramatic events in arenas where I appeared on stage in "leading actor" roles.

## Chapter Notes

1. According to Singh (2004, pp. 103-104), "The great promise of World War II)...was that black aspirations for justice and the interests of American world-ordering power would coincide...the global rationale for fighting World War II upped the ante of the promise of American universalism in ways that had unprecedented implications for blacks in the U.S."

# CHAPTER 5

## 1960: The Year The Methodist Church Failed to Cross the Rubicon

The General Conference Organization convened in Denver, Colorado in the spring of 1960 for its quadrennial meeting There were clear signals and credible supporting evidence of a dramatic shift in public policy in the United States of America—with respect to an orientation toward civil rights and basic human freedoms, both in this Nation and around the world.

The United States Supreme Court had provided a new juridical foundation for this public policy shift:

- **Sixteen years before the 1960 meeting of the denominational legislature the Court had ended the exclusion of Blacks from participation in southern primary elections (*Smith v. Allright*).**

- **Fourteen years before the 1960 convening of the denominational legislature the Supreme Court had opened up interstate travel to Blacks on a non-segregated basis (*Morgan v. Virginia*).**

- **Twelve years prior to the beginning of the 1960 session of the denominational legislature the Supreme Court had guaranteed to Blacks equal access to housing opportunities by invalidating government enforcement of restricted covenants (*Shelly v. Kraemer*).**

- **Ten years before the 1960 session of the denominational legislature began the Supreme Court had ordered the admission of Blacks to southern law schools on a non-segregated basis (*Sweatt v. Painter*). The Court recognized the critical role of "intangibles" in legal education.**

- **Six years before the 1960 session of the denominational legislature opened the Supreme Court had jettisoned the notorious juridical doctrine of "separate but equal"(*Brown v. Board of Education*).**

- **In 1948 (twelve years before the beginning of the 1960 session of the denominational legislative body), thanks to the undaunted leadership of Eleanor Roosevelt, the General Assembly of the United Nations adopted a Universal Declaration of Human Rights that articulated norms applicable to inter-ethnic relationships in the United States of America.**

One researcher for the Gunnar Myrdal study of **An American Dilemma** noted the tendency in America for the Protestant churches not to lead the broader society with respect to determining *operative* norms that govern relationships between Blacks and Whites. Conversely, mainline Protestant churches quite often follow the patterns set by secular institutions.

In the case of the "racially" segregated Central Jurisdiction Organization of The Methodist Church, the members of the denomination's legislative body, at its 1960 quadrennial session, had an opportunity to figuratively "cross the Rubicon."

They could have taken bold legislative actions to bring "race" relations practices of The Methodist Church into conformity with the new norms manifest in public policy.

*Unfortunately, the legislative body failed to rise to the occasion!*

## I. Commission of Seventy's "No Basic Change" Recommendation

In Chapter 3, we discussed in some detail the establishment in 1956 of the Commission of Seventy. That group was expected to recommend effective measures to remove involuntary "racial" segregation from the structures and institutions of The Methodist Church. The "racially" defined Central Jurisdiction Organization was, without doubt, the most visible symbol and system of involuntary "racial" separatism that existed at the time.

Concomitantly with the establishment of the Commission of Seventy in 1956, the Church's legislative body also enunciated and embraced a problematic concept of *voluntarism* for dealing with the economic, political and social power that had created the Central Jurisdiction Organization seventeen years earlier, and had ensured its existence since 1939.

The paradoxical nature of the denomination's "voluntarism" concept is revealed by the following fact: **It presumed that the *imposed*[1] system of apartheid in The Methodist Church polity would be changed fundamentally and in a timely manner by the *voluntary* actions of those**

**non-Blacks who were responsible for its creation, who had sustained it over the years, and who perceived some *value* in its continued existence.**

In its 1960 *Report*, the Commission of Seventy explained that it had devoted a lot of time and energy to studying the "problem" presented by the Central Jurisdiction Organization and its status within the polity of The Methodist Church. After consideration of "differences of opinion" at many points, the Commission members had agreed on the following recommendation:

> **That the 1960 General Conference [Organization] undertake no basic change in the Central Jurisdiction [Organization]. We urge that the [legislative body] take cognizance of the action of the 1956 [legislative body] in adopting Amendment IX...which we feel is *a definite beginning in the direction of the abolition of the Central Jurisdiction* [Organization], and any action by the 1960 General Conference [Organization] regarding the Central Jurisdiction [Organization] be *in the direction of the implementation of Amendment IX. Report*, p. 12.** (Emphasis added.)

### A. Power Dynamics of Amendment IX

Chapter 3 of this book explained that Amendment IX established a very complex process for accomplishing two types of *inter-organizational* transfers: (1) a **local church** and (2) an entire **annual conference component** of the Central Jurisdiction Organization. Both could be transferred into a geographical jurisdiction organization. Three stages of voting were involved and a two-thirds affirmative vote was required at each stage. (See section 2(a) of Chapter 3.)

In 1960, it was very troubling for active anti-segregationist members of The Methodist Church that the Commission would rely on Amendment IX as *the* primary instrument for eliminating involuntary "racial" segregation.[2] The fact was known that in 1956 some of the drafters and active proponents of Amendment IX had manifested a hidden or unspoken purpose. It was to make fundamental and positive change in *structured* inter-"racial" relationships in The Methodist Church very difficult, if not impossible, to achieve. The inclusion of a two-thirds voting requirement at all stages of the Amendment IX process was in pursuit of that purpose.

**The whole procedure allowed control of fundamental change to remain with groups in the denomination who had an interest, for whatever reason, in maintaining the status quo.**

As I discuss in more detail in the following chapter, this motivation was revealed very clearly when Blacks sought to use the Amendment IX process to prevent what I referred to then as the "Balkanization" of the Central Jurisdiction Organization. I was referring to a situation where the Central

Jurisdiction Organization would be dissolved in a manner that allowed distribution and maintenance intact of its "racially" segregated annual conference organizations as operating entities within the geographical jurisdiction organizations.

I helped some Central Jurisdiction Organization leaders to use Amendment IX to frustrate such Balkanization. Our use of Amendment IX procedures for that purpose was resisted by groups of Methodists in the Southeastern Jurisdiction Organization.[3]

The Commission of Seventy reported several of its *Findings* to the 1960 quadrennial meeting of the Church's legislative body. The pertinent parts of one "Finding" are stated as follows:

> ***To legislate the immediate elimination of the Central Jurisdiction would be harmful to the Church, and especially disastrous to the Negro Methodists.*** **Many life-long members of The Methodist Church would be without full fellowship in a local church or Annual Conference... in large sections of our Methodist Church, Negro Methodists would be left without opportunity to be included in interracial churches and interracial conferences. ...We are agreed in this report that the Church cannot now abolish the racial jurisdiction. Drastic legislation will not accomplish the fully inclusive Church we all desire.** ***Report.*** **P. 22.** (Emphasis added.)

Most of the Central Jurisdiction Organization's delegates to the 1960 quadrennial meeting of the Church's legislative body either strongly disagreed with this finding or had serious misgivings regarding the validity of its *assumptions* and *premises*. They were not aware of anyone in The Methodist Church who was so naïve as to believe that it was legally possible "To legislate the immediate elimination of the Central Jurisdiction." That idea was simply a "straw person" created disingenuously by the Commission.

More serious, however, was the Commission's premise that legislative action would be powerless to prevent "Negro Methodists [from being] left without opportunity to be included in *interracial churches* and *interracial conferences*." (Emphases added.) This premise ignored the extra *moral power* and *sense of legitimacy* that would have flown from legislative actions of The Methodist Church designed to bring the body of its ecclesiastical law on "race" relations into closer harmony with the new norms of public policy. In 1960 there were changes that could have been made in the body of church law, as it existed then, which would have produced significant positive benefits for efforts to resolve what the Commission called "the Central Jurisdiction problem."[4]

## II. Decisions of the 1960 Session of The Legislative Body

When the 1960 quadrennial session of the Church's legislative body began, its basic approach to changing undesirable structures of relationships between Blacks and Whites in The Methodist Church may be described as *voluntary permissiveness*. That same stance was manifest at the close of the session.

The Commission of Seventy had stated, "Drastic legislation will not accomplish the fully inclusive Church we all desire. We must give ourselves to education and experimentation in the creating of a climate—spiritual and psychological—in which an inclusive Methodist Church will be a reality" (*Report*, p. 22). After extensive and wide-ranging discussions and debates, a majority of the delegates agreed with the Commission of Seventy.

### A. New Commission Created

To coordinate and direct educational and related activities aimed at fostering a more favorable climate for creating "an inclusive Methodist Church," the 1960 session of the legislative body established a **Commission on Interjurisdictional Relations**. Composed of thirty-six members, the group became popularly referred to as the "*Commission of Thirty-Six.*" [5]

### B. Critical Issues Surfaced

***1. Transferring entities into the Central Jurisdiction Organization.*** The Commission of Seventy's *Report* contained a statement with far-reaching implications that had not been seriously examined before. The *Report* stated (p. 12):

> **It should be noted that Amendment IX makes possible transfers of churches or conferences into the Central Jurisdiction [Organization] where circumstances make this an advisable change. *A substantial number of such transfers would result in a Central Jurisdiction [Organization] that is racially inclusive.*** (Emphasis added.)

This notion was reflected in the mandate of the new Commission of Thirty-Six, as implied in Paragraph 2(d) of the statement of its "responsibilities and authority." During the discussion of this matter in a plenary session at the 1960 meeting of the Church's legislative body, an issue was raised concerning the legality of the following:

> **An entire annual conference organization of the Central Jurisdiction Organization, or of a geographical jurisdiction**

> **organization transferring into another entity in which it *is not geographically located.***

On April 29, 1960, the legislative body petitioned the Judicial Council for a ruling on the constitutionality of such a transfer. The ruling of the Judicial Council was as follows:

> **An Annual Conference [organization] may be transferred from one Jurisdiction [organization] into another...*without regard to the geographical boundaries of the Jurisdictions involved*, and such procedure under...Amendment IX is constitutional.** *Decision No. 169* (May 2, 1960). Emphasis added.

In Chapter 3 we noted Thelma Stevens' 1956 criticism of Amendment IX as a procedural device *whose primary purpose was to serve as an instrument for moving The Methodist Church away from "the most visible national expression of racism" in its polity.* As the Church's legislative body debated at length what should be done, either to facilitate or require Amendment IX transfers, the stark fact became obvious that Thelma Stevens's 1956 assessment was correct.

The ruling of the Judicial Council in Decision No. 169 meant that it would be constitutionally proper for The Methodist Church to get rid of "the most visible national expression of racism" by a process of Balkanization of the Central Jurisdiction Organization—through the use of Amendment IX procedures.

Chapter 4 elaborated upon the fact that The Methodist Church was "in the public eye" partly because its polity included the "racially" segregated Central Jurisdiction Organization. For an increasing number of denominational leaders, both in the United States of America and overseas, that was a painful embarrassment. For some of them it would have been a temporary palliative, at least, if they could have said, "the Central Jurisdiction Organization is 'racially' inclusive."

It should be noted that the Commission of Seventy apparently perceived no paradox or moral dilemma in the fact that a "racially" segregated Central Jurisdiction Organization was relied on to assure what the Commission described as "racial integration in the highest echelons of our Church—in the Council of Bishops, in the Judicial Council and in all boards, commissions and committees of the Church" (*Report*, p. 10). That Commission proudly boasted, "There is no other denomination in America where this degree of racial integration in the governing bodies of the Church has been achieved" (*Ibid.*).

This is a disingenuous comment by the Commission. The Central Jurisdiction Organization as well as the five geographical jurisdiction organizations had a right to have representation "in the Council of Bishops, in the Judicial Council and in all boards, commissions and committees [at the denominational level] of the Church." Blacks from the Central Jurisdiction Organization were representatives on these "governing bodies of the Church." They ensured the "degree of racial integration" that the Commission proudly referred to.

2. ***What are the limits of "voluntary" action within a fellowship of believers in Christ?*** In all of the debates on "the Central Jurisdiction problem" at the 1960 meeting of the Church's legislative body, the principle of *voluntarism* was strongly advocated and defended. The point was emphasized again and again that in The Methodist Church the existent patterns of relations between Blacks and Whites were the result of voluntary mutual agreement.

Unfortunately, the critical issue of the limits of voluntary behavior within the parameters of a *fellowship* of "believers in Christ" was not prominently highlighted and given the examination that its importance deserved.

**What kinds of voluntary action are inherently incompatible with the fundamental nature of any fellowship of "believers in Christ?"**

My understanding of the New Testament standards affirmed by major denominations is that these standards proscribe all *voluntary* interactions among communicants that are based on considerations of "race" and color. In 1960, many Methodists, including both Blacks and Whites, shared this understanding of New Testament standards.

Surprisingly, debates and discussions at the 1960 meeting of the Church's legislative body did reveal a promising sign. An increasing number of people throughout "the connection" were becoming aware for the first time that "the Central Jurisdiction problem" involved a great deal more than simply abolishing a large—and constitutionally prescribed—"racially" defined organizational *structure*.

Eliminating the Central Jurisdiction Organization posed another critical issue for the legislative body. It was fundamentally a moral question: Should the legislative body amend the existing body of Church law to include *ecclesiastical rules stating that for Methodist communicants, acting within the bounds of The Methodist Church fellowship, voluntary behavior of any kind based on "race" or color was totally unacceptable?*

In 1960, if the legislative body had answered that question affirmatively, then The Methodist Church would have crossed the Rubicon. Failure to do so meant waiting four years for another opportunity to ensure that the law of The Methodist Church governing relations between Blacks and Whites paralleled the emerging new norms of public policy in the United States of America.

## CONCLUDING SUMMARY

The fact that the 1960 session of The Methodist Church's legislative body did not act boldly and decisively, with respect to amending the body of church law so as to *prohibit* involuntary "racial" segregation, put Central Jurisdiction Organization leaders under enormous pressure. That pressure is evident in the following statement by Dr. James P. Brawley, then president of Clark College:

> **The climate, the temper, and the revolutionary character of the current general struggle for human dignity, and removal of every vestige of segregation and discrimination from our American life demand that the same reform be effected within the Church. The members of the Central Jurisdiction are not only in accord with this demand, but are a part of the struggle that undergirds this demand. *The Negro in The Methodist Church could not with prudence be a part of such a struggle for desegregation in the community life outside of the Church, and at the same time not favor or urge the same reform within the Church.* (Emphasis added.)**

Failure of The Methodist Church to cross the Rubicon at its 1960 quadrennial legislative meeting precipitated an unprecedented, organized and well-directed *civil rights* movement within the denomination. A "new breed" of Blacks in The Methodist Church provided leadership for this movement. Like the civil rights movement in the broader society, this newly energized denominational *anti-segregationist* movement had an immediate paramount goal: **To rid The Methodist Church of involuntary "racial" segregation.**

The Central Jurisdiction Organization's own leaders of this movement were able to creatively and skillfully exploit changes in inter-ethnic relations that had occurred in the secular society since the creation of The Methodist Church in 1939.

Their strategy involved methodically creating a set of circumstances in which the *disvalue* of the Central Jurisdiction Organization to The Methodist Church as a whole would far exceed the *value* of that "racially" segregated organization to denominational special interest groups.

The walls of The Methodist Church's Jericho (i.e., its constitutionally mandated "Jim Crow" or apartheid system) could not withstand our well organized and carefully directed assaults against them; they had to come "tumbling down."

The delegates to the 1960 quadrennial meeting of the Central Jurisdiction Organization established a special committee—the **Committee of Five**—to plan a denomination *civil rights* strategy and to lead a broad-scale, coordinated and sustained assault on the bastions of involuntary "racial" segregation in The Methodist Church. Chapter 6 discusses in detail the *foundational* work of that group.

## Chapter Notes

1. The Commission of Seventy indirectly acknowledged the "involuntary" nature of the Central Jurisdiction Organization by stating that it viewed appointment of the Commission as an indication of The Methodist Church's seriousness in "seeking a practical and fair method of doing away with *forced* segregation" (*Report*, p. 22). Emphasis added.

2. "Your Commission now feels that transfers should remain optional with the Annual Conferences rather than be forced by abolition of their jurisdiction" (*Report*, p. 10).

3. The mechanism that the author devised for Central Jurisdiction *sub*units to use was the insertion of an "Annual Conference merger or consolidation clause" in the proposed transfer agreement or contract. The Advisory Council on Interjurisdictional Affairs of the Southeastern Jurisdiction attacked such clause before the Judicial Council, contending that it was not legal under Amendment IX. In the following chapter I will discuss the cases that were involved and the decision of the Judicial Council.

4. In the following chapter I will discuss the twelve (12) specific changes in the body of church law that Central Jurisdiction leaders recommended to the 1960 quadrennial meeting of the denominational legislature.

5. The Commission was given the following duties and responsibilities:

   1. **The continuing program of The Methodist Church to abolish the Central Jurisdiction, promote interracial brotherhood through Christian love, and achieve a more inclusive church shall be entrusted to a quadrennial Commission on Interjurisdictional Relations. The General Conference of 1960 shall elect on nomination of the College of Bishops of each Jurisdiction a commission composed of the following representatives of each Jurisdiction: one bishop, two ministers, and three laymen. Officers shall be elected from the ministerial or lay membership.**

   2. **The responsibilities and authority of this commission shall be as follows:**

      a. **To study and recommend courses of action which shall implement the use of Amendment IX on all levels of church structure.**

b. To study the possibilities and problems inherent in the transfer of local churches, districts, Annual Conferences, and areas as provided in Amendment IX, and to give such information, guidance, and other assistance as may be possible and proper to those considering such transfer.

c. To make an immediate study of the reasons for reluctance to make use of Amendment IX, where such reluctance exists, and to bring together responsible churchmen, ministerial and lay, to expedite action.

d. Where such transfers cannot be made in either direction at present, to recommend the immediate development of a long-range program designed to create better understanding of mutual problems.

e. To give special attention and study to such matters as may impede the speedy implementation of Amendment IX, including the adjustment of ministerial requirements, pension and apportionment differentials, minimum support, church extension, and ministerial itinerancy.

f. To make progress reports to the Council of Bishops, and to the church through the church press.

g. To present an inclusive report to the General Conference of 1964 containing findings and recommendations which shall be printed and distributed to the delegates at least three months prior to the convening of the conference.

h. To work closely with the General, Jurisdictional, and Annual Conference Boards of Christian Social Concerns, with the Department of Christian Social Relations of the Woman's Division of Christian Service, and with all other agencies having information and facilities for expediting the use of Amendment IX and for promoting interracial brotherhood and Christian love.

3. The Commission shall consider the duly elected representatives of each jurisdiction on its membership as jurisdictional commissions, and delegate them such responsibilities as may properly and expeditiously be fulfilled by them.

4. **The general commission shall make specific delegation of responsibilities wherever possible, on local, district, conference, and area levels of church structure:**

   a. **In cooperation with existing agencies to formulate and promote programs of education and courses of action to develop greater interracial understanding and brotherhood on all levels of church life.**

   b. **To study the policies, programs, and activities of the church, its agencies, and related institutions with respect to the practices of interracial brotherhood.**

   c. **To assist church extension through the establishment, wherever possible, of preaching places, and the organization of new congregations characterized by interracial brotherhood.**

5. **The Commission shall be given adequate financing to carry out fully and efficiently the responsibilities assigned to it.**

6. The Commission shall meet before the conclusion of the 1960 General Conference.

# CHAPTER 6
# The Committee of Five: Building A Foundation

In 1940, when Bishops of Central Jurisdiction Organization organized that "racially" defined structure of The Methodist Church's polity, they expressed a **"hope [that] in the near future our Methodism may become sufficiently Christian in character and maturity to find a more excellent way"** (Kirk, 1963, p.1). (Emphasis added.)

It took twenty-eight years for "a more excellent way" to be realized—that is, for the Central Jurisdiction Organization to be eliminated and for a denominational polity free of *involuntary "racial" structures* to come into existence.

The Central Jurisdiction Organization's own Committee of Five was primarily responsible for making this event, in apt biblical phraseology, "come to pass."

The 1960 quadrennial meeting of the Central Jurisdiction Organization was held in Cleveland, Ohio in July 1960. That was just two months after the adjournment of the Church's legislative body.

I was a delegate to the 1960 meeting of the Central Jurisdiction Organization. It was my first time attending such a meeting.

Those individuals who had served as delegates to the recent quadrennial session of the Church's legislative body expressed a lot of disappointment, discontentment, frustration and resentment. They deplored that body's decision to **"undertake no basic change"** in the *law* of The Methodist Church with respect to eliminating involuntary "racial" segregation in the Church, especially the segregated Central Jurisdiction Organization. Several of these individuals had served on the Commission of Seventy. They expressed their concern regarding the general lack of understanding of their former colleagues on the Commission of Seventy that the primary interest of Blacks was the elimination of what the Commission finally acknowledged as "forced segregation" (*Report*, p. 22).

In organizing the 1960 meeting, the delegates established an Ad Hoc Committee on eliminating the Central Jurisdiction Organization. This

Committee was composed of Dr. James P. Brawley (Chairman), Attorney Richard C. Erwin, Mrs. Louis R. Fields, Reverend Dennis R. Fletcher, Mrs. Martin L. Harvey, Reverend C. M. Luster, Dr. John T. King, and Dr. Richard V. Moore. All petitions, resolutions and reports dealing with the matter of abolishing the Central Jurisdiction Organization were directed to the Ad Hoc Committee for analysis and study.

In a plenary session of the conference, during the process of establishing the Ad Hoc Committee, there was free-flowing, unfocused discussion of "the Central Jurisdiction problem." The delegates, including myself, recognized that the Church's legislative body had established a denominational Commission on Interjurisdictional Relations ("*Commission of Thirty-Six*") with very broad responsibilities and authority.

We also knew that the six members of the Commission of Thirty-Six from the Central Jurisdiction Organization would constitute a jurisdictional sub-commission. But there was a general feeling that the sub-commission would not be free to explore a legislative option during the 1960-1964 quadrennium. It was part of a larger group that had rejected any consideration of changing the *body of law* of The Methodist Church. In any event, the Central Jurisdiction Organization needed its own study entity.

During the opening plenary session of the conference I made some notes pertaining to the nature and responsibilities of an appropriate study committee that the delegates might establish. At the conclusion of the plenary session, I discussed my ideas with Dr. James P. Brawley. He suggested that I draft a resolution for the consideration of the Ad Hoc Committee. My "draft" resolution is included in the book's **Appendix 2.**

After adding some procedural provisions and necessary funding authority to the document, the Ad Hoc Committee recommended the adoption of the resolution I proposed. As amended at a subsequent plenary session of the conference and adopted almost unanimously by the delegates, my resolution provided for a five-member Quadrennial Study Committee, the members of which were to be appointed by the College of Bishops "without regard to orders." The committee became popularly known as the *Committee of Five.*

## Part I. Organization and Preparation for Work

In the fall of 1960, the College of Bishops appointed the following persons to the Central Jurisdiction Study Committee ("*Committee of Five*"): Dr. James S. Thomas (now bishop, retired), Dr. W. Astor Kirk, Dr. John H. Graham, Reverend John J. Hicks, and Attorney Richard C. Erwin, Jr. The Committee of Five held its organizational meeting in January 1961. Committee member Thomas was selected as chairman. Although I was unable to attend the first meeting, I was chosen as secretary.

A letter to me from the chairman under date of February 8, 1961 indicated the range of discussions, decisions and related activities covered at the initial meeting of the Committee of Five on January 24, 1961. Dr. Thomas' letter indicated that the Committee "spent the entire day on January 24 trying to define our task, explore definitions, and determine our relationship with the Commission on Inter-Jurisdictional [Relations]."

The 1961 spring meetings of the Committee were devoted to a thorough review and analysis of (1) the far-reaching ramifications of "the Central Jurisdiction problem" and (2) the advantages and disadvantages of using Amendment IX as a tool to effectively address the problem. We had the good fortune of having Dr. James P. Brawley present at our meetings. He was a member of the Commission of Thirty-Six. His presence enabled the Committee to gain a perspective on the thinking and strategies of the Commission of Thirty-Six.

Dr. Brawley gave the Committee a copy of a 16-page paper he had presented to the Commission of Thirty-Six. The paper was entitled *The Central Jurisdiction: The Problem Stated* (hereafter referred to as the "1961 Brawley Paper"). It noted that for many Blacks in the Methodist Church the Central Jurisdiction Organization had long posed an agonizing dilemma.

> **The members of the Central Jurisdiction are caught in a dilemma—The two horns of the dilemma are: (1) the advantages of the structure of the Central Jurisdiction, which advantages are common in all six jurisdictions; and (2) the undesirable racial character of the Central Jurisdiction, which not only makes it a symbol of segregation, but in fact draws such lines of separation as to prohibit the relationships, associations and programs necessary for the realization of an inclusive Christian fellowship in the Methodist Church.** (*1961 Brawley Paper*, p. 3.)

The *1961 Brawley Paper* became an invaluable reference document for the Committee. It represented a forthright and scholarly analysis of the advantages and disadvantages, for Blacks in The Methodist Church, of the Central Jurisdiction Organization. That governance institution, Brawley pointed out, afforded some "distinct advantages" that were not only desirable but also "essential" at that point in time. They needed "to be retained and safeguarded so long as conditions for Negroes and attitudes toward them [were] so different from those exhibited toward other people of the Church." The "distinct" advantages included a "guarantee of representation at the policy and program making levels of the general church."

Brawley emphasized that the importance of such representation "does not rest in office holding and positions, as desirable as they are, but rather in the necessity of being a part of policy and program making bodies at the top levels where decisions are made and destinies are determined" *(1961 Brawley Paper*, p.4).

Brawley insisted that the "other side of the dilemma" must not be ignored or minimized. It consisted of the "recognized and admitted...symbol of segregation in The Methodist Church" that the Central Jurisdiction Organization represented. Moreover, that organization was "an obstruction to the achievement of the kind of Christian fellowship which the Church has declared to be its goal" *(ibid.)*.

As a Committee, we believed it was necessary early on for us to develop a strongly shared philosophy of how we should address the dilemma, as conceptualized by Dr. Brawley. After many hours of discussion, during long meeting sessions of the Committee in the spring of 1961, we agreed on an ultimate goal:

> Leaders of the Central Jurisdiction Organization should seek to achieve *"an inclusive Methodist fellowship at all levels of Church life"*!

We defined such a fellowship as one in which organizational structures, policy-making processes, administrative procedures, managerial practices, and program operations—at all levels of The Methodist Church—are free of differentiations or distinctions based on "race" or color.

A critical implication of this normative stance soon became clearly obvious. As a Committee, we should not embrace any strategy, plan or program for eliminating the Central Jurisdiction Organization that would prevent or unduly delay the achievement of an inclusive Methodist fellowship.

Or stated positively, the Committee should propose, endorse or support initiatives specifically designed to move The Methodist Church, in demonstrable ways and in a timely manner, toward realization of our goal of an inclusive fellowship.

### A. Considerations of Strategy and Tactic

With an agreement on an inclusive Methodist fellowship as the fundamental goal to be achieved, the Committee was in a position to turn its attention to crucial considerations of strategies and tactics.

The Committee recognized that a sound program of strategy and tactics to achieve the goal of transforming The Methodist Church into an inclusive fellowship had to be based on adequate and accurate empirical data. The Committee asked me to undertake three research efforts during the summer:

- To analyze the potentials of Amendment IX as a vehicle for eliminating the Central Jurisdiction organization in a desirable manner.

- To examine the *First Report and Recommendations* of the Commission of Thirty-Six. (In April 1961 the Commission of Thirty-Six issued a *First Report*, which included several recommendations regarding transferring annual conference organizations of the Central Jurisdiction Organizations into four of the five geographical jurisdiction organizations.)

- To develop an *organizational profile* of the Central Jurisdiction, both as an ecclesiastical body and a corporate entity.

The expectation behind this request was that I would be able to provide as much information as possible to guide the fall meetings of the Committee.

### *1. Potentials of Amendment IX*

In mid-June 1961 I transmitted to the Committee and to the College of Bishops of the Central Jurisdiction Organization a *Memorandum Analysis of the Provisions of Amendment IX Regarding Transfers of Annual Conferences* (hereafter referred to as "*1961 Amendment IX Analysis*"). Chapter 3 of this book includes an extensive discussion of the Amendment IX transfer procedures. Much of the material presented there was taken from the *1961 Amendment IX Analysis*, and I will not repeat that presentation here.

One of the important findings I reported in my *1961 Amendment IX Analysis* memorandum was that Amendment IX did not afford a basis for real optimism regarding its practicality as an effective instrument for realigning the jurisdictional structure of The Methodist Church, through the transfer of annual conference organizations from one jurisdiction to another. The Amendment IX transfer process was entirely too cumbersome and too complex.

A second, and more critical, finding was that "only *non-controversial* transfer proposals [had] any real chance of adoption." This was especially true where transfer proposals initiated by annual conference entities of the Central Jurisdiction Organization had to be voted on by Southeastern and South Central annual conference organizations. Moreover, it even appeared doubtful that a Delaware Annual Conference Organization transfer proposal involving substantial steps toward an *inclusive fellowship*—as the Committee defined "inclusiveness" for The Methodist Church—would be adopted at that time by the Northeastern annual conference organizations

The *First Report* of the Commission of Thirty-Six recommended an immediate transfer of the Delaware Annual Conference Organization into the Northeastern Jurisdiction Organization. There is a statement in the recommendation that probably supported my conclusion regarding *non-controversial* transfers. The Commission stated that its recommended transfers of Central Jurisdiction annual conference organizations "will be *voluntary and shall proceed at a schedule and in a manner dictated by the individual needs and desires* of the...units involved" (p. 1). (Emphasis added.)

For Blacks serving as ministers in The Methodist Church, "open itineracy" was clearly a necessary component of *an inclusive Methodist fellowship*. Yet in 1961, for example, it was doubtful that the "needs and desires" of Northeastern annual conference organizations would have coincided with *open itineracy* for clergy members of the Delaware Annual Conference Organization.

My *1961 Amendment IX Analysis* noted that Amendment IX provided a basis for Central Jurisdiction annual conference organizations "to take significant initial steps toward the abolition of the Central Jurisdiction [Organization], within a framework of *understandings, planning, timing, and programming* designed to enlarge the possibilities of achieving the desired goal of a Christian fellowship without regard to distinctions based on race and color." *Ibid.*, pp. 10-11. (Emphasis in the original.) The *1961 Amendment IX Analysis* concluded with the following recommendation to the Committee and to the College of Bishops of the Central Jurisdiction Organization:

> **A Central Jurisdiction [annual conference organization], or a group of such [organizations]...*desiring to transfer* into one or more of the regional [organizations], should formulate, after careful study and discussion, transfer resolutions expressing that desire. The resolutions should clearly set forth the *understandings, circumstances, and conditions* on the basis of which the transfer proposal is being made. This approach is essential in order that the other [annual conference organizations] of the Central Jurisdiction, and the [annual conference organizations] of the receiving [geographical jurisdiction organization], all of whom must vote to approve or disapprove the transfer resolutions, may have a clear understanding of what is actually being proposed. In other words, wherever an [annual *conference organization*] is transferred...under Amendment IX, the responsibilities, privileges, and obligations of all parties concerned should be definitely understood by them. *1961 Amendment IX Analysis*, p. 11.** (Emphasis in the original.)

### *2. First Report of the Commission of Thirty-Six*

In the preceding chapter I noted that although in 1960 the Church's legislative body failed to make any changes in ecclesiastical law governing inter-"racial" relations, it did create a new thirty-six member Commission on Interjurisdictional Relations. The mandate of that Commission is included in **Appendix 3**.

When the Commission of Thirty-Six met in the spring of 1961, high visibility and internationally prominent leaders of The Methodist Church had begun to feel self-conscious distress over the failure of the denomination to cross the Rubicon a year earlier. Among these dominant leaders were

- six Methodist Bishops,
- one university president,
- one college president,
- two deans of theological seminaries, and
- three nationally prominent corporate attorneys.

They were also members of the Commission of Thirty-Six. The existence of the "racially" segregated Central Jurisdiction Organization was a painful embarrassment to them—as they associated with their colleagues at conferences and meetings of such renowned organizations as the World Methodist Council, the National Council of Churches and the World Council of Churches.

The members of the Commission of Thirty-Six had become wary of having to apologize for an *apartheid* system within the constitutional framework of The Methodist Church. In their *First Report* they sought to hastily eliminate that system by Balkanizing it within four of the five geographical jurisdiction organizations. The seventeen *micro*-Central Jurisdiction Organizations distributed among four geographical jurisdiction organizations would not be as visible as the existing *macro*-Central Jurisdiction Organization, which stretched from New England to Florida, from the Great Lakes to the Gulf of Mexico, and from the East Coast to the Rockies.[1]

Immediately after mailing its *First Report* to the "Council of Bishops and the Annual Conferences of The Methodist Church," the Commission of Thirty-Six initiated a campaign to get the report's transfer recommendations adopted. Calling for *"no new legislation but urg[ing] that transfers be voluntary and under the provisions of [Amendment] IX,"* the Commission asked the Central Jurisdiction annual conference organizations and the annual conference organizations of the Northeastern, Southeastern, North Central, and South Central Jurisdiction Organizations to vote *"favorably"* on the transfer proposals. The Commission thought it possible that "the transfer of Bishop Love's Baltimore Area to Northeastern Jurisdiction [Organization] *could be accomplished before the end of 1962*" (*First Report*, Transmittal Letter. Emphasis added.)

Leaders of the Central Jurisdiction Organization sought counsel and guidance from the Committee of Five. The Committee asked me to examine the *First Report* of the Commission of Thirty-Six. I did so within three contexts:

- The unstated ecclesiastical policy involved.
- The "inclusive Methodist fellowship" standard of the Committee.
- The legal requirements of Amendment IX.

***(a) Ecclesiastical Policy.*** The transfer recommendations of the Commission of Thirty-Six encompassed an unstated ecclesiastical policy for The Methodist Church that I viewed as unwise and fundamentally immoral. The policy involved enlarging geographical jurisdiction organizations by including annual conference organizations with "racially" defined boundaries as well as annual conference organizations with geographically defined boundaries.

Chapter 3 of this book discussed the fact that in 1952 the Judicial Council (in Judicial Decision No. 85) gave constitutional legitimacy to an ethically suspect concept of "racial boundaries" of *annual conference organizations* of The Methodist Church. In Chapter 5 I noted that Judicial Decision No. 169 (1960), in effect, extended this concept by declaring: "An Annual Conference [Organization] may be transferred from one Jurisdiction [Organization] into another Jurisdiction [Organization] *without regard to the geographical boundaries of the Jurisdictions involved*, and such procedure under...Amendment IX is constitutional." (Emphasis added.)

A policy of extending the notorious "separate but equal" principle, which had been eliminated from American civil law seven years earlier, to geographical jurisdiction organizations of The Methodist Church might not offend the denomination's constitution. But that policy could hardly be judged morally or ethically correct.

The anomaly of the policy the Commission recommended is highlighted by the fact that (a) both the Northeastern and North Central Jurisdiction Organizations would have responsibilities for "racially" defined annual conference organizations situated geographically within the Southeastern Jurisdiction Organization and (b) the North Central Jurisdiction Organization would have responsibility for a "racially" defined annual conference organizations situated geographically within the Western Jurisdiction Organization.

After a careful reading of the text of the Commission of Thirty-Six's *First Report*, one of its unstated premises was clear to me. **The Commission was intentionally advocating a policy under which bishops serving in the Central Jurisdiction Organization would provide presidential and residential services only in the "racially" segregated *annual conference organizations transferred* into four geographical jurisdiction organizations of The Methodist Church.** I advised the Committee that I would not support such a policy.

**(b) "Inclusive Methodist Fellowship" Standard.** As explained earlier in this chapter, during its spring 1961 meetings the Committee had agreed on a clearly defined "inclusive Methodist fellowship" standard as a fundamental goal to be achieved in eliminating the Central Jurisdiction Organization. This Committee standard comprised the second context for my examination of the *First Report* of the Commission of Thirty-Six.

The Commission stated that its *First Report* provided for "*re-alignment of the Jurisdictions* by the merging of the present Jurisdictions with appropriate Episcopal Areas, Conferences, or other units of the present Central Jurisdiction [Organization]...*to form new and enhanced jurisdictional structures*" (p. 1). (Emphasis added.) I did not find any credible evidence in the Commission's *First Report* that might create a reasonable presumption that adoption and implementation of its transfer recommendations would move The Methodist Church substantially—in tangible ways and in a timely manner—toward a fellowship absent of considerations of "race" and color.

The "new and enhanced jurisdictional structures" the Commission proposed included no internal dynamics or built-in mechanisms to effect self-destruction of "racially" segregated *annual conference organizations* that would be newly established in four geographical jurisdiction organizations of The Methodist Church.

No new legislation was proposed. The operating premise was *voluntarism*. The "racially" defined annual conference organizations "within the re-constituted Jurisdictions" would not be eliminated until "*all Conference [organizations] affected are ready for this move*" (*First Report*, p. 2). (Emphasis added.)

In this connection, I reminded the Committee of Five and the College of Bishops that (a) eight of the sixteen Central Jurisdiction annual conference organizations, (b) 1,567 of its 2,843 local churches and (c) 174,363 of its 372,922 church members were located within the Southeastern Jurisdiction Organization. As I viewed the situation in 1961, it was certainly unreasonable to condition elimination of any new "racially" segregated components of the Southeastern Jurisdiction Organization upon a *voluntary process*—one that would "*proceed at a schedule and in a manner dictated by the individual needs and desires of [all the] units involved*" (*Ibid.* p. 1). (Emphasis added.)

**(c) Legal requirements of Amendment IX.** The *First Report* of the Commission of Thirty-Six was based on a flawed concept of Amendment IX provisions and requirements. The Commission assumed that it had set forth a valid *Annual Conference* transfer proposal to effect "re-alignment of the Jurisdictions by the merging of the present Jurisdictions with appropriate Episcopal Areas, Conferences, or other units of the present Central Jurisdiction [Organization], *as authorized by Amendment IX*, to form *new and enhanced Jurisdictional structures*" (p. 1). (Emphasis added.)

In the first place, Amendment IX did not directly or indirectly address "Episcopal Areas." Secondly, and more importantly, under Amendment IX the Commission of Thirty-Six had no authority to develop and submit a legally binding transfer proposal for a vote of annual conference organizations of the Central Jurisdiction Organization, or of geographical jurisdiction organizations.

I reported to the Committee of Five and to the Central Jurisdiction Organization's College of Bishops that, as I read Amendment IX, a valid Central Jurisdiction annual conference organization transfer resolution or proposition *must originate with the particular entity desiring to be transferred* to a geographical jurisdiction organization. The relevant provision of Amendment IX was as follows:

> **An Annual Conference may be transferred from one Jurisdiction to another upon approval by:... (a) *The Annual Conference desiring transfer*, by a two-thirds majority of those present and voting.** (Emphasis added.)

The Commission of Thirty-Six was not an "Annual Conference." It was not constitutionally competent to initiate formally a bona fide instrument under which annual conference organizations of the Central Jurisdiction Organization might be transferred to a geographical jurisdiction organization of The Methodist Church.

It was my view in 1961, and I so advised the Committee of Five and the Central Jurisdiction College of Bishops, that the "plan" the Commission proposed was merely a suggestion or recommendation. It had the useful advantage of serving as an alternative concept for study and discussion by the Council of Bishops, the six Colleges of Bishops, and the Northeastern, Southeastern, North Central, and South Central Jurisdiction Organizations. If the "plan" as a whole, or any portion of it, were to be judged as having sufficient merit to commend adoption, *initiation of the appropriate transfer resolution or other instrument* would have to come from one or more of the annual conference organizations of the Central Jurisdiction Organization.

On June 5, 1961, the Chairman of the Commission of Thirty-Six forwarded an *Interim Report* to the other Commission members. The *Interim Report* described the action on the Commission's "plan" that had been taken by a number of annual conference organizations of the Northeastern and North Central Jurisdiction Organizations, and of the Central Jurisdiction Organization.

Earlier in this chapter I alluded to high profile members of the Commission of Thirty-Six who had grown wary of having to apologize to their World Methodist Council colleagues for the "racially" segregated Central Jurisdiction Organization within The Methodist Church polity. Chairman Charles C. Parlin, a nationally and internationally prominent attorney, was one of those Commission members. His *Interim Report* summary statement represented an instance of a full court press to alleviate his self-conscious distress through a process of Balkanizing the Central Jurisdiction Organization.

### *3. Central Jurisdiction Organization Profile*

At the time the Committee of Five asked me to do the research for a profile of the Central Jurisdiction Organization, we did not have sufficient data to make reasonably informed decisions regarding operational objectives and strategies. Initially, my intention was to conduct a comprehensive study of the Central Jurisdiction Organization, as it existed in 1961. My idea was to draw upon the social science research capabilities of several historically Black colleges related to The Methodist Church.

Before I could formulate a research prospectus or even develop an outline of a research project, events came crashing down on us. The Commission of Thirty-Six had published a shallow "plan for the elimination of the Central Jurisdiction" and was aggressively marketing it. For me, therefore, my first research priority became that of compiling the data and information that the Committee of Five and the Central Jurisdiction College of Bishops needed to meet the challenge posed by the aggressive strategy and tactics of the Commission of Thirty-Six.

I joined the staff of the denominational Board of Christian Social Concerns (now *Board of Church and Society*) in mid-July 1961. That was a propitious move. It meant that I had the services of a secretary, and the research materials I needed were easily accessible through the Board's library facilities. By the time the Committee of Five began its meeting schedule for the fall of 1961, I had assembled and organized a small database. At the first fall meeting that year, I was able to produce a document that included the following information:

1. Number of Central Jurisdiction annual conference organizations.
2. Boundaries of each annual conference organization.
3. Extent Central Jurisdiction overlaps geographical jurisdictions.
4. Number of local churches in each annual conference organization.
5. Aggregate membership of all Central Jurisdiction local churches.
6. Number of Central Jurisdiction district superintendents.
7. Number Methodist-related colleges in the Central Jurisdiction.
8. Extent of the Central Jurisdiction's support of the benevolent programs of The Methodist Church.

My limited research document enabled the Committee to make some preliminary judgments about future strategy development. As we began our fall meetings we could draw upon the following accomplishments:

- **We had agreed that in eliminating the Central Jurisdiction Organization the pursuit of an "inclusive Methodist fellowship," at all levels of Church life, was our fundamental goal.**

- **We understood the advantages and limitations of Amendment IX as a tool for eliminating the Central Jurisdiction Organization within a framework designed to ensure the absence of involuntary "racial" segregation.**

- **We had a heightened awareness of the aggressiveness of the Commission of Thirty-Six in "selling" a plan of action that we viewed as detrimental to our interest in an "inclusive Methodist fellowship."**

- **We had broadened our knowledge and understanding of the Central Jurisdiction Organization, as an intermediate *governance structure* within the larger polity of The Methodist Church.**

## Part II. Adopting and Implementing Strategy

The fall 1961 series of Committee of Five meetings began at a time when there was much confusion throughout The Methodist Church regarding the April 1961 *First Report* and the June 1961 *Interim Report* of the Commission of Thirty-Six. The Commission's *First Report* was a classic example of mediocre work by a denominational ad hoc body. It did not include any documentary, reference or other background material. No rationale for or explanation of the Commission's basic assumptions and premises was set forth in the report. Addressed to the "Council of Bishops and the Annual Conferences of The Methodist Church," the report professed to be the Commission's "first step towards fulfillment of its task to ***accept*** 'The continuing program of The Methodist Church to abolish the Central Jurisdiction, promote interracial brotherhood through Christian love, and achieve a more inclusive church'" (p. 1). (Emphasis added.)

The *Interim Report* of June 5, 1961 made matters worse. The summary statement by the Commission's chairman was a classic case of deliberate deception and misrepresentation of fact. It was the source of widespread misunderstanding throughout The Methodist Church. The Bishops of the Central Jurisdiction Organization were bombarded with questions not only from the religious press but also from secular media representatives.

I was secretary of the Committee of Five. Religious News Service had carried a story about my new staff position at the Board of Christian Social Concerns. And the same day I arrived at the Board, I had to respond to Washington, DC media representatives, who wanted an explanation of the statement by the chairman of the Commission that the "Delaware Annual Conference [Organization] has approved the Plan."

During my first day of duty at the Board I also took telephone calls from two members of the Commission—Dr. James P. Brawley and Reverend

Dennis Fletcher—who were from the Central Jurisdiction Organization. They informed me that the chairman and secretary had not fairly represented their position when these two Commission officers stated in the Transmittal Memorandum that the *First Report* "received the unanimous support of the Commission members from the Central Jurisdiction [Organization]." The callers stated that the Transmittal Memorandum failed to indicate they supported the *First Report* "with serious reservations." Subsequently, the late Bishop Charles F. Golden confirmed the reservations in a private conversation with the author.

The members of the Committee of Five had communicated with each other regularly by telephone during the summer.[2] When we met in the fall of 1961 we were fully aware of the confusion, unrealistic expectations, and unnecessary anxiety that the Commission of Thirty-Six had caused. We devoted very little discussion to that matter. We all knew, kind of instinctively, so it seemed, that the Committee had to take charge of the whole "*eliminate the Central Jurisdiction Organization*" movement. Failure to do so might very well result in a situation far more troublesome than the Great Compromise of 1939, which produced the Central Jurisdiction Organization.[3]

We recognized that as things stood in September 1961, the College of Bishops, the Committee of Five and other leaders of the Central Jurisdiction Organization were really in a *defensive* posture, relative to the Commission of Thirty-Six. Our discussions focused on how we might effectively become proactive rather than reactive. We concluded that the Committee of Five *could take charge of the whole movement* if, within the next six to eight months, the Committee could get broad agreement among the leaders and rank-and-file members of the Central Jurisdiction Organization with respect to the following matters:

- **The fundamental goal that the Committee must seek to achieve through any efforts to eliminate the Central Jurisdiction Organization, as a "racially" segregated entity of The Methodist Church polity;**

- **The basic strategy that the Committee should follow in attempting to achieve the fundamental goal involved in eliminating the Central Jurisdiction Organization; and**

- **A reasonable timetable for critical actions to be taken by the annual conference organizations of the Central Jurisdiction Organization.**

When I joined the staff of the Board of Christian Social Concerns, the Committee agreed that its "operations" office would be at the Board. Hence during the summer, as interest in the Commission of Thirty-Six's *First* and *Interim* reports increased, I received a lot of mail and messages from Central Jurisdiction members, and from Methodists across the denomination. Many suggestions and recommendations were made. I shared all of them with my Committee colleagues.

Faced with so many suggestions, recommendations and divergent points of view, the Committee decided that one approach to getting the Central Jurisdiction Organization "to speak with one voice" (in the words of chairman Thomas) would be to convene a study conference. Consequently, we agreed to request the Central Jurisdiction College of Bishops to call a conference of representative leaders of the Central Jurisdiction Organization to explore various points of view and, if possible, to arrive at some consensus regarding fundamental goals, basic short-term objectives, and operational strategies.

The College of Bishops, in a joint meeting with the Committee, expressed the view that such a conference would probably prove to be a very useful approach. The Bishops agreed to schedule a Central Jurisdiction Organization Study Conference for March 26-28, 1962. Bishop Charles F. Golden would serve as General Chairman of the Conference, and Dr. James S. Thomas would serve as Conference Director. Dr. Graham and I were requested to serve as conference research directors. Both Bishop Golden and Dr. Thomas agreed to solicit the assistance of persons on board and agency staffs who were associated with the Central Jurisdiction Organization.

### A. Central Jurisdiction Study Conference

On March 26-28, 1962 just over 200 men and women from all walks of life throughout the Central Jurisdiction met in Cincinnati, Ohio. They were conferees to the Central Jurisdiction Study Conference. They included district superintendents, women, youths, pastors, executive secretaries of Christian education, college presidents, and representatives of denominational boards and agencies. In addition, each of the five geographical jurisdiction organizations of The Methodist Church had representatives on the conference program.

- **Recognizing that elimination of the Central Jurisdiction Organization was only a means to the achievement of more fundamental ends, the conferees came to the Conference to help determine what those ultimate ends should be. They also were expected to help the Committee of Five decide the most desirable and effective strategies for achieving chosen ends.**

The major work of the conference was accomplished in thirteen work groups whose reports were compiled and incorporated in the body of materials that were presented in plenary sessions. Points were debated freely and openly. Suggestions were made in the final plenary session. A Findings-Steering Committee coordinated the mass of details. The Conference was an extraordinary event. It achieved a remarkable consensus.

Published under the title **The Central Jurisdiction Speaks**, the report of the Conference was widely distributed throughout The Methodist Church by the Woman's Division of Christian Service of the denominational Board of Missions and the Service Department of the denominational Board of Christian Social Concerns. The *Statements and Recommendations of the Central Jurisdiction Study Conference* gave the Committee of Five the direction and guidance it needed in order to take charge of a "civil rights" movement in The Methodist Church aimed at eliminating not just the Central Jurisdiction Organization but also all involuntary "racial" separatism. The entire document is included in **Appendix 4** of the book.

### B. Developing Strategies To Implement Conference Recommendations

By any standards used to evaluate professional meetings, the Central Jurisdiction Study Conference was a turning-point event. The formal product of the conference—a document of **Statements and Recommendations**—provided the means and the momentum whereby the Committee of Five, the College of Bishops and other leaders of the Central Jurisdiction Organization could take charge of the "*elimination of the Central Jurisdiction Organization*" movement. They could now exert a powerful influence in directing that movement toward achieving their fundamental objective—an *inclusive Methodist fellowship*

- **Henceforth they could state with *authority* that Blacks within the Central Jurisdiction Organization would work cooperatively to realize their vision of a Methodist Church "composed of persons who respond to the call of Christ in love and obedience and who are, therefore, members of a new kind of fellowship, which transcends all ethnic, racial, and class barriers."**

The outcome of the Study Conference gave their position a special *legitimacy* that it might not have acquired otherwise.

We noted earlier the Commission of Thirty-Six's claim that its transfer recommendations had the support of "the Commission members from the Central Jurisdiction [Organization]." Following the publication of that claim there were baseless rumors of a serious rift between the Committee of Five and the Commission members from the Central Jurisdiction Organization.

The Study Conference put to rest any speculation that the Commission members from the Central Jurisdiction Organization did not support the position of the Committee of Five. In that connection, it is worthy of note that five of the six Commission members from the Central Jurisdiction Organization served on the Findings-Steering Committee of the Study Conference. They were in complete agreement with the conclusion of the Findings-Steering Committee (1) that the Commission's "letter accompanying the *First Report* was embarrassing to the Central Jurisdiction" and (2) that "no annual conference [organization] of the Central Jurisdiction [Organization] be transferred into a regional jurisdiction in which it is not located geographically."

## C. Joint Declaration

Since the Study Conference was convened at the request of the Committee of Five, its recommendations were directed to us. We had to decide how to incorporate the recommendations into a Committee action plan. Meanwhile, the College of Bishops was seeking an appropriate and effective way to signify its agreement with (1) the findings of the Study Conference and (2) the basic recommendations that the Committee intended to include in a strategic action plan.

During informal discussions between the Committee chairman and the Bishops, someone suggested the appropriateness of a joint declaration between the College of Bishops and the Committee of Five. In a Committee telephone meeting arranged by the chairman, we agreed that a joint declaration was a very good idea. The Committee chairman, Bishop Golden and I were assigned the task of developing and circulating a "draft" of a joint declaration, which would be formally considered at the September 1962 joint meeting of the Committee and the College of Bishops. The resultant **Joint Declaration of the College of Bishops of the Central Jurisdiction and the Central Jurisdiction Study Committee** *("Joint Declaration")* became a most useful document. It played a critical role in important subsequent events. The Joint Declaration is included in the book as **Appendix 5.**

The College of Bishops' and the Committee of Five's adoption of the Joint Declaration was both a defining moment and a course-setting event. Subsequently, the Joint Declaration became a *foundational* document for several reasons.

**First,** it removed any basis for rational doubt that the Committee and the College of Bishops would *collaboratively* lead, guide and direct the "eliminate-the-Central-Jurisdiction Organization" movement. The two groups shared a common dislike for the sinister nature of the "unholy alliance" that produced the *First Report* of the Commission of Thirty-Six, and then used the report surreptitiously to tarnish the reputation of Blacks whose impeccable integrity was widely acclaimed throughout The Methodist Church

**Second,** it strengthened the position of those members of the Commission of Thirty-Six who were from the Central Jurisdiction Organization. In creating the Commission, the Church's legislative body had directed that "the duly elected representatives of each jurisdiction [be considered] as a jurisdictional commission, and [be delegated] such responsibilities as may properly and expeditiously be fulfilled by them" (*Discipline*, 1960, Par. 2013). The Joint Declaration provided the Commission members from the Central Jurisdiction Organization with a *policy document* and broad outlines for the execution of the policy thus declared.

**Third,** more frequently than might have been expected, the College of Bishops and the Committee of Five were asked the question "What do Negro Methodists want?" The Joint Declaration answered that question clearly. It said, as Methodists we wanted "a fellowship in which all Methodists may enjoy the responsibility, privilege, and opportunity of making [our] contributions to our church's ministries of preaching, teaching, witnessing, and serving solely on the basis of [our] ability, competence, and depth of understanding of the Christian faith and our Methodist heritage."

**Fourth,** and of critical importance, the Joint Declaration declared to The Methodist Church as a whole that the top leadership of the Central Jurisdiction Organization was unified in its determination to remove a centralized structure of "racial" segregation in a way that would not inhibit progressive movement toward an *inclusive* Methodist fellowship. For this leadership, the crucial issue of removing that structure was not a matter of symbolism; it was fundamentally about substance—about Christian morality.

**Fifth,** the Joint Declaration notified the leadership of the Northeastern, Southeastern, North Central, South Central, and Western Jurisdiction Organizations that henceforth the College of Bishops of the Central Jurisdiction Organization and the Committee of Five intended to use Amendment IX creatively to achieve the pattern of abolition of the Central Jurisdiction Organization that the Cincinnati Study Conference recommended. To facilitate such use of Amendment IX the boundaries of Central Jurisdiction annual conference organizations would be realigned.

**Sixth,** by endorsing the recommendations of the Cincinnati Study Conference, the Joint Declaration signaled the determination of the Committee of Five and the College of Bishops to seek changes in some basic provisions of existing ecclesiastical law of The Methodist Church. At a minimum, they would petition the 1964 quadrennial meeting of the General Conference Organization *to declare in unequivocal terms that The Methodist Church in its entirety, and all of its supported and related institutions, should be desegregated, and they must pursue an employment policy of equal opportunity without regard to color or "racial" identity.*

**Seventh,** and most importantly, the Joint Declaration was based on solid principles of Christology. *The Methodist Church* was, to be sure, a human institution. But to the extent it was truly part of the Church Universal, it was an instrument of God's purpose. As such an instrument, the requirements for its membership and the nature of its mission were set by God. *The Methodist Church* could not truly be part of the House of God and segregate persons, or discriminate against them, on the basis of "race" and color.

One final comment should be made before we proceed to another dimension of this chapter's discussion. The Cincinnati Conference's **Statements and Recommendations** and the College of Bishops and Committee of Five's **Joint Declaration** were clear indications that in 1962 Blacks in The Methodist Church were certainly not in as *powerless* a position as they had appeared to be in 1939, when a segregated governance structure was imposed on them.

In 1962, the leaders of the Central Jurisdiction Organization had significant leverage on the sinews of The Methodist Church. They were determined to prayerfully exercise that leverage to secure the abolition of the Central Jurisdiction Organization *within a framework of overall planning and programming* designed to facilitate progressive movement toward an inclusive Methodist fellowship. They had the knowledge, the sophistication, the connections, and the associations within and outside The Methodist Church to carry out their intentions. The fact that their principal goal paralleled basic human rights goals of the larger society was a definite plus.

### D. Committee's Two-Year Work Program

In September 1962, following the adoption of the Joint Declaration, the Committee of Five agreed on a work program for the remainder of quadrennium 1960-64. The program included these major components.

1. Develop and promote a plan to realign the annual conference organizations of the Central Jurisdiction Organization.

2. Establish and market a set of guidelines to govern annual conference organization and local church transfers under Amendment IX.

3. Formulate a set of petitions for modifying the basic law of The Methodist Church on "race" relations.

4. Develop and circulate a Final Report of the Committee for the 1964 quadrennial meeting of the Central Jurisdiction Organization.

## Part III. Realignment Work

In 1962, four annual conference organizations of the Central Jurisdiction organization had boundaries that extended into the territory of more than one geographical jurisdiction organization. The Cincinnati Study Conference recommended, "no annual conference of the Central Jurisdiction be transferred into a regional jurisdiction in which it is not located geographically" (*Central Jurisdiction Speaks*, p. 8). This recommendation was incorporated in the Joint Declaration.

In adopting the Joint Declaration the Committee of Five was obligated to submit to the College of Bishops by November 1, 1962 "a proposed plan of realignment." The College of Bishops was committed to adopting a proposed realignment plan by the end of the1962 calendar year. There was an expectation that during calendar year 1963 the recommended realignment plan would be "discussed thoroughly by all parties and groups within The Methodist Church who may be affected directly or indirectly by the final adoption of the plan at the 1964 Central Jurisdictional Conference" (*Central Jurisdiction Speaks*, p. 12).

In approaching the task of devising a plan the Committee of Five never lost sight of the controlling purpose of realignment: *To facilitate structural changes that would be compatible with the principle of an inclusive Methodist fellowship.* Therefore, in developing proposed adjustments of the boundaries of Central Jurisdiction annual conference organizations, we felt that it was essential to carefully examine the following factors, as they were manifest in 1962:

1. Major social, economic, political and religious forces that may be expected to have a continuing effect on inter-group relations in the United States of America.

2. Recent trends in population changes, especially the migration of people from the south to the north and west, and from rural areas to urban centers.

3. Natural travel patterns of the American people as determined by the major national highways, railroads, and other means of travel.

4. The desirability of maintaining, in the process of realignment, existing conference relationships as much as possible.

5. The existence of many relatively small local churches that are dispersed over a vast geographical area of the country.

6. Wherever possible, the desirability of Central Jurisdiction Organization clergy personnel gaining the experience of serving

churches in communities with different ecological patterns, social structures, and demographic characteristics.

7. The need to strengthen several annual conference organizations before they could effectively initiate action to transfer into a regional organization under circumstances that would promote a truly inclusive Methodist fellowship.

8. Matters relating to (a) the legal status of annual conference organizations under the civil laws of the different states and (b) the property that the annual conference organizations owned.

9. Relationships of annual conference organizations with Methodist-related institutions of higher education established historically for the education of Blacks.

10. The rights of ministerial members of the annual conference organizations under existing ecclesiastical law of The Methodist Church.

After consultation with the members of the Commission of Thirty-Six from the Central Jurisdiction Organization, and other leaders of The Methodist Church, both within and outside the Central Jurisdiction Organization, the Committee of Five drafted and submitted to the College of Bishops a proposed plan to realign the annual conference units of the Central Jurisdiction Organization. The Bishops accepted the plan for the purpose of publication of a **Study Document on Realignment of the Central Jurisdiction** ***("Realignment Study Document)***. As published for study during calendar year 1963, the Realignment Study Document proposed the following changes in Central Jurisdiction annual conference organization boundaries:

**Delaware**

The existing Delaware *Annual Conference Organization*, *minus* all churches located on the eastern shore of the State of Virginia.

**Washington**

The existing Washington *Annual Conference Organization*, *plus* those churches in West Virginia that were then in the East Tennessee *Annual Conference Organization*, *minus* all the churches in Virginia.

**East Tennessee-Virginia**

The existing Tennessee *Annual Conference Organization*, *plus* the churches in Virginia that were then in the Washington and Delaware *Annual Conference Organizations*, and any churches in the counties on the eastern border of Kentucky.

**Tennessee-Kentucky**

The existing Tennessee *Annual Conference Organization*, *plus* all churches in Kentucky, except any in the counties on the eastern border of the State.

**Southwest**

The existing Southwest *Annual Conference Organization*, *plus* all churches in the States of Nebraska, Kansas, and Missouri.

**Lexington**

The existing Lexington *Annual Conference Organization*, *minus* all churches in the State of Kentucky; *plus* all churches in the State of Illinois that were then in the Central West *Annual Conference Organization*.

**Central West**

The Central West *Annual Conference Organization* would be *dissolved*.

The *Realignment Study Document* directed attention to two *special situations*. **First,** the three Central Jurisdiction Organization's local churches in Colorado Springs, Denver, and Pueblo, Colorado, respectively, were located within the territory of the Western Jurisdiction Organization. Therefore, they could not be included in the boundary of any Central Jurisdiction annual conference organization proposed in the *Realignment Study Document*. The Committee of Five recommended that these churches be encouraged to transfer into the Rocky Mountain Annual Conference Organization, in accordance with the local church transfer provision of Amendment IX. The Committee thought it might be possible to effect such transfers during the 1960-64 quadrennium.

**Second,** the proposed Southwest Annual Conference Organization would cover the States of Arkansas, Kansas, Missouri, Nebraska, and Oklahoma. It might not be possible in the near future for this redesigned Central Jurisdiction annual conference organization as a whole to transfer into the

South Central Jurisdiction Organization under circumstances that would promote the ultimate goal of a truly inclusive Methodist fellowship. However, it might be possible for the four churches in Nebraska and the twelve churches in Kansas to effect a desirable transfer. Therefore, the Committee of Five recommended that a special effort be made during calendar year 1963 to transfer these churches into annual conference organizations of the South Central Jurisdiction Organization in which they were geographically located. The transfers should be accomplished in accordance with the local church transfer provision of Amendment IX.

Table 6-1 presents relevant statistical data applicable to the realigned annual conference organizations proposed by the Committee of Five.

**Table 6-1**

**Central Jurisdiction Membership That Would Be Within Regional Organizations Under Committee of Five's Realignment Plan**

| Realigned Conference Organization | Membership Within Regional Organization |
|---|---|
| Delaware (259) [A] | 47,771—NEJ |
| Washington (246) | 37,007—NEJ |
| | |
| Tennessee-Kentucky (210) | 17,504—SEJ |
| North Carolina-Virginia (225) | 22,257—SEJ |
| | |
| Central Alabama (116) | 15,017—SEJ |
| Florida (97) | 9,160—SEJ |
| Georgia (195) | 28,657—SEJ |
| Mississippi (224) | 22,398—SEJ |
| South Carolina (322) | 45,370—SEJ |
| Upper Mississippi (178) | 14,000—SEJ |
| | |
| Lexington (124) | 40,419—NCJ |
| | |
| Louisiana (164) | 20,518—SCJ |
| Southwest (151) | 17,968—SCJ |
| Texas (182) | 19,987—SCJ |
| West Texas (150) | 19,889—SCJ |

**(A) Figures in parentheses represent the number of local churches.**

**DATA SOURCE:** ***General Minutes of the Annual Conferences of The Methodist Church for 1962*** **(Chicago: Department of Research and Statistics, The Council on World Service and Finance). In 1962, Dr. W. Astor Kirk compiled the figures in Table 6-1 for the Committee of Five and the College of Bishops of the Central Jurisdiction**

---

I should direct the reader's attention to the fact that the plan the Committee developed was substantially more logical and rational than the one the Commission of Thirty-Six proposed in its *First Report*. (See *Chapter Notes*, Note 1.)

As shown in Table 6-1, the realignment plan the Committee of Five recommended to the 1964 quadrennial meeting of the Central Jurisdiction Organization consisted of fifteen (15) annual conference organizations.

- Two (2) would be located wholly within the bounds of the Northeastern Jurisdiction Organization;
- Eight (8) would be situated entirely within the bounds of the Southeastern Jurisdiction Organization;
- One (1) would be completely within the geographical territory of the North Central Jurisdiction Organization; and
- Four (4) would be wholly embraced by the South Central Jurisdiction Organization.

Three local churches in Colorado would transfer to the Rocky Mountain Annual Conference Organization of the Western Jurisdiction Organization.

In the *Realignment Study Document*, the Committee of Five reminded all members of The Methodist Church that

> **The abolition of the racially segregated Central Jurisdiction [Organization] of The Methodist Church is not an end in itself. Removal of this unit from the organizational structure of the church** ***is of real significance only as this action will clearly promote a truly inclusive Methodist fellowship.***
>
> **There can be no justification for abolition of the Central Jurisdiction [Organization] in such a way as to prolong unduly the existence of racially segregated annual conferences or limit, solely on the grounds of race or color, opportunities for**

> **spiritual and intellectual growth and Christian service.** (P. 2. Emphasis added.)

Thanks to support from and work of the Literature Headquarters of the Woman's Division of Christian Service (denominational Board of Missions) and the Service Department (denominational Board of Christian Social Concerns), over 8,000 copies of the *Realignment Study Document* were distributed to individuals and groups throughout The Methodist Church. During calendar year 1963 they were used in study-discussion groups not only in the Central Jurisdiction Organization but also in geographical jurisdiction organizations.

I was an invited participant (i.e., *resource person*) in over a dozen of these study-discussion groups that were sponsored by local boards of Christian Social Concerns and local groups associated with the Woman's Division of Christian Service. At several such meetings I had to defend my active and widely known opposition to the *First Report* of the Commission of Thirty-Six, which was being marketed aggressively as the "first step" in eliminating the Central Jurisdiction. I dealt with this issue quite candidly and forthrightly in an address to the Philadelphia Conference Board of Christian Social Concerns May 17, 1963. Included here are the pertinent paragraphs from my address.

> **In 1961, the Commission on Inter-Jurisdictional Relations recommended abolition of the Central Jurisdiction by what I regard as an irresponsible use of the procedures of Amendment IX. In the *first* place, the basic model proposed by the Commission would have made a mockery of the jurisdictional system by seriously breaching the geographical integrity of the regional jurisdictions. *Secondly,* it involved a questionable shift of major responsibility for dealing with fundamental problems of racialism in The Methodist Church. Thus, the task of resolving these problems would be shifted from the general church to four of the five regional jurisdictions. The two regional jurisdictions, namely, Southeastern and South Central, which would be given the greatest share of the total task, are the two jurisdictions in which one finds the most intractable forces opposing a racially undifferentiated Methodist Church. *Thirdly,* while the Commission's plan would eliminate the Central Jurisdiction nationally, it would actually result in seventeen "little Central Jurisdictions" masquerading as constituent units of four regional jurisdictions. In the *fourth* place, the plan ignored entirely the crucial issue of normative patterns of relations at**

**intermediate and local levels among Methodists of different racial backgrounds.**

**After a careful study of the Commission's plan, I concluded that its adoption would not represent a responsible exercise of social power by The Methodist Church. I do not hesitate to acknowledge publicly that I advised the Committee of Five to oppose the model proposed by the Commission. Also, I make no apology for suggesting to the Central Jurisdiction annual conferences that they ought not commit themselves to this proposal. The reason that underlies my decision in this matter is a simple one: *We now stand at the threshold of another critical period not only in the institutional life of The Methodist Church but also in the history of this country. In such a period The Methodist Church cannot afford to turn its back on history and revert to a pattern of race relations that prevailed prior to Unification in 1939.***

A later chapter of this book will discuss the 1964 quadrennial meeting of the Central Jurisdiction Organization. It will suffice for our purpose here to state that the delegates to that meeting approved the Committee of Five's realignment plan by an overwhelming majority. Only minor adjustments, which were agreeable to the Committee, were made in the states of Kentucky, Tennessee and Virginia.

### Part IV. Guidelines for Amendment IX Transfers

The Joint Declaration expressed the firm conviction of the signatories thereto that the Central Jurisdiction Organization should adopt "basic standards" relating to transfers of its annual conference organizations under Amendment IX into regional organizations of The Methodist Church. The Committee of Five was requested to develop a set of "recommended standards" for the consideration of the 1964 quadrennial session of the Central Jurisdiction Organization.

As the Committee of Five began to focus on this task Chairman Thomas reminded us that since Amendment IX "makes no reference to conditions or bases upon which transfers are to be made, a great responsibility is left upon [Central Jurisdiction annual conference organizations] and local churches to state these conditions—very clearly and in advance of voting." He felt that this was crucially important for three reasons:

1. There are "certain points of information" that must be in hand before intelligent transfers can be made.

2. There are important matters of relationship. For example, what will be the status of transferring ministers, and what relationship will an annual conference organization have to the geographical jurisdiction organization into which it is transferring?

3. There is the important matter of always having enough of a Central Jurisdiction Organization to negotiate with strength.

We also had a reminder from Dr. James P. Brawley that some key sociological and political dynamics must not be overlooked in developing recommended transfer standards under Amendment IX. He was especially concerned that we seriously address the following related question:

> **(a) To what extent will any given transfer (or transfers) contribute to the solution of the main problem of segregation, and the achievement of an "inclusive church?"**
>
> **(b) How can we prevent any first steps taken, whether satisfactory or not, from becoming crystallized so as to prevent next steps, because first steps were interpreted as "the solution" to the problem of the Church, or because of the development of a tendency not to "trouble the waters" any more?**
>
> **(c) What should be written into the small print?**

In Part II of this chapter the fact was noted that I was asked to undertake three research projects. One was to undertake an analysis of the potentials and limitations of Amendment IX as a vehicle for accomplishing the dissolution of the Central Jurisdiction Organization *within a framework of overall planning and programming* that would facilitate rather than impede achieving an inclusive Methodist Church.

The research work that I performed for the Committee and for the College of Bishops of the Central Jurisdiction Organization gave me an insight into more than just the potentials and limitations of Amendment IX. It also revealed the very inadequate concept of an *annual conference organization* that leaders of The Methodist Church had, as they contemplated making use of a key provision of Amendment IX.

It is true, of course, that the constitution of The Methodist Church declared annual conference organizations of the Central Jurisdiction Organization and of geographical jurisdiction organizations to be "the basic body" in The Methodist Church (*Discipline*, 1960, Par, 22). Ecclesiastically speaking, these entities were "the reservoir of all powers not specifically delegated to the [Church's legislative body]" (Judicial Council, Decision No. 38).

But such entities were more than merely traditional ecclesiastical bodies. **They were also important societal structures of power, privilege,**

**duties, obligations, and opportunities.** Most, if not all, of them were *bodies corporate* under the civil laws of the countries, states, and territories within whose bounds they were located. As corporate entities they could sue and be sued, receive, hold, manage, control and dispose of property, and incur debt.

In other words, they were not just institutions of The Methodist Church. They were also institutions of the larger society. As such, they were employers of labor; providers of social services; educational entrepreneurs; and sponsors of recreational, entertainment, and cultural enterprises. They were landlords as well as tenants. And they consumed natural resources, collected, expended, and invested money, and enjoyed the many benefits that were derived from the civil society.

This was the kind of entity that was involved in all of the processes set forth in Amendment IX. The Committee of Five had to ask and answer the tough question "What basic principles or norms should guide any use of Amendment IX processes involving Central Jurisdiction annual conference organizations and entities of geographical jurisdiction organizations?"

**Our sense of ethical duty, our moral integrity, and our intellectual honesty compelled us to go beyond the Commission of Thirty-Six's shallow focus on the mere procedural mechanics of voting.**

We recognized that in the final analysis a vote, in the "Amendment IX context," was only a means of registering one's decision to help bring about *some desired result*. All members of the Committee of Five had a strong belief that everyone voting in any Amendment IX process should know up front the fundamental *proposed results* that were involved.

In the real world, crucial circumstances and situations could vary among sections of the country, from state to state and, in some instances, between different parts of a particular state. Urban settings were certainly different from rural ones. The existence of such variations posed great difficulties with respect to developing detailed Amendment IX guidelines that could apply across the board.

One distinguishing or unique characteristic of The Methodist Church (now United Methodist Church) is the concept and related principles of "connectionalism." The Committee of Five thought it prudent to concentrate on guidelines that Methodist *connectionalism* seemed to require.

### A. Transfers of Annual Conference Organizations

We believed, and therefore we recommended, that actual instruments (i.e., *contracts of transfer*) to achieve Central Jurisdiction annual conference organization transfers under Amendment IX should specifically stipulate:

1. **That the Central Jurisdiction annual conference organization involved shall be merged, joined, amalgamated or otherwise**

**combined with one or more existing (or newly created) annual conference organizations of the receiving geographical organization as soon as possible during the 1964-68 quadrennium. The objective of that requirement was to preclude a policy of The Methodist Church of merely terminating the Central Jurisdiction Organization, as such, and distributing and maintaining in tact its "racially" segregated entities among the geographical jurisdiction organizations. We wanted to guard against what I called a "Balkanization policy."**

2. **That all ministerial members of the Central Jurisdiction annual conference organization transferring into a geographical jurisdiction organization shall be an inseparable part or component of such *transferring* entity, and that they shall enjoy the same status, rights, and privileges (under the same conditions) as are or may be enjoyed by other ministers in the annual conference organizations of the geographical jurisdiction organization.**

3. **That all lay men and women of local churches transferred along with the transfer of Central Jurisdiction annual conferences shall have rights and opportunities to participate in all aspects of programs and enterprises in the geographical jurisdiction organization involved, which rights and opportunities shall not be limited and abridged on grounds of "race" or color.**

4. **That when all Central Jurisdiction annual conferences comprising an Episcopal Area transfer into geographical jurisdiction organization in which they are geographically located, the resident bishop of that Episcopal Area shall also be transferred into the same geographical jurisdiction organization.**

5. **That any geographical jurisdiction organization into which a Central Jurisdiction annual conference organization(s) shall transfer, shall indicate a willingness to assist The Methodist Church in coping with the problems resulting from (a) the transference of the annual conference organization(s) and (b) the relation of such transfer to the over-all programmed abolition of the Central Jurisdiction Organization.**

The Committee of Five recognized the limited scope and purpose of Amendment IX. However, we believed that its use to transfer Central Jurisdiction annual conference organizations into geographical jurisdiction organizations should conform to at least the standards outlined here. We were confident that if Amendment IX were used in this manner, then our concept of "inclusiveness" would find concrete expression and practical application in the institutional structures of The Methodist Church polity. It was our conviction that utilization of Amendment IX in this creative way was a task not of the Central Jurisdiction Organization alone but of The Methodist Church as a whole.

### B. Transfers of Local Churches

The transfers of local churches under Amendment IX could not give rise to boundary problems. However, we considered such transfers in the light of the "inclusiveness" standard to which the Committee of Five and the College of Bishops of the Central Jurisdiction were committed under the Joint Declaration. In that context, broad policy questions were inescapably involved in transferring local churches from a Central Jurisdiction annual conference organization into a similar entity of a geographical jurisdiction organization. In 1960, the Commission of Seventy called attention to the fact that

> **Transfers may be voted without full knowledge of what will be required either of the transferring church or the receiving conference, with respect to such problems as freedom of mobility of membership transfers, ministerial recruitment and standards, salary and pension differentials, and clerical and lay leadership opportunities in Districts, Conferences and Areas... Members of local churches and ministers need to be prepared spiritually and psychologically for the proposed transfer. Transferring churches should measure their relative strength in leadership, finance, membership growth, participation in and responsiveness to the general church program (*Report*, p. 11).**

The Committee of Five urged such transfers wherever *contracts of transfers* followed proper planning. We stated that "proper planning" involved at least giving careful consideration, at both the local church and annual conference stages of the transfer process, to the following factors:

1. The relative advantages of a group of local churches, if possible, in a given geographical area transferring rather than a single church in that area.

2. The future conference status (including privileges of itineracy) of the minister or ministers involved.

3. The obligations and responsibilities the church will have as a member of a given annual conference organization of a geographical jurisdiction organization.

4. The opportunities that lay men and lay women will have for participation, without regard to "race" or color, in all aspects of the programs and enterprises of the annual conference organization of the geographical organization involved.

In 1963, the Committee of Five gained some actual experience in working with the local church transfer process of Amendment IX. The New York Area of the Northeastern Jurisdiction Organization developed a plan to consolidate the New York and New York East Annual Conference Organizations to form a new metropolitan New York City Annual Conference Organization. Within the boundaries of the projected new annual conference organization were eight churches and three mission stations of the Central Jurisdiction's Delaware Annual Conference Organization. Through its Board of Christian Social Concerns, the Delaware Annual Conference Organization participated in the planning that resulted in a proposal that the Central Jurisdiction churches become an integral part of the new entity in metropolitan New York City. The Committee of Five recognized the advantage to these churches of becoming part of the new annual conference organization at the time of its organization, rather than transferring into it later after its structure had been completed. Therefore, we assisted the Delaware Board of Christian Social Concerns with respect to securing approval for the transfer of the eight churches involved.

The Committee gave similar assistance to the Board of Christian Social Concerns of the Central West Annual Conference Organization in its planning, which was directed toward the transfer of a number of local churches in Kansas and Nebraska. Both the Committee and the Board hoped that acceptance of basic standards to ensure inclusiveness would be achieved in 1963, and that transfers would follow thereafter as soon as possible. We also helped to pave the way for the three Central Jurisdiction churches in Colorado to transfer into the Rocky Mountain Annual Conference Organization of the Western Jurisdiction Organization.

## CONCLUDING SUMMARY

In this chapter we have discussed how Blacks reacted to the 1960 decision of the legislative body of The Methodist Church to **not** make any substantive changes in the "racially" segregated governance structures of the Church's polity.

The Sixth Quadrennial Session of the Central Jurisdiction Organization met shortly after the adjournment of the Church's legislative body. The delegates to the 1960 session of the Central Jurisdiction Organization established a Committee of Five. The Committee was directed to study and report on any matters that, in its judgment, "have or may be expected to have a significant bearing on the status of the Central Jurisdiction [Organization]."

Through a national study conference the Committee of Five obtained agreement on broad goals and strategies for achieving the elimination of involuntary "racial" segregation in the polity of The Methodist Church. The principal elements of this agreement were incorporated in a **Joint Declaration** between the College of Bishops of the Central Jurisdiction Organization and the Committee of Five.

Chapter 7, which immediately follows, is devoted to a discussion of the Committee of Five's decisions and actions with respect to the initial implementation phases of the **Join Declaration.**

These phases involved (1) developing proposed modifications of Church law for the consideration of the 1964 quadrennial meeting of the legislative body of The Methodist Church and (2) planning and directing a church-wide "legislative change" advocacy campaign.

## Chapter Notes

1. At a meeting in Washington, DC on April 28-29, 1961, the Commission of Thirty-Six approved its *First Report*, which recommended to leaders of The Methodist Church the following transfers under Amendment IX:

    (A) From the Central Jurisdiction Organization to the Northeastern Jurisdiction Organization, the-

    (1) Delaware Annual Conference Organization
    (2) Washington Annual Conference Organization
    (3) North Carolina Annual Conference Organization

    (B) From the Central Jurisdiction Organization to the North Central Jurisdiction Organization, the-

    (1) Central West Annual Conference Organization
    (2) Lexington Annual Conference Organization
    (3) Southwest Annual Conference Organization

    (C) From the Central Jurisdiction Organization to the South Central Jurisdiction Organization, the-

    (1) West Texas Annual Conference Organization

(2) Texas Annual Conference Organization
(3) Louisiana Annual Conference Organization

(D) From the Central Jurisdiction Organization to the Southeastern Jurisdiction Organization, the-

(1) South Carolina Annual Conference Organization
(2) Georgia Annual Conference Organization
(3) Florida Annual Conference Organization
(4) East Tennessee Annual Conference Organization
(5) Tennessee Annual Conference Organization
(6) Upper Mississippi Annual Conference Organization
(7) Annual Conference Organization
(8) Central Alabama Annual Conference Organization

See **Commission of Thirty-Six, *First Report*** (1961), pp. 1-2.

2. Richard C. Erwin was practicing attorney in North Carolina; John J. Hicks was a local church pastor in St. Louis; John H. Graham was a staff member at the denominational Board of Missions; James S. Thomas was a staff member of the denominational Board of Education; and I was a new staff member of the denominational Board of Christian Social Concerns.

3. Assume, for example, that the Commission of Thirty-Six had been successful in effecting transfers of the Central Jurisdiction's Washington and North Carolina Annual Conference Organizations—as they existed in 1961—into the Northeastern Jurisdiction Organization. That would have resulted in a Northeastern geographical regional organization with twenty-two (22) *annual conference entities*—twenty with geographically defined boundaries and two with "racially" defined boundaries. The "racially" defined entities would include 250 local churches in Virginia and North Carolina. Both states are in the Southeastern regional organization. There would have been no constitutional way for the Northeastern Jurisdiction Organization, acting alone, to make these local churches part of its *geographically defined* administrative structures.

   An even more frightening prospect was the possibility that the Commission of Thirty-Six might successfully exploit the desire "to remove an embarrassing symbol of racial segregation from The Methodist Church," and secure the transfer of all Central Jurisdiction annual conference organizations, as proposed in its *First Report*. We would then have had to confront a number of little Central Jurisdictions, and we would have lacked tools to deal with the resulting problems. We might have faced the prospect of enduring the painful effects of Balkanization of the Central Jurisdiction for many years.

# CHAPTER 7
## Committee of Five: Advocate For Legislative Action

Chapter 6 focused on one aspect of the work of the Committee of Five. It dealt with the Committee's development of a framework of concepts, principles and strategies for taking charge of desegregating the polity of The Methodist Church.

A dimension of the framework established was an outgrowth of a recommendation of the 1962 Cincinnati Study Conference. The conference recommended that the Committee of Five memorialize the 1964 quadrennial meeting of The Methodist Church's legislative body

> **...to declare in unequivocal terms that the entire Methodist Church and all of the institutions related to it, such as educational institutions, homes, hospitals, assembly grounds, etc., should be desegregated and that no person should be denied admission or employment because of color or racial identity (*Central Jurisdiction Speaks*, p. 9).**

The Committee of Five developed twelve memorials for the consideration of the 1964 quadrennial session of The Methodist Church's legislative body. The memorials were published in a pamphlet document entitled **Creative Pursuit of an Inclusive Church** (referred to hereafter as "*1964 Memorials Document*"). In the Introduction the Committee stated:

> **The Methodist Church has now arrived at a point in its history, and in the history of the world, when our Church must become a prominent witness, within its own institutional life, to the principles of equality, brotherhood and "oneness of all Christians in Christ," which have been affirmed as essential elements of the Christian faith.**
>
> **To achieve this goal, it seems urgently necessary that the**

**[Church's legislative body] enact fundamental additions to the main body of law of The Methodist Church.**

Our memorials proposed changes in, and addition to, the body of law of The Methodist Church. The major ones, and the Committee's reasons for proposing them, are summarized and included in the book's **Appendix 6.**

## The 1964 Meeting of the General Conference Organization

In late April 1964, the "eliminate-the-Central-Jurisdiction " movement within The Methodist Church moved to the legislative arena again. That was when the Church's legislative body convened its quadrennial meeting in Pittsburgh, Pennsylvania.

The Commission of Thirty-Six, representing the general church, came to the legislative body with a report that urged continued use of Amendment IX transfer processes as the primary means of eliminating the "racially" segregated Central Jurisdiction Organization. The Commission submitted a number of proposals designed to remove acknowledged procedural impediments to a wider and more expeditious use of Amendment IX mechanisms.

The Committee of Five contended that the Commission's proposals were insufficient. They failed to provide general church protection against the indefinite continuation of "racially" segregated annual conference organizations within geographical jurisdiction organizations.

The Committee of Five *strongly advised the delegates that a reversion to the Northern ME Church pattern of "racially" segregated constituent units of regional organizations was totally unacceptable to Blacks.*

Representing the Central Jurisdiction Organization, the Committee of Five lobbied for an **anti-racial-segregation rule *("ARS Rule")*** that would be binding on geographical jurisdiction organizations.

The Commission's position on this issue was that the legislative body and the general church should continue to rely on the principle of *voluntarism.* Inherent in that principle was an implication that the Committee of Five found unacceptable:

- **Dissolution of "racially" segregated annual conference organizations transferring from the Central Jurisdiction Organization into geographical jurisdiction organizations would occur only when all affected parties mutually agreed that this step should be taken.**

On the eve of the convening of the church's legislative body, Charles C. Parlin, chairman of the Commission of Thirty-Six, and the author, as secretary of the Committee of Five, discussed in much detail the contrasting approaches of the two groups. Their discussions appear side-by-side in the denominational Board of Christian Social Concern's magazine. (See Charles C. Parlin, "Implement Amendment IX" and W. Astor Kirk, "Modify Church Law," ***Concern***, April 15, 1964, pp. 7-9.)

In the previous chapter of this book I emphasized the ultimate goal of the Committee of Five, which the Cincinnati Study Conference affirmed. It was to achieve genuine *cross-"racial," cross-cultural and cross-class inclusiveness* at all levels of the community of believers known institutionally at the time as The Methodist Church. To promote tangible progress toward realizing that goal during the 1960-64 quadrennium, we had a critical legislative objective:

> We wanted to put in place a legal and policy framework designed to ensure the discontinuance, *as "racially" defined entities*, of Central Jurisdiction annual conference organizations transferring into geographical jurisdiction organizations.

**We believed some substantive changes in the body of Methodist Church law were imperative. We did not consider our task finished merely with the development and submission of twelve memorials (i.e., legislative proposals) for the consideration of the Church's legislative body. We believed that the Committee of Five also had a crucial responsibility to influence the legislative process toward producing outcomes that would be supportive of the Committee's urgent legislative objective.**

Our first formidable challenge was to find a way to get the Committee's total legislative package to **all of the delegates** to the 1964 quadrennial meeting of the Church's legislative body. That body had standing legislative committees, each of which had jurisdiction over specified subjects. Under the rules of procedure then in effect, each memorial had to be limited to a single subject matter. Upon receipt of a memorial the legislative body's secretariat would send it to the standing committee that had jurisdiction over the subject matter involved. Our twelve memorials would be sent to at least five (and possibly seven) different legislative committees. No delegate would get our legislative package in its totality.

**More importantly, delegates would not be aware of the underlying rationale for the package as a whole!**

The Committee of Five assigned to the author the task of steering our memorials through the legislative process. To overcome the barrier to a *multi-subject* memorial, and to get all of our memorials in the hands of each delegate, I decided to create a single, consolidated memorial-petition. The document would include (1) an introductory statement, including an explanation of our *fundamental goals* and (2) the twelve separate memorials and the reason for each. The document was entitled **Creative Pursuit of an Inclusive Church: *Memorials to the General Conference of The Methodist Church*.**

When the memorial-petition documents arrived at the site of the meeting, we faced another challenge. It was the challenge of getting them distributed to the delegates. The most reliable and efficient way would be to have one document put in the assigned seat of each delegate. In order for me to do that, I would have to get a special permission from the Commission on Entertainment. At the close of the evening session, I took 1500 copies of the document to the office of the person in charge of the distribution of literature. I requested that office to hold the documents until I could get permission for them to be distributed to the delegates.

Some delegates already had copies of the memorial-petition document, which they had received from the Committee of Five in other connections. For example, we had given in advance a copy to each member of the Commission of Thirty-Six. Similarly, the head of the delegation from each Central Jurisdiction annual conference organization had received a courtesy copy.

When the session began the next morning I had not gotten approval for the distribution of the document to all delegates. However, in the plenary session debates some delegates quoted from the document, and one used some language in one of the memorials as his amendment to a motion before the body. At the request of a majority of the delegates, the presiding officer had the documents distributed.

With that decision of the legislative body the Committee of Five's memorial-petition document was officially given to each of the delegates. The task now was to work with key delegations. We wanted to achieve the best possible legislative outcomes from the use of the document, regardless of what the standing legislative committees did with the separate memorials referred to them.

The Committee had its members to schedule conferences with delegations from the Central Jurisdiction Organization. The purpose of the conferences was to explain our legislative package and to answer any questions or respond to any concerns that individual delegates might have. I represented the Committee at four such conferences. That experience suggested to me the need to prioritize our twelve memorials, and then concentrate on "pushing" the one or two with the highest priority.

For me, completing the prioritizing exercise identified Memorial #2 as the one that should have top priority—in terms of both immediate and long-term substantial impact. Memorial #2 is the one that sought enactment of an ARS Rule. It would require that in the exercise of their "powers and duties" a geographical jurisdiction organization "shall take only such action or authorize and sanction only such activities, programs and practices as are in harmony with the policy of The Methodist Church to eliminate racial segregation and discrimination."

Adoption of this proposal by the Church's legislative body would have established an ARS Rule. I believed that prevention of the Balkanization of "racially" defined Central Jurisdiction annual conferences should take precedence over all other issues dealt with in our memorial-petition. Moreover, the resulting delegates' discussion and debate of this critical issue would give our Committee some guidance with respect to recommendations to the forthcoming 1964 quadrennial meeting of the Central Jurisdiction Organization. I consulted with the other four members of the Committee and found them in agreement with giving Memorial #2 the highest priority.

I had no information that indicated what the standing legislative committee might do with our Memorial #2, or any similar ones from other petitioners.[1] Delegates' consideration of the Report and recommendations of the Committee of Thirty-Six was the order of the day for May 1, 1964. Therefore, it seemed to me that we might get legislative consideration of our Memorial #2 by having it presented by some delegate as an appropriate "amendment" of some pertinent recommendation of the Commission. As the "legislative manager" of our memorial-petition effort, that was the tactic I chose to pursue.

I was in constant contact with several delegates who had agreed to offer our Memorial #2 as an amendment to the Commission's recommendations in case the presiding officer recognized them. Allen M. Mayes of the Central Jurisdiction's Texas Annual Conference Organization was one of them. When the presiding officer recognized him, Mayes proposed the Committee of Five's Memorial #2 as an amendment to the report of the Commission of Thirty-Six. The Mayes Amendment stated that in the exercise of its powers and duties, a geographical jurisdiction organization

> **shall take only such action, including creation and maintenance of annual conferences, and authorize or sanction only such activities, programs and practices as are consistent with the policy of The Methodist Church, to eliminate from its organizational structure all patterns of racial discrimination and segregation."** (1964 General Conference *Journal*, Vol. I, p. 309.)

Mayes told his fellow delegates he believed that "we must do everything in our power to keep from reverting to a pattern that prevailed in the Methodist Episcopal Church prior to 1939. ***Without the direction which this proposed amendment would give to The Methodist Church, we could conceivably still end up in 4 years, 8, or even 25 years with racially segregated Annual Conferences, in regional jurisdictions as a consequence of the dissolution of the Central Jurisdiction."***

Mayes' poignant and concise statement went to heart of the basic problem, about which the Central Jurisdiction Organization had spoken eight years earlier.[2] Therefore, most of the debate on Mayes' Amendment is included in **Appendix 7.** I strongly recommend reading it for insights otherwise unavailable.

A vote was taken on the Mayes amendment. The amendment was lost. *(Daily Christian Advocate, page 165.)*

## SUMMARY APPRAISAL

The Committee of Five and the Central Jurisdiction Sub-Commission of the Commission of Thirty-Six held a joint meeting March 1-2, 1963 at the Interdenominational Theological Center in Atlanta. The group revisited the Cincinnati Conference's request that certain anti-segregation memorials be presented to the Church's legislative body in 1964. I was assigned the task of developing draft proposals.

In presenting draft proposals to the joint meeting in the spring of 1963, I expressed my be_has that we should craft a legislative package designed to help delegates to the 1964 session of the General Conference Organization *understand and internalize* four crucial issues, regardless of whether any specific memorial might be adopted. I listed the four issues as follows:

1. With respect to institutionalized or formalized inter-'racial" relationships in The Methodist Church, the overriding or paramount concern of Blacks was *involuntary* "racial" segregation.

2. The Central Jurisdiction Organization within The Methodist Church polity was both a *structural symbol* and an *institutional fact* of involuntary "racial" segregation in a multi-ethnic, worldwide denomination.

3. It was entirely possible to eliminate the Central Jurisdiction *structural symbol* without eradicating the *institutional fact* of involuntary "racial" segregation within The Methodist Church.

4. There was a need for a legal and policy framework that would ensure the removal of the Central Jurisdiction Organization, both as a structural symbol and as an institutional fact of involuntary "racial" segregation.

As noted earlier, at the 1964 session of the Church's legislative body I chose to give top priority to the Committee of Five's Memorial #2, which was presented for plenary consideration as the "Mayes Amendment" to the report of the Commission of Thirty-Six.

There is a simple explanation of why I include most of the debate on the Mayes Amendment as **Appendix 7** of this book. It is to present a document that will enable readers to make their own appraisal of the impact of the discussion on the delegates—in terms of the delegates' *understanding* and *internalizing* the four crucial issues I identified in 1963.

It has been over forty years since that debate occurred. I still have not changed my overall assessment of that historic moment in the Committee of Five's *transformational and moral* leadership of the "eliminate-the-Central-Jurisdiction" movement. Although the Mayes Amendment was not adopted, the debate on it was a behavioral-change event.

- **An enigmatic contradiction was exposed.** George Atkinson had been quite vocal publicly in accusing leaders of the Central Jurisdiction Organization of "foot-dragging." Now he was publicly telling delegates "our Central Jurisdiction brethren...are going too fast."

- **Kelly Jackson** not only **highlighted the "dragging feet/going too fast" contradiction**, but he also challenged the Church's legislative body not to "go on record as dragging its feet."

- **No delegate would be able to forget the subtle humor of William T. Handy**, a Central Jurisdiction delegate, whom the South Central Jurisdiction Organization later elected to the episcopacy. Nor would they forget his urgent plea to "do what I believe the world is demanding us to do in the social revolution of which we are a part, to rid ourselves of segregation in all of its insidious forms."

- **Stanley S. McKee spoke for a lot of delegates** when he said "it was very difficult for me to understand this a few years ago; our good friend Dr. Brawley, and others, called to our attention that the real problem is not the doing away with the Central Jurisdiction Organization; the real problem, which we face as a church, is the doing away with racial discrimination... this amendment is the most important thing we have before this General Conference and as far as I can see, it is the most important issue we will have before us while we are here"

- **Leonard Slutz**, a North Central delegate, stated his "complete sympathy with the purpose" of the Mayes Amendment, but could not vote for it for certain practical reasons. He **verbalized the agony of many delegates** when he said "we are dealing on the one side with emotion, and what we would like to do, and on the other side we are trying to deal with intellect and what we think we ought to do." More importantly, perhaps, was his deep involvement, as a socially conscious lawyer, in really trying to make things happen with respect to the Central Jurisdiction's Lexington Annual Conference Organization.

- ***Only non-Central Jurisdiction delegates*** spoke against the Mayes Amendment. Stanley S. McKee from the Western Jurisdiction Organization was the ***only non-Central Jurisdiction delegate to speak in favor of this Amendment.***

- **Charles C. Parlin**, chairman of the Commission of Thirty-Six, had the right to close debate after the previous question was ordered. He **exploited a parliamentary tactic** of waiting until the previous question had been ordered to raise an issue of the constitutionality of the Mayes Amendment. That meant no one could counter his disingenuous argument.

I did some unscientific opinion sampling after the adoption of the "programming" amendment offered by James S. Thomas, which followed the debate on the Mayes Amendment. The results indicated to me that no serious-minded delegate read **Creative Pursuit of An Inclusive Church** and failed to realize the goals the Committee of Five was attempting to accomplish.

On the positive side, the legislative body did make some incremental changes in the ecclesiastical law and policy of The Methodist Church. Those changes included:

1. Ensuring that whenever a ministerial member of an annual conference organization of the Central Jurisdiction was transferred to any geographical jurisdiction organization the minister would have the same rights and obligations as the other members of the geographical jurisdiction organization to which the minister was transferred.
2. Requesting the Council of Bishops to declare its willingness to transfer a bishop from the Central Jurisdiction Organization to a geographical jurisdiction organization when such transfer is requested by a geographical jurisdiction organization.
3. Urging each geographical jurisdiction organization to vote to request the Council of Bishops to transfer to it bishops from the Central jurisdiction Organization effective upon transfer of the annual conference organization(s) and to constitute their Episcopal Areas in accordance with a formula established by the legislative body—and make appropriate plans to receive them, and assign them to their respective residences.
4. Requesting each geographical jurisdiction organization to act, as promptly as details could be worked out and it was mutually agreeable,

to discontinue Central Jurisdiction annual conference organizations, transferred as "racially" segregated entities, and in the process establish a new Episcopal area or areas, and assign the bishop who came from the Central Jurisdiction Organization to an area.

5. Establishing a new 24-member Commission on Interjurisdictional Relations with a directive "that if, by September 1, 1967, for any reason the Central Jurisdiction [Organization]shall not have been dissolved pursuant to the procedures provided in Amendment IX, the Commission shall draft a report to the General Conference of 1968 on a plan for the termination of the Central Jurisdiction."
6. Declaring that "The Methodist Church is a part of the Church Universal" and affirming the right of "all persons, without regard to race, color, national origin, or economic condition...to attend its worship services, to participate in its programs, and, when they take the appropriate vows, to be admitted into its membership in any local church in the connection" (*Book of Discipline*, Par. 106.1).[3]
7. Establishing a rule that officials of a local church shall not give preference to any state or local law that conflicts with the policy of The Methodist Church "that the services of worship of every local Methodist Church shall be open to all persons without regard to race, color, or national origin" (Ibid, Par. 156).
8. Adoption of a provision of church law directing that in its determination of policies for the church school, the Commission on Education in the local church shall insure "that the educational program of the church be open to all persons without regard to race, color, nationality, or class" (Ibid. Par 233.1).
9. Enactment of a rule requiring that before a candidate for the traveling ministry is admitted on trial, the candidate shall be asked the following question: "Are you willing to relate yourself in ministry to all persons without regard to race, color, or national origin, including receiving them into the membership and fellowship of the Church?" (Ibid. Par. 322.5).
10. Incorporation in Methodist Church law of a provision that in the exercise of the powers and duties given to it by the General Conference Organization, a jurisdiction organization "shall act in all respects in harmony with the policy of The Methodist Church with respect to elimination of discrimination on the basis of race" (Ibid. Par. 527).
11. Promulgation of a rule that "in the exercise of the powers granted by the General Conference [Organization] each Annual Conference [Organization] shall act in all respects in harmony with the policy of The Methodist Church with respect to elimination of discrimination on the basis of race" (Ibid. Par 634).

12. Amending Methodist Church law to require that a bishop, "bearing in mind the stated goals of an inclusive church...shall seek the co-operation of the Cabinet and congregations in the appointment of pastors without regard to race or color" (Ibid. Par. 432.1).

It is interesting that one fascinating outcome of the Committee of Five's legislative initiative seems to have remained unnoticed over the years. In exploring ways to utilize Amendment IX creatively and innovatively, we decided *to establish a nexus between appropriate actions by geographical jurisdiction organizations and proposals to transfer annual conference organizations out of the Central Jurisdiction Organization.* We used our "transfer contract" principle to make geographical jurisdiction organizations, as well as their annual conference organizations, a party to transfer actions. (See Part IV of Chapter 6 for a discussion of this approach.)

The actions of the legislative body in 1964 gave the Committee of Five sufficient insights and policy premises to make reasonable and prudent recommendations to the 1964 quadrennial meeting of the Central Jurisdiction Organization.

## Chapter Notes

1. Under the rules of the legislative body a standing legislative committee could take one of the following actions on a memorial referred to it: (a) report it out with a vote of "non-concurrence," (b) report it out with a vote of "concurrence," or (c) make changes in it and report the amended version out with a "concurrence" vote.

2. **"There is general agreement that the crucial problem faced by The Methodist Church is the elimination of segregation...There are those who assume that the elimination of the Central Jurisdiction will solve the problem of segregation. There are others who point out that segregation is possible and likely after the elimination of the Central Jurisdiction even as there was segregation before the Central Jurisdiction or before Unification. There is a danger of giving too much attention to the framework of the organization and missing the heart of the problem."** Central Jurisdiction, *Report of the Commission to Study the Central Jurisdiction* (1956), P. 36.

To a large extent this action was a direct response to nationally and internationally embarrassing events involving local Methodist congregations in Jackson, Mississippi. Over a period of several months inter-"racial" teams had attempted to worship at two Methodist congregations in that city. Ushers would block entrance to these visitors, who were mainly local college students. Occasionally, however, Methodist ministers from northern and midwestern cities would accompany the visiting students. In several instances the ushers had them arrested. On Easter Sunday before the denominational legislative body convened in Pittsburgh, Pennsylvania, Central Jurisdiction Bishop Charles F. Golden and Northeastern Bishop James K. Matthews attempted to worship at Galloway Methodist Church. The chair of the official board barred them from entering the church and denied an opportunity to meet with the pastor of Galloway Church. As they gathered in Pittsburgh, many delegates were shocked by the scene of two bishops of The Methodist Church being turned away from a local congregation on Easter Sunday morning. The story of this incident was carried in the *New York Times on March 30, 1964.*

# CHAPTER 8
## Committee of Five: Managing *Inter-Organization* Conflict

Chapter 7 included a limited discussion of differences between the Committee of Five and the Commission of Thirty-Six, with respect to legislative action to rid The Methodist Church polity of involuntary "racial" separatism.

In the present chapter of the book we will examine more fully, from my perspective, fundamental differences of philosophy and viewpoint between the Committee of Five and the Commission of Thirty-Six (and between the Commission's chairman and myself, as the Committee's secretary).

Excluding the permanently established program agencies of The Methodist Church, two groups were specifically concerned with the "eliminate-the-Central-Jurisdiction Organization" *movement* during the 1960-1964 quadrennium. They were the general Church's Commission of Thirty-Six and the Central Jurisdiction Organization's Committee of Five.

The viewpoints of both organizations had become known among most leaders of The Methodist Church by the end of 1962.

The basic orientation of the Commission of Thirty-Six was that the Central Jurisdiction Organization was an *independent* phenomenon. The Commission did not view it as a complex structure of *human relationships* that formed a part of the fabric of other institutional and social phenomena.

The Committee of Five, on the other hand, viewed the Central Jurisdiction Organization as both a symptom and an expression of a deeply rooted *ideology and practice of "formalized racism"* in the polity of The Methodist Church. Unlike the Commission, we recognized that instituted "racism" was unsettling the fragile legitimacy of the Church's claim to be an instrument of peace, reconciliation and human freedom in a revolutionary world.

With such fundamental difference in perception of the nature of the "problem" presented by the Central Jurisdiction Organization, it was inevitable that there would be a basic difference in the remedies prescribed by the two groups. The Committee of Five was determined to address the *structural* aspects of the problem in ways that would substantially weaken and eventually eliminate "institutional racism" within The Methodist Church polity. This approach required significant changes in church law, in program processes, and in executive management practices.

The top priority of the Commission of Thirty-Six was to first remove an embarrassing "racially" defined and constitutionally prescribed organizational structure—by distributing its annual conference components among geographical jurisdiction organizations. The Commission seemed unperturbed that its approach to the problem would strengthen "institutional racism" within the polity of The Methodist Church. The Commission eschewed dealing with "institutional racism" through legislative interventions, opting instead for *voluntary* remedial processes.

The Commission laid out in its *First Report* a master plan for the elimination of the Central Jurisdiction Organization. The *First Report* was released in April 1961. The details of this plan were discussed in Chapter 6 of this book.

After a careful reading and analysis of the Commission's plan, I had no reasonable choice but to conclude that adoption of the plan would represent a tragic backward step—for Blacks in particular and for The Methodist Church in general.

**If the Commission's recommendations had been adopted, The Methodist Church would have reverted to the formalized pattern of relations between Blacks and Whites that existed in the Northern ME Church at the time of Unification in 1939.**

I reported my analysis and conclusions to the other members of the Committee of Five and to the Central Jurisdiction College of Bishops. I also told them that I was going to *personally* oppose the Commission's Amendment IX transfer recommendations even if we, as a Committee, chose not to take such opposition. The Committee wisely decided that before we took any public position we should ascertain the views of a much broader segment of the leaders of the Central Jurisdiction Organization. That decision was what immediately triggered the Committee's request that the Central Jurisdiction Bishops call a national study conference, (See **Appendix 4**.)

Meanwhile, the Commission of Thirty-Six was busy aggressively "selling" its Amendment IX transfer recommendations throughout The Methodist Church. However, the March 1962 recommendations of the Cincinnati Study Conference and the September 1962 Joint Declaration of the Committee of Five and the College of Bishops of the Central Jurisdiction effectively put the Commission's plan on hold until the Central Jurisdiction Organization could realign the boundaries of its annual conference organizations. The realignment would take place at the 1964 quadrennial meeting of the Central Jurisdiction Organization.

The Commission of Thirty-Six became quite displeased with the Committee of Five and the College of Bishops (a) for causing its plan of Amendment IX transfers to be put on hold and (b) for not honoring the Commission's request for a special meeting of the Central Jurisdictional Organization. With respect to these two issues, the historical records of the Committee of Five and of the Commission of Thirty-Six reveal the following events:

- **The recommendation of the Cincinnati Study Conference was as follows: "With regard to the matter of transfers of annual conferences under Amendment IX, no annual conferences of the Central Jurisdiction be transferred into a regional jurisdiction in which [they are] not located geographically (*Central Jurisdiction Speaks*, p. 8). The Joint Declaration requested the Committee of Five "to submit a proposed plan of realignment...to the College of Bishops by November 1, 1962."**

- **The Commission of Thirty-Six requested the College of Bishops of the Central Jurisdiction to call a special session of the Central Jurisdiction organization in 1963 to realign the boundaries of its annual conference organizations. This request was not honored for two principal reasons: (a) there was reasonable doubt that a special session could be legally convened in 1963 under existing church law and (b) it would negate the orderly process of planning and preparation for realignment actions to which the College of Bishops and the Committee of Five were committed under the Joint Declaration.**

- **At the October 5, 1962 meeting of the Executive Committee of the Commission, "A motion was made by Dr. James, seconded by Dr. Bosley, and passed, that: The Executive Committee transmit to the Central Jurisdiction College of Bishops and the Committee of Five our regret that they have disagreed with our recommendation for a special session of the Central Jurisdiction, and express our sense of urgency for such a session before the 1964 General Conference."** *Minutes of the Executive Committee of the Commission on Inter-Jurisdictional Relations* (October 5, 1962).

- **At the September 1963 Joint Meeting of the Committee of Five and the Central Jurisdiction Sub-Commission of the Commission of Thirty-Six, "It was reported that the Commission on Inter-Jurisdictional Relations has again requested the College of Bishops of the Central Jurisdiction to call a special session of the Jurisdictional Conference, this time *to meet at the same time and place of the General Conference.* After much discussion, a MOTION was adopted that the College of Bishops be advised of the groups' judgment that a special session should not be called, for the following reasons: (A) It would disrupt the planned schedule of activities and events outlined by the Committee of Five; (B) a special session of the Jurisdictional Conference at the same time and place of General Conference would be illegal under present church law; and (C) confusion would arise concerning delegates, as the *Discipline* does not determine which delegates—those elected in 1959 or those elected in 1963—would be eligible to attend such a special session of the Jurisdictional Conference."** *Minutes of Joint Meeting of Committee of Five and Central Jurisdiction Sub-Commission of the Commission on Inter-Jurisdictional Relations for September 26-27, 1963*

The Executive Committee of the Commission met in Chicago on October 5, 1962 (on my 40th birthday). Following that meeting I received the following note from Dr. John T. King, chairman of the Commission's Central Jurisdiction Sub-Commission.

> **"Bill:**
>
> **[These] questions were raised at our Executive Committee Meeting. They attempted to rake me over the coals and charged us with delaying. They are asking for a meeting of the Committee of Five and the Executive Committee at the Morrison [in Philadelphia] at 9:00 a.m., January 11, 1963, at the Commission's expense. They authorized our two groups, the Five and the Six, to meet prior to that if we want to. I think that we should. *We must come up with something.*"** (Emphasis in the original.)

King's note listed the following ten questions that the Executive Committee of the Commission wanted us to answer:

1. What additional elements of the program are desired?

2. What specific minority rights do we want preserved? Spell out.

3. What is meant by "overall planning and programming?" Spell out. Be very specific.

4. What does the statement mean that Amendment IX is inherently limited in scope?

5. Why do we refuse to call a session of the Jurisdictional Conference to realign *now?* Of what are we afraid?

6. What is meant by "adopt Basic Standards?"

7. What is meant by "An orderly fashion?"

8. What is meant by a "General study?" Why not specific study and specific action?

9. What Churches or conferences are ready for transfer now? What have we done to encourage such transfers?

10. What is meant by the statement on page 13 of the **Central Jurisdiction Speaks,** "The future conference status, etc.?" Of what are we afraid?

**It has been forty plus years since I received that note from John King. But I still have vivid recollections of my emotional reactions the first time I read these ten questions.**

**Suddenly, I became angry—very, very angry!**

It appeared to me at the time—and it still does today—that the Executive Committee of the Commission was blatantly attempting to exercise *directive* or *supervisory* authority over both the Committee of Five and the College of Bishops of the Central Jurisdiction Organization.

I immediately recalled that four months earlier (on June 21, 1962) the chairman of the Commission of Thirty-Six, Charles C. Parlin, had written a letter to Dr. James S. Thomas (chairman of the Committee of Five) and me, which included the following statements:

> **"The [First] Report of the Commission was well received by the church—I could almost say joyfully—and Annual Conferences went into action.**
>
> **Then came unilateral action by the Central Jurisdiction, the Committee of Five calling an unofficial, non-disciplinary**

> **meeting which recommended action against the Commission's report and urged a further period of study to be followed by realigning of boundaries."** Letter from Charles C. Parlin to James S. Thomas and W. Astor Kirk, June 21, 1962.

**I thought the Commission's Executive Committee was belittling our intelligence, our integrity, our commitment to The Methodist Church—even our Christian faith. After forty plus years I still believe the feelings I had in 1962 were grounded in reality.**

I experienced some of the same painful emotions that I had endured a decade earlier, when officials of the University of Texas responded to my application for admission to the graduate school to pursue doctoral studies. They offered me what they described as an "opportunity" to enroll in an *off-campus, "racially" segregated, single-student class* at the local YMCA. The class was to be taught by a "distinguished" professor of the University of Texas.

To sum up, I was shocked by the nature of the questions the Executive Committee wanted the Committee of Five and the Central Jurisdiction Bishops to answer.

After several days of meditative reflection, I recalled that Niccolo Machiavelli once said "There is nothing more difficult to take in hand, more perilous to conduct or more uncertain in its success than to take the lead in the introduction of a new order of things."

The Committee of Five had boldly taken the lead in "the introduction of a new order of things" within The Methodist Church.

I gained further calming insights from also recalling a statement that a noted architect was reported to have made a few years earlier. He said that he always designed a thing "by considering it in its next largest context—a chair in a room, a room in a house, a house in an environment, an environment in a city plan."

The Committee of Five, with strong encouragement and support from the College of Bishops and other leaders of the Central Jurisdiction, had courageously designed a plan to eliminate the Central Jurisdiction Organization—"by considering the next largest context," an *inclusive Methodist Church at all levels of the Church's life*, in a world in revolution.

The Executive Committee of the Commission of Thirty-Six had merely designed a plan to eliminate the Central Jurisdiction Organization, *not to achieve a higher moral end but simply as a means of relieving Commission members' feelings of self-conscious distress.*

As I revisit in this book the October 5, 1962 extraordinary demands that the Executive Committee of the Commission made, I do so in the context of insights gleaned from re-reading James MacGregor Burns' (1978) classic work on **Leadership**.

I now realize that the Commission of Thirty-Six was offering The Methodist Church what Burns calls *transactional* leadership. In its *First Report* the Commission did not offer Methodists a vision of a Church in which there would be no involuntary "racial" segregation. Rather, the Commission painted a picture of a denomination in which "forced segregation" (Commission of Seventy, *Report*, p. 22) would still exist—but in much less visible forms.

In contrast, the Committee of Five and the College of Bishops of the Central Jurisdiction were offering The Methodist Church what Burns characterizes as *transforming* and *moral* leadership. We challenged Methodists to take a courageous and significant step toward achieving a future Methodist fellowship that would be *undifferentiated on the basis of "race" and color.*

In October 1962, the new *understandings* that came from several days of meditation and reflection gave me the strength and determination to move forward toward the New Jerusalem envisioned in the **Statement and Recommendations** of the Cincinnati Study Conference and in the **Joint Declaration** of the Committee of Five and the Central Jurisdiction College of Bishops.

Most of the ten questions the Executive Committee posed are regrettably disingenuous manifestations of picayunish mind-sets. They require no serious attention here. However, there are several basic issues that I should briefly comment on for the benefit of readers who are unfamiliar with the dynamics of the movement in the 1960s to abolish the Central Jurisdiction Organization.

## Geographical Integrity of Regional Organizations

As I have previously stated, the Commission of Thirty-Six was aggressively promoting a plan for the elimination of the Central Jurisdiction Organization that the Committee of Five strongly opposed. The plan involved a significant and serious breach of the territorial integrity of geographical jurisdiction organizations. For example, under the plan the Northeastern Jurisdiction Organization would be given policy authority and program oversight responsibility for "racially defined" annual conference organizations operating in the states of Virginia, North Carolina and Kentucky. These states are in the territory of the Southeastern Jurisdiction Organization.

Likewise, the Commission's plan would assign to the North Central Jurisdiction Organization similar authority and responsibility with respect to "racially" defined annual conference organizations operating in Kentucky, Colorado, Kansas and Nebraska. As noted, Kentucky is in the territory of the Southeastern Jurisdiction Organization. Kansas and Nebraska are in the territory of the South Central Jurisdiction Organization, and Colorado is in the Western Jurisdiction Organization's territory.

Under such an arrangement there would have been no way for any one of those geographical jurisdiction organizations, *acting alone or independently*, to abolish the "racial boundaries" (Judicial Council Decision No. 85) of annual conference organizations transferred into it from the Central Jurisdiction Organization.

**This prospect posed a very serious problem for Blacks, not only in The Methodist Church but also throughout the United States of America.**

Yet the Commission of Thirty-Six was strongly opposed to any change in the law of The Methodist Church aimed at providing an effective legislative remedy. *Involuntary* "racial" segregation in The Methodist Church polity would have existed indefinitely in annual conference organizations of the Northeastern, North Central and Southeastern Jurisdiction Organizations—as a consequence of the dissolution of the Central Jurisdiction Organization.

> In an America that had made reasonable adjustments to the Supreme Court's *Brown v. Board of Education*" decision, it was incredibly naïve of the Commission to presume that Blacks in The Methodist Church would tolerate a concealed apartheid system resulting from the dissolution of the Central Jurisdiction Organization.

## Committee of Five's Boundary Realignment Plan

To address the matter of "racial boundaries" overlapping the territory of two or more geographical jurisdiction organizations, the Cincinnati Study Conference requested the Committee of Five to draft and submit a plan for realigning boundaries of certain Central Jurisdiction annual conference organizations. The draft plan was to be submitted to the College of Bishops of the Central Jurisdiction by November 1, 1962. The College of Bishops was expected to approve a proposed plan by the end of calendar year 1962.

It was the intention of the Committee of Five and the College of Bishops that the proposed realignment plan would be "discussed thoroughly by all parties and groups within The Methodist Church who [might] be affected directly or indirectly by the final adoption of the plan at the 1964 Central Jurisdiction Conference" (*Central Jurisdiction Speaks*, p. 12). See **Appendix 4.**

In the fall and winter of 1962, the Commission of Thirty-Six subjected the College of Bishops of the Central Jurisdiction and the Committee of Five to intense pressure. Their objective was clearly and forcefully articulated. The Commission wanted us:

1. To abandon our plans for *church-wide promotion in 1963 of the Committee of Five's boundary realignment proposals, and*

2. To immediately call a special meeting of the Central Jurisdiction organization *for the purpose of voting on the realignment proposals.*

With respect to the ten questions that the Commission asked us to answer, Question No. 5 was part of the pressure for an immediate vote on realigning boundaries of Central Jurisdiction annual conference organizations. It was this motivation that prompted the adoption of a motion "by Dr. Trigg James, seconded by Dr. Harold Bosley," directing the Commission's Executive Committee

> **"to the Central Jurisdiction College of Bishops and the Committee of Five our regret that they have disagreed with our recommendation for a special session of the Central Jurisdiction, and express our sense of urgency for such a session before the 1964 General Conference."** *Minutes of the Executive Committee of the Commission on Inter-Jurisdictional Relations for October 5, 1962.*

The Commission was either naively unaware of, or deliberately chose to ignore, the enormity and complexity of the task of providing the consultations and developing the understandings, *at the grass roots level,* that would be necessary to secure favorable action on the boundary realignment proposals. The realignment plan that the Committee of Five proposed involved disruption and severing of long-standing relationships among and between (a) individuals, both clergy and lay; (b) entities such as congregations, circuits, districts, and bi-conference enterprises; (c) program organizations such as Woman's Society schools of mission, inter-conference and inter-district Methodist Men's fellowships.

Moreover, some of the ongoing programming of denominational boards and agencies would be materially affected by the new structure of Central Jurisdiction annual conference organizations that the boundary realignments would create. Existing pension assets and liabilities of annuity funds of annual conference organizations would be affected.

In cooperation with the Woman's Division of Christian Service of the Board of Missions, the Human Relations Division of the Board of Christian Social Concerns, and the Division of the Local Church of the Board of Education, the Committee of Five had planned to conduct in 1963 a series of boundary realignment seminars, conferences, special presentations at schools of missions, and Methodist Men's retreats—not only within the Central Jurisdiction Organization but also throughout the Northeastern,

Southeastern, North Central and South Central Jurisdiction Organizations. Over 5,000 copies of the **Study Document on Realignment of the Central Jurisdiction** had been ordered for these meetings. And major presentations were to be made at the Second Methodist Conference on Human Relations.

**It was incomprehensible to me then how the Commission of Thirty-Six could conclude that it would be *wise and prudent* for us to (1) abandon all of these boundary-realignment promotion plans, (2) unilaterally cancel major inter-agency commitments, and (3) precipitously call a special session of the Central Jurisdiction Organization to vote immediately on the realignment proposals.**

We may never know the *real* reason why the Commission of Thirty-Six insisted that leaders of the Central Jurisdiction call a special session of the Central Jurisdiction Organization without proper planning and preparation.

Did they really want to diminish and jeopardize the *post-Cincinnati Conference* enhancement of the credibility and legitimacy of the Committee of Five? The Commission's only publicly articulated rationale was that it wanted some action that *"would enable the General Conference to know whether or not the plan of annual conference realignment will be adopted"* (*Second Report*, p. 3)

In this connection I should emphasize that the Committee of Five and the College of Bishops of the Central Jurisdiction committed themselves to a plan of action without knowing whether the Church's legislative body would enact the basic changes in church law needed to ensure the success of the plan. That is to say, we were going to move ahead aggressively to get the Committee of Five's realignment proposals approved even though the Commission of Thirty-Six strongly opposed our complementary legislative package.

The Central Jurisdiction College of Bishops, with the strong support of the Committee of Five, successfully resisted the misguided pressures of the Commission. We carried out our 1963 boundary-realignment promotion plans. The *transformational* and *moral* leadership that we provided paid off handsomely at the 1964 quadrennial meeting of the Central Jurisdiction Organization. With three modifications that the Committee felt had substantial merit, the plan of realigning the boundaries of Central Jurisdiction annual conference organizations was overwhelmingly adopted.

### Creative Use of Amendment IX

In the Joint Declaration, the Committee of Five and the College of Bishops of the Central Jurisdiction acknowledged that

> **The only existing procedural machinery for abolishing the Central Jurisdiction is Amendment IX of the Constitution of The Methodist Church.** ***This amendment is inherently limited in***

> ***scope*. Nevertheless, it may be used creatively to achieve the pattern of abolition of the Central Jurisdiction to which we are committed, provided Methodists in all jurisdictions are willing to use for that purpose.**

The Executive Committee of the Commission of Thirty-Six wanted the Committee of Five to respond to the question "What is meant by the statement that Amendment IX is inherently limited in scope?"

*It is unlikely that most readers of this book know that, as posed by the Commission's Executive Committee, this apparently simple and innocent question is a surrogate for reference to an issue of fundamental difference of viewpoint between the Committee of Five and the Commission.*

If that were not the case, I would not devote any time and space to the Executive Committee's question, which has an appearance of sandbox silliness, given the 1956 legislative history of Amendment IX. The record of the proceedings of the 1956 quadrennial session of the Church's legislative body reveals that officers and prominent members of the Commission of Thirty-Six played major roles in shaping Amendment IX. They intended for it to be what Burns (1978) describes as a *transactional* document rather than a *transformational* instrument.

**What the Commission really wanted to know was why the Committee of Five intended to facilitate and support the utilization of Amendment IX to achieve objectives that the Commission was unwilling to embrace or be identified with publicly.**

The Committee of Five had informed the dominant "power elites" of The Methodist Church that the Committee intended to use Amendment IX to achieve transfers of "racially" defined Central Jurisdiction annual conference organizations into geographical jurisdiction organizations, *in ways and under conditions that would ensure their discontinuance as "racially" defined annual conference organizations.*

In other words, the Committee had vowed to legally and morally use Amendment IX to prevent the institutionalization within geographical jurisdiction organizations of The Methodist Church polity of "separate but equal" governance entities based on "race" and color.

The Commission of Thirty-Six did not approve of this strategy. The strategy was not consistent with the Commission's concept of "voluntarism." Hence the question posed by the Commission was part of a search for a way to oppose the strategy without triggering damaging public reaction.

Part IV of Chapter 6 of this book outlined the broad set of principles the Committee of Five adopted to govern transfers under Amendment IX. The Committee then assigned me the task of working out implementation details. I developed the concept of a *"transfer contract,"* which I will discuss in detail in a later chapter. Suffice it to state here that one provision of the contract was that the transferring annual conference organization "shall no longer continue to exist as a racially segregated entity."

The Committee of Five incorporated this "transfer contract" concept in one of its recommendations to the 1964 quadrennial session of the Central Jurisdiction Organization. That recommendation was adopted.

- Both the Commission of Thirty-Six and the Committee of Five were familiar with the limitations of Amendment IX.

- Both groups knew it was inherently limited in terms of the scope of its initial objectives.

The members of the Commission's Executive Committee posed their question to the Committee of Five not because they did not understand that the basic objective sought in 1956, when Amendment IX was conceived, was to provide a means whereby Central Jurisdiction local churches and annual conference organizations might transfer into geographical jurisdiction organizations, **as "racially" segregated entities of The Methodist Church polity**. The Commission's Executive Committee also knew that in 1956 it was assumed that ultimately the Central Jurisdiction Organization might be eliminated through such transfers.

In 1962, for some undisclosed reason, the Commission became frightened by the Committee of Five's determination to prevent Amendment IX from being used in ways that would result in The Methodist Church's reversion to the pre-Unification pattern of "racially" segregated annual conference organizations in otherwise geographically defined governance structures. Once we understood that dynamic, the Committee of Five was able to deal with the Commission's fears constructively, compassionately and civilly

.

## Meetings

Of necessity, the work that the Committee of Five had to perform on behalf of the Central Jurisdiction Organization involved consideration of issues and problems that concerned the Commission of Thirty-Six, which operated under a mandate from the Church's legislative body. In creating the Committee of Five the 1960 quadrennial meeting of the Central Jurisdiction Organization specifically directed the Committee to "analyze the proposals, recommendations, and actions of the Commission on Inter-Jurisdictional Relations as they relate to or involve the Central Jurisdiction [Organization]."

From the beginning the Committee of Five recognized the desirability of consultations with the Commission of Thirty-Six on matters of mutual concern to both groups. On June 20, 1962, an informal consultation was held in New York City between the officers of the Committee and the officers of the Commission. Also present at this meeting were the executives of (a) the Division of Human Relations and Economic Affairs of the denominational Board of Christian Social Concerns and (b) the Department of Christian Social Relations of the Woman's Division of Christian Service of the denominational Board of Missions. Both of these executives had responsibilities with respect to promotion of The Methodist Church's Quadrennial Emphasis on Race Relations.

The note from John King, chairman of the Central Jurisdiction Sub-Commission, (shown above) revealed an interest in a joint meeting of the Committee of Five and the Executive Committee of the Commission of Thirty-Six. The note suggested January 11, 1963. I wrote the secretary of the Commission expressing my view that a joint meeting of the two groups would probably be useful and productive. I advised that on January 11th we would be in Atlantic City, New Jersey. However, I was sure that we could arrange our schedule to provide time for a joint meeting in Atlantic City. I indicated that I would recommend such a course of action to my Committee of Five Colleagues.

**On October 25, 1962 the Commission's secretary, Dr. D. Trigg James, wrote advising me of the difficulty of getting to Atlantic City from Philadelphia. After consulting with the other members of the Committee of Five, I accepted the suggestion that the meeting be held in Philadelphia.**

On January 11, 1963, the Committee of Five and the Executive Committee of the Commission of Thirty-Six held a joint meeting in Philadelphia, Penn_hases_a. At this meeting there were free and frank exchanges of viewpoints and concerns. The officers of the Commission strongly expressed their understanding that the mandate given the Commission in 1960 by the Church's legislative body was grounded in the principle of *voluntary action*. The Commission could not propose courses of action that were inconsistent with that mandate. Hence the Amendment IX transfer proposals in the *First Report* were within the bounds of the Commission's mandate.

A point was made that my vocal and aggressive opposition to those transfer proposals had the effect of thwarting the operation of the principle of *voluntary* action. In 1960 the Church's legislative body intended that the principle of voluntary action apply to the Amendment IX transfer process, when it directed the Commission to promote transfers of Central Jurisdiction annual conference organizations into geographical jurisdiction organizations. The implication of the point was that once Central Jurisdiction annual conference organizations were transferred, they would continue as "racially" segregated entities of The Methodist Church polity until all parties "affected [were voluntarily] ready" for a different status (*First Report*, p. 2).

In response, I recalled that six months earlier Dr. A. Dudley Ward, the chief executive of the denominational Board of Christian Social Concerns, gave me a draft copy of a manuscript on "Voluntarism within Methodism" and requested my comments on it. I shared with the group my written Statement on the Principle of Voluntarism, which is included in this book as **Appendix 8.**

I expressed to the Commission's Executive Committee my strong feelings that the most obnoxious form of "racial" segregation, especially within the fellowship of a Christian church, is *involuntary* separation on the basis of "race" and color—what the Commission of Seventy referred to as "forced segregation" (*Report*, 1960, p. 22).

I stated that within The Methodist Church, the constitutional provisions, laws, structures, processes, rules, regulations, and official practices that are based on "race" and color **are not results of historically defined and understood "voluntary action." They are the product of conscious behavioral choices of men and women in their exercise of the social power of The Methodist Church, as a social institution. The Central Jurisdiction organization and all of its annual conference entities represent *involuntary*, not *voluntary*, "racial" segregation.**

I told the two groups the fundamental question that each member of the Commission of Thirty-Six and each member of the Committee of Five must ask and answer for herself or himself is-

- **"What *formalized and institutionalized* patterns and structures of relationships between Blacks and Whites—within The Methodist Church fellowship—am I going to help establish through my participation in the processes of eliminating the Central Jurisdiction Organization?"**

I concluded my comments by saying that my Christian conscience would not allow me to support a process of eliminating the Central Jurisdiction organization that would resurrect from the institutional graveyard the pre-Unification patterns of "race" relations of the Northern ME Church.

Another delicate matter surfaced at the joint meeting. It related to issues about specifying "minority rights," which was referenced in question Number 2 of the note from John King. A member of the Commission alluded to a perception that the Committee of Five opposed the Commission's Amendment IX transfer proposals in order to preserve "Negro" staff positions on denominational boards, agencies and commissions. The implication was subtle but nonetheless clear to members of the Committee of Five. It was that we were attempting to protect certain special interests.

For the benefit of readers who may not be familiar with certain staffing practices of The Methodist Church forty years ago, I include here the following brief explanation.

One of the practices of church boards and agencies at that time was to recruit and employ certain staff to serve what I referred to in 1962 as "associated clientele groups," of which the Central Jurisdiction Organization was one. The positions held by Blacks were commonly called "Negro" staff jobs. The Commission member's comment about a perception that the Committee of Five was interested in protecting "Negro" staff jobs was made in that context.

**In the 1960s there were both a "new generation" and a "new breed" of Blacks serving in staff positions at denominational boards and agencies of The Methodist Church. (E.g., Dr. James Thomas and I were two of them.) This was a phenomenon that top management and volunteer officers of governing bodies did not fully recognize or appreciate.**

- **Talented, well educated, sophisticated, comfortable at serving *inter*-racially as well as *intra*-racially, these Blacks did not view themselves in "racial" terms or as "Negro" staff members. Their self-understanding was that they were staff servants of The Methodist Church as a whole and not just the Central Jurisdiction Organization of the denomination.**

At the joint meeting of the Committee of Five and the Commission's Executive Committee, Dr. James S. Thomas, chairman of the Committee of Five, responded to this concern—calmly, brilliantly, concisely and prophetically. He emphasized the point of the *Joint Declaration* that affirmed the desire of Blacks to "enjoy the responsibility, privilege, and opportunity of making their contributions to our church's ministries of preaching, teaching, witnessing, and serving solely on the basis of their ability, competence, and depth of understanding of the Christian faith and our Methodist heritage"(*Central Jurisdiction Speaks*, 1962, p. 11). See **Appendix 5.**

Chairman Thomas made his response against the backdrop of an in-depth and professional analysis of the issue involved. The Committee of Five and Blacks on the staffs of denominational boards and agencies were well aware of the erroneous perceptions of the Commission's Executive Committee.[1]

At the conclusion of the period of exchanging personal viewpoints, we reported that the College of Bishops had recently approved the Committee of Five's plan for realigning boundaries of Central Jurisdiction annual conference organizations. We also outlined in detail our boundary-realignment promotion plans for 1963. The Commission's Executive Committee reported that the **Second Report** of the Commission was in the final stages of preparation. The report would probably be issued by the end of January 1963.

While fundamental differences of viewpoint remained, the January 11, 1963 joint meeting of the Committee of Five and the Commission's

Executive Committee opened up fruitful channels of communication. On July 29, 1963 I received a letter from the Commission's chairman requesting a copy of my report on the "*Central Jurisdiction Membership Which Will Be Within Regional Jurisdictions Under Committee of Five's Realignment Plan.*" I sent the report to Mr. Parlin August 1st. On August 13th Mr. Parlin wrote thanking me for my report. He stated, "The data concerning the Committee of Five's plan for realignment of boundaries...is exactly what I needed."

The Committee of Five met with the full Commission of Thirty-Six in Chicago, Illinois on October 16, 1963. There was a general review of the impact of the Second Methodist Conference on Human Relations, which was held in Chicago August 26-30, 1963. The issue of the Commission's desire for a special meeting of the Central Jurisdiction Organization at the time and place of the 1964 quadrennial session of the Church's legislative body was discussed. The Committee of Five explained the three reasons why it strongly advised the College of Bishops of the Central Jurisdiction not to attempt to convene such a special session.

The two groups engaged in a lengthy discussion of the Commission's draft report for the consideration of the 1964 quadrennial session of the denominational legislature. The fundamental difference of viewpoint involved the issue of "racially" segregated annual conference organizations of geographical jurisdiction organizations. The Committee of Five was strongly committed to ensuring that Central Jurisdiction annual conference organizations transferring under Amendment IX would not exist indefinitely as "racially" segregated entities of The Methodist Church. We wanted the Church's legislative body to enact what I called an "anti-racial-segregation rule" (" **ARS Rule**"). As we read the draft report, it did not specifically and categorically renounce "racially" segregated annual conference organizations.

> We wanted to establish a new ecclesiastical, cultural and cross-"racial" trajectory for Blacks in The Methodist Church.

Members of the Commission declined to join us in seeking at least legislative affirmation that "racially" segregated annual conference organizations are incompatible with policies and principles of The Methodist Church with respect to institutional relationships between Blacks and Whites within the church. They regarded any general church ARS Rule or principle as incompatible with the basic premises of *voluntarism*. Some members of the Commission expressed the view that any action by the Church's legislative body to impose an ARS Rule upon geographical jurisdiction organizations would violate the constitution of The Methodist Church.

We shared with the Commission my draft of a Committee of Five memorial to the 1964 session of the Church's legislative body, which would expand existing church law to include an ARS Rule. I explained to the group that if the Church's legislative body failed to directly address this issue, our only practical recourse would be to advise Central Jurisdiction annual conference organizations to do the "Adam Clayton Powell thing" [2] and incorporate an ARS Rule in every Amendment IX transfer proposal.

During the 1960-64 quadrennium there were six joint meetings of the Committee of Five and the Central Jurisdiction Sub-Commission of the Commission of Thirty-Six. The Sub-Commission rendered invaluable assistance in the planning for the Cincinnati Study Conference and in the drafting of the Study Document on Realignment. We consulted extensively with the Sub-Commission regarding the substance of our Final Report to the 1964 quadrennial meeting of the Central Jurisdiction organization.

In retrospect, it is quite evident that the Central Jurisdiction Sub-Commission of the Commission of Thirty-Six occupied a delicate and very difficult "in between" position. (See statement of John King that appears at the end of this chapter.)

It was part of a larger organization with a general church mandate that the organization's top leaders construed from a "transactional" mind-set. Yet the Sub-Commission had to relate to and participate in the work of the Committee of Five whose members operated from a "transformational" view of their mission.

One thing that facilitated the close cooperation of the two groups was the fact that the chairman of the Sub-Commission, Dr. John T. King, and I were (a) former professional colleagues, (b) members of the same Central Jurisdiction West Texas Annual Conference Organization and (c) delegates to the 1960 and 1964 quadrennial meetings of the Central Jurisdiction Organization.

---

## Special Statement of John T. King
## At A Session of the 1964 Legislative Body
## During Consideration of the Report of the Commission of Thirty-Six

"Bishop Corson, members of the General Conference, and my friends. I am sure each of you can envision what an extremely difficult assignment this Commission has assumed. Also, I am sure that some can appreciate the fact that six of the members of the Commission have had to wear two hats, one as Commission members representing the church at large, and one as members of the minority group which has been seriously affected through the years by the matters and concerns that have been the major consideration of the Commission.

**"These are not hats identical to those worn by our colleagues and brethren from the regional jurisdictions. However, in the wearing of these two hats, it is my own belief that there have been no divided loyalties for we each hold first allegiance to The Methodist Church while representing this Commission....**

**"To wear my alternate or companion hat, we of the Central Jurisdiction obviously wished to see it eliminated as soon as possible, but be it remembered that we did not create it ourselves. We cannot accept a proposal simply calling for us to abolish the Central Jurisdiction....we must have a plan so that we can see, or at least anticipate, where we are going to land, those adhering to the old admonishment 'Look before you leap'."** *Daily Christian Advocate, May 1, 1964, p. 145.*

---

## Chapter Notes

1. Dr. Thomas' transformational and moral leadership in dealing with the issue of *mischaracterizations* of the roles of Blacks on the staffs of denominational boards and agencies is clearly reflected in the following Memorandum to those staff associates.

Board of Education * Division of Higher Education
The Methodist Church
P. O. Box 871
Nashville 2, Tennessee
November 30, 1962

| | |
|---|---|
| Dr. John H. Graham | Dr. L. Scott Allen |
| Rev. R. Fletcher | Dr. T. E. Echols |
| Rev. Dewitt E. Dykes | Dr. Ernest T. Dixon |
| Miss Theressa Hoover | Dr. W. D. Lester |
| Miss Dorothy Barnette | Dr. J. H Touchstone |
| **Mr. George N. Daniels** | **Dr. W. Astor Kirk** |

Dear Colleagues:

On November 2, the Committee of Five to Study the Central Jurisdiction met in joint session with the College of Bishops at Dillard University in New Orleans, Louisiana. Many of you were present. We also met jointly with the six members of the Central

Jurisdiction on the Commission on Interjurisdictional Relations. This provided an opportunity to discuss many of the important issues which face us in this transitional period. After a rather long discussion of procedures by which these issues could be intelligently discussed, the Committee of Five and the Committee of Six agreed that we should hold a consultation of our joint group and all members of the field staff of the Central Jurisdiction.

One of our colleagues, Ernest Dixon of the Board of Education, presented a paper to the College of Bishops indicating the need for each of us to think through our specific work and develop a rationale for our continuing work against the background of the changes which are likely to take place. In other words, we shall have to justify our positions as staff members first, and "Negro staff members" secondly, or even incidentally. This is not necessarily a difficult process, but it is certainly one which no group can carry on at long range.

Therefore, pursuant to the action of the joint group, I am fulfilling their request to each of us to prepare a paper outlining our work, the rationale for our work, and the rationale for our continuing work within The Methodist Church. The joint group felt that all of us should prepare these papers and have them ready for presentation at a session which will be held in Atlanta, Georgia on March 1, 1963. Each staff member is asked to be able to present the details concerning his work and discuss his work with reference to the changes which are expected in the future. All of us have been assured that this is not to be a "defense" of our position. We hope to do this in a completely objective atmosphere so that each of us can share with the other some of the plans which we have in mind.

Please consider this a very urgent request to clear your schedules for this meeting, which we may be able to hold before the end of the quadrennium. If this can be done properly, the Committee of Five would like to include some of these insights in its quadrennial report to the Seventh Central Jurisdictional Conference which will be held at Bethune-Cookman College, Daytona Beach, Florida, in June of 1964.

With best wishes, I am
Sincerely yours,

/s/ James S. Thomas

2. In the 1960s, before Congress enacted a general anti-discrimination law, Congressman Adam Clayton Powell would attach "anti-discrimination riders" to every education grant-in-aid bill that came to the House

Education and Labor Committee.. That legislative tactic was popularly referred to as the "Adam Clayton Powell thing."

# CHAPTER 9
# Committee of Five: Quadrennial Performance Report

The Seventh Quadrennial Session of the Central Jurisdiction Organization was held in Daytona Beach, Florida on June 16-21, 1964. The delegates to this session were definitely more hopeful and upbeat than those four years earlier. They manifested a feeling of "we're in control of our own destiny." Part of this positive and proactive attitude was due to the dedicated and imaginative work of the Committee of Five during the quadrennium from 1960 to 1964.

At the 1964 session, the Committee of Five had three major tasks; they were:

- To give an oral account of its stewardship during the quadrennium;
- To present the Committee's final report and recommendations; and
- To facilitate the delegates' consideration of and action on the recommendations of the Committee.

Dr. James S. Thomas, Committee chairman, gave an oral overview of the work of the Committee since its organization meeting in January 1961. He began by stating that fundamentally the title of the Committee's report epitomized its work. For throughout the quadrennium the Committee worked, indeed, to build **Bridges to Racial Equality in The Methodist Church.** Dr. Thomas informed the delegates that the bridge-building work of the Committee was decisively influenced and shaped by basic beliefs, which members of the Committee shared. A statement of these beliefs, he noted, introduces the printed report. The Committee's statement of basic beliefs is such a powerful affirmation that even today it resonates with Methodists who are intentionally committed to a radically inclusive fellowship within the current United Methodist Church.[1]

The chairman then briefly described the various facets of the Committee's work during the quadrennium—**(a)** research; **(b)** meetings, including joint meetings with the College of Bishops and with the Central Jurisdiction Sub-Commission of the Commission of Thirty-Six, the Commission's

Executive Committee and the full Commission, **(c)** analyzing the "proposals, recommendations, and actions" of the Commission of Thirty-Six as they related to or involved the Central Jurisdiction Organization **(d)** planning the Cincinnati Study Conference, **(e)** developing a plan to realign the boundaries of Central Jurisdiction annual conference organizations, **(f)** drafting memorials for the consideration of The Methodist Church's legislative body, **(g)** working with and providing assistance to annual conference organizations and local churches, **(h)** attending conferences throughout the denomination and making major presentations regarding the elimination of "racial" segregation in the polity of The Methodist Church, and **(i)** writing articles for publication in religious periodicals.

All of the members of the Committee participated in the question-and-answer period and the general discussion that followed Dr. Thomas's overview presentation. Generally, the Committee of Five was highly praised for planning the Cincinnati Study Conference, for developing and publishing the Study Document on Realignment of the Central Jurisdiction, and for the memorial-petition document **Creative Pursuit of an Inclusive Church.** Delegates expressed the view that these materials were very helpful.

## Recommendations of the Committee

The Committee of Five presented 16 recommendations for the consideration of the delegates. All were adopted, several with minor modification by the delegates. The most important policy and procedural ones are briefly discussed here.

**Fundamental Goal.** There were three recommendations pertaining to fundamental goals for the transition period ahead. The ***first*** was reaffirmation of a "commitment to the fundamental goal of a society and fellowship of Methodist Christians *completely uncircumscribed*, at all levels of church life, by distinctions based on race or color."

***Second***, the pursuit of Christian inclusiveness should "be clearly reflected in all plans and programs of the Central Jurisdiction [Organization] aimed at implementing Amendment IX."

***Third***, recognizing that "racially segregated annual conference organizations in geographical jurisdiction organizations are incompatible with a truly inclusive Methodist Church," the Central Jurisdiction Organization should "unequivocally" oppose "racially" segregated annual conference organizations.

With little discussion or debate, the delegates unanimously approved these three recommendations.

**Realignment of Boundaries.** Under the Committee of Five's boundary realignment plan, each of the fifteen Central Jurisdiction annual conference organizations would be situated entirely within the territory of a geographical jurisdiction organization. With the agreement of the Committee, the delegates made minor changes in the boundaries proposed for the North Carolina-Virginia and Tennessee-Kentucky Annual Conference Organizations. The delegates adopted the plan as modified. They also approved the recommendation authorizing any two annual conference organizations "within the same State to merge and form a single annual conference [organization], *provided* the boundaries of the new conference shall coincide with the geographical boundaries of that State."

**Criteria for Annual Conference Transfers.** The delegates established the following criteria to govern transfers of Central Jurisdiction annual conference organizations into geographical jurisdiction organizations:

1. Agreement by the receiving geographical jurisdiction organization that all of its annual conference organizations shall be so constituted as to include *all* local Methodist churches in a designated geographical area, regardless of the "racial" characteristics of the membership of the local churches.

2. Agreement of the annual conference organizations of the receiving geographical jurisdiction organization that they will implement the law of The Methodist Church that guarantees to ministers in full connection in the Central Jurisdiction transferring annual conferences the same status, rights, privileges and responsibilities under the same conditions as other ministers in full connection in those annual conference organizations within the geographical jurisdiction organizations.

3. Agreement of the annual conference organizations of a receiving geographical jurisdiction organization that opportunities for lay participation in the enjoyment of the benefits of all programs, activities, and institutions of those annual conference organizations will be provided without regard to "race" or color.

4. Agreement that each geographical jurisdiction organization involved, will request the Council of Bishops to transfer to that geographical jurisdiction organization for presidential and residential supervision the bishop of the Central Jurisdiction Organization assigned to preside over the transferring annual conference organization(s).

**Continuing Committee of Five.** The final three recommendations that the delegates adopted involved authorizing a continuing Committee of Five for the 1964-1968 quadrennium. The work envisioned for a continuing Committee included:

1. Serving in an executive capacity to the Central Jurisdiction Advisory Council to the new denominational Commission of Twenty-Four.[2]

2. Giving guidance and assistance to Central Jurisdiction annual conference organizations and local congregations as they developed plans to transfer into geographical jurisdiction organizations in accordance with established criteria.

3. Representing to the denominational Commission for Ecumenical Affairs and the Ad Hoc Committee on EUB Union the genuine concern that no "racially" segregated structures be included in the Plan of Merger of The Methodist Church and the Evangelical United Brethren Church.

## Immediate Steps To Be Taken

In 1956, delegates to the quadrennial meeting of the Central Jurisdiction Organization affirmed not only the "desirability" but also the "inevitability" of the dissolution of that "racially" constituted governance entity within The Methodist Church polity. Delegates again reaffirmed that position in 1960 and in 1962 the Cincinnati Study Conference did likewise. The only procedural machinery available to the Committee of Five was Amendment IX of the constitution of The Methodist Church.

The delegates to the 1964 session of the Central Jurisdiction Organization directed the continuing Committee of Five and the 15 Central Jurisdiction annual conference organizations to "give the highest priority to a *programmed implementation* of the annual conference transfer provision of Amendment IX." The immediate steps for the future would include the following actions:

(a) Each Central Jurisdiction annual conference organization would be encouraged to initiate an appropriate resolution to transfer into the geographical jurisdiction organization within whose bounds it was located. The resolution should be presented to the agency of the annual conference organization that has responsibility for studying all matters related to transfers under Amendment IX.[3]

(b) At the earliest practicable date in the 1964-1968 quadrennium the Central Jurisdiction's Lexington Annual Conference Organization would transfer into the North Central jurisdiction Organization. Likewise, the Delaware and Washington Annual Conference Organizations would transfer into the Northeastern Jurisdiction Organization.

(c) Annual conference organizations of the Central Jurisdiction that could not be transferred during the 1964-1968 quadrennium to the geographical jurisdiction organizations in which they were located, fully in accordance with established criteria, would remain as the Central Jurisdiction *in transition* until proper transfers could be made. No Central Jurisdiction annual conference organization would become established as a "racially" segregated unit of a geographical jurisdiction organization. Delegates to the Central Jurisdiction Organization's 1964 session were firm in their conviction that at that moment in history there was no justification for a system of "racially" segregated annual conference organizations in the polity of The Methodist Church.

## Intermediate Action Programs

The delegates recognized the likelihood that not all 15 Central jurisdiction annual conference organizations would be able to transfer into geographical jurisdiction organizations in the 1964-1968 quadrennium. They supported specific and positive intermediate programs to help pave the way for eventual transfers consistent with the criteria the session adopted.

With respect to specific and positive intermediate programs, the delegates recommended that the bishops of the Central Jurisdiction initiate a Cooperative Programming of Methodist Concerns (CPMC); which would include at least the following elements:

(a) Joint cabinet meetings of conferences in overlapping Episcopal areas,

(b) Joint meetings of boards, commissions and other conference agencies,

(c) Joint planning and administration of evangelistic efforts, pastor's schools, and leadership training enterprises, and

(d) The exchange of pulpits and reciprocal family and group visitations for worship and fellowship between different congregations.

### Summary of Committee of Five Accomplishments

During the 1960-1964 quadrennium the Committee of Five facilitated and supported innovative planning, and risky but reasonable institutional-change enterprises. As a result delegates to the Central Jurisdiction Organization were able to put in place in June of 1964 an overall framework of policy and procedures for the elimination of this "racially" segregated governance institution in an orderly and responsible manner. They proved the skeptics, "doubting Thomas's" and cynics wrong.

We had not engaged in "foot dragging." We had tried to intelligently carry out "consistent planning" to implement "the procedures duly authorized in Amendment IX of the constitution of The Methodist Church," as we and others were asked to do. (See *General Conference Journal*, 1960, p. 1511).

The new Central Jurisdiction leadership that coordinated and directed this effort had, indeed, put Blacks in The Methodist Church in a position where they could, in the words of Dean Richardson, "bargain collectively" to ensure that Central Jurisdiction annual conference organizations would "not enter into a merger in disorder and disarray." ( Dean E. Richardson's comments in a letter to Charles C. Parlin dated July 6, 1962.)

The four principal publications of the Committee of Five contributed immensely to this outcome. **The Central Jurisdiction Speaks** (report on the Cincinnati Conference); **The Study Document on Realignment of the Central Jurisdiction; Creative Pursuit of An Inclusive Church** (memorial-petition document for delegates to the Church's legislative body); and **Bridges to Racial Equality in The Methodist Church**—these four publications focused on both issue analysis and policy-change advocacy. As James S. Thomas (1992, p.113) has stated:

> **By the publication and distribution to bishops, district superintendents, and pastors of the Central Jurisdiction of these documents, the people of a wide and diverse jurisdiction became knowledgeable about the basic issues of the Central Jurisdiction. What Amendment IX sought to do by *general permission*, the Central Jurisdiction sought to do by *clearly outlined procedures and policies*.** Emphasis added.

The chairman and secretary of the Committee of Five also carried on the "clearly outlined procedures and policies" approach through articles that they wrote for several religious periodicals. The articles included the following:

- "Central Jurisdiction Actions Since the Cincinnati Conference," James S. Thomas, ***CONCERN***, October 15, 1962.

- "Steps Toward An Inclusive Methodist Church," James S. Thomas, ***CONCERN***, February 15, 1964.

- "The Central Jurisdiction: *Dilemma and Opportunity*," James S. Thomas, ***MOTIVE***, March 1964.

- "Decisions of the Central Jurisdiction Study Conference," W. Astor Kirk, ***CONCERN***, May 1, 1962.

- "What Will Follow the Central Jurisdiction?" W. Astor Kirk, ***CHRISTIAN ADVOCATE***, January 17, 1963.

- "Another View of the Plan," W. Astor Kirk, ***CHRISTIAN ADVOCATE***, April 23, 1964.

- "Modify Church Law," W. Astor Kirk, ***CONCERN***, April 15, 1964.

Upon completing action on the report and recommendations of the Committee of Five, the 1964 quadrennial session of the Central Jurisdiction Organization turned to its second important agenda item. That was to elect a person to the episcopacy to replace retiring Bishop Matthew W. Clair, Jr. The general understanding among Central Jurisdiction Organization leaders and leaders of the North Central Jurisdictional Organization was that the new bishop would be transferred, under Amendment IX procedures, to the North Central Jurisdiction Organization before the end of 1964.

At the conclusion of a long balloting process, the delegates elected Dr. James S. Thomas to the episcopacy. He became the thirteenth bishop to be elected by the "racially" defined Central Jurisdiction Organization since its establishment in 1939. Bishop Thomas was assigned to the realigned Lexington Annual Conference Organization.

### First Round of Transfers After 1964 Central Jurisdiction Organization Meeting

For over a year the Committee of Five had worked with lay and clerical leaders of the Delaware, Washington and Lexington Annual Conference Organizations and with their counterparts in the Northeastern and North Central Jurisdiction Organizations. A shared vision of and a commitment to geographical jurisdiction organizations without any "racially" segregated *sub*units had emerged.

We planned for and expected the first round of annual conference organization transfers from the Central Jurisdiction Organization into geographical jurisdiction organizations to take place before the end of 1964. They would involve the Lexington, Delaware and Washington.

***Delaware And Washington Annual Conference Organizations***

After the 1964 realignment actions, the Delaware and Washington Annual Conference Organizations jointly had slightly over 500 local congregations. The combined membership of these congregations was 80,000 plus. One bishop and eleven district superintendents provided supervisory leadership for the local churches and their pastors.

Effective July 25, 1964, the Central Jurisdiction Organization membership of the Delaware and Washington Annual conference Organizations came to an end. They became constituent units of the Northeastern Jurisdiction Organization. On that day, at the quadrennial meeting of the Northeastern Jurisdiction Organization, Bishop W. Vernon Middleton announced that the 20 annual conference organizations of the Northeastern Jurisdiction Organization had overwhelmingly voted to approve the transfer of Delaware and Washington. Thereafter, Bishop Prince A. Taylor, Jr. reported that the other annual conference organizations of the Central Jurisdiction Organization had voted by substantial majorities to approve the transfer of Delaware and Washington into Northeastern.

In accordance with procedures enacted at the 1964 session of the denomination's legislative body, Bishop Taylor was transferred from the Central Jurisdiction College of Bishops to the Northeastern College of Bishops. Bishop Taylor was assigned to the Northeastern Jurisdiction Organization's New Jersey Area for residential and presidential duties. Thus, Bishop Taylor became the first episcopal leader who is Black to be assigned to an area of The Methodist Church comprised primarily of local congregations whose members and pastors were mostly Whites.

Several months before the 1964 quadrennial meeting of the Northeastern Jurisdiction Organization, leaders of the Delaware and Washington Annual conference Organizations and their Northeastern counterparts had entered into a mutual agreement. It provided that when the Delaware and Washington became constituent units of the Northeastern Jurisdiction Organization, all annual conference organizations of Northeastern would be reconstituted so that none would be "racially" segregated. In light of this commitment to "racial" inclusiveness, the Delaware and Washington annual conference Organizations remained intact for one year until all of the details of amalgamation and consolidation could be worked out. These details included such matters as pension rates, minimum salary of pastors, transfer of property, establishing new district boundaries, and interchange of pastoral appointments.

All of the local churches involved were placed under the supervision of Bishop John W. Lord. Geographically, more than 400 of the 500 churches of the Delaware and Washington Annual conference Organizations, with a combined membership of about 50,000, fell within the boundaries of the

Northeastern Jurisdiction Organization's Washington Episcopal Area. Prior to the temporary addition of Delaware and Washington, that Episcopal Area included only the Peninsula and Baltimore Annual Conference Organizations.

In assuming episcopal responsibilities for this temporarily enlarged Episcopal Area, Bishop Lord addressed a pastoral letter to all the churches. His challenge to the churches included the following statement

> **There are times when God "bares his arm" and is seen to be redemptively at work in current happenings. Men call such hours turning points; historians call them "hinges of history." The very forces of history call us now to a new devotion, a new dimension, and a new dynamic....**
>
> **We must now go to work in our communities and in our churches and in the depths of our hearts to eliminate the final strongholds of intolerance and hatred. The entire church and the world will be watching.**

During the entire transition process, both before and after the transfer, the Committee of Five cooperated with and supported the efforts of the inter-conference planning groups as they worked out the details of necessary amalgamations and consolidations of annual conference organizations.

Earlier in the transition process, I had a productive private conference with the bishop. I emphasized the crucial importance of the pastoral appointments at four Washington, DC churches. They were Capitol Hill Methodist Church, Mt. Vernon Place Methodist Church, Foundry Methodist Church and Metropolitan Methodist Church. These churches had experienced some incidents involving Blacks that needed to be assessed by senior pastors who were committed to proactive implementation of the denomination's policy of "an inclusive fellowship at all levels of the church's life."

### *Lexington Annual Conference Organization*

In 1964, the Central Jurisdiction Organization assigned the newly elected bishop, James S. Thomas, to the Chicago Episcopal Area for supervision of the Lexington Annual Conference Organization. As realigned, Lexington included the seven states of Illinois, Indiana, Iowa, Michigan, Minnesota, Ohio, and Wisconsin. We were confident that Bishop Thomas had the leadership experience and skills, and the denomination-wide affection and respect, needed to put the finishing touches on plans to transfer the Lexington Annual Conference Organization to the North Central Jurisdiction Organization. We were also confident that he would be an excellent episcopal leader for any of the annual conference organizations in the North Central geographical region.

Early in the transition planning process, key lay and clergy leaders of the North Central Jurisdiction Organization had informed the Committee of Five of their views regarding the continued existence of the Lexington Annual Conference Organization as a "racially" segregated entity of North Central. They stated that such an arrangement "would seem unreasonable and inadvisable." In a draft document dated July 17, 1963, they advised the leaders of all North Central annual conference organizations that:

> **"It clearly appears preferable for the bishop to be assigned to one of the Areas of the Jurisdiction and the churches to become part of the various other Annual Conferences within whose boundaries they are located.**

Thus the Committee of Five was confident that the North Central regional organization would not continue Lexington as a "racially" segregated entity. Hence we recommended to Central Jurisdiction annual conference organizations that at their spring 1964 annual meetings they vote advance approval for the transfer of the Lexington Annual Conference Organization into North Central, *subject to the adoption of the realignment plan of the Committee of Five.* Giving such advance approval would enhance the chances of Lexington's transfer in 1964, following adjournment of the 1964 quadrennial session of the Central Jurisdiction Organization. Annual conference organizations of the Central Jurisdiction followed the Committee's advice.

As explained earlier here, the delegates to the 1964 quadrennial session of the Central Jurisdiction Organization adopted the realignment plan the Committee of Five recommended. The other Central Jurisdiction annual conference organizations voted substantially in favor of the transfer of the Lexington into North Central. Lexington's own annual meeting was held in Chicago June 10-14, 1964. A mutually agreed upon plan of **transfer and consolidation** had been carefully worked out in numerous meetings and consultations. A resolution that incorporated the plan was presented to the delegates. The resolution was overwhelmingly adopted. This was a historic moment in the lifecycle of a proud and glorious ninety-five year old ecclesiastical body of The Methodist Church. Central Jurisdiction annual conference organization transfers under Amendment IX, according to the model developed by the Committee of Five, required geographical jurisdiction organizations to take certain actions. On July 9, 1964, Leonard Slutz presented the Lexington transfer and consolidation resolution to the quadrennial session of the North Central Jurisdiction Organization. He reported that the plan had received 5,746 affirmative votes and only 9 negative votes in the annual conference organizations of North Central. He also reported that the other Central Jurisdiction annual conference organization had taken all of the necessary actions required for the transfer and consolidation of

Lexington as the plan proposed. When the plan was presented for a vote, the delegates to the North Central Jurisdiction Organization voted 370 to 0 to adopt it. After the vote was taken, Bishop Richard C. Raines told the body:

> **It is one thing to talk about history; it is another thing to make it. You have just done that and now we ratify and welcome that which future historians of The Methodist Church will be writing about and talking about.**

Bishop Rains presented Bishop James S. Thomas to the assembled delegates at the 1964 quadrennial session of the North Central Jurisdiction Organization. And so, on January 9, 1964, Bishop Thomas ceased to be a bishop of the Central Jurisdiction Organization and became a bishop of the North Central Jurisdiction Organization. He was assigned to the Iowa Area. Along with Bishop Prince A. Taylor, he became the second former Central Jurisdiction bishop to be assigned to supervise annual conference organizations composed primarily of local churches that were never part of the Central Jurisdiction Organization.

## Central Jurisdiction *In Transition*

In several places in previous chapters of the book, I have alluded to what was, in effect, a "non-negotiable" stand of the Committee of Five. It was that *no arrangement would be acceptable if it provided for or allowed indefinite continuance of "racially" segregated subunits in regional organizations as a consequence of the dissolution of the Central Jurisdiction Organization.*

We insisted on explicit commitments from the key leaders of the Northeastern, Southeastern, North Central, South Central, and Western Jurisdiction Organizations that local churches of the Central Jurisdiction Organizations would, within a specified period of time, become part of the geographically defined annual conference organizations in which they were located.

The Committee of Five had presumed that early in the 1964-1968 quadrennium four of the sixteen realigned Central Jurisdiction annual conference organizations—Central West, Delaware, Lexington and Washington—would be transferred into geographical jurisdiction organizations. Based on mutual agreements and understandings, we were confident that they would be consolidated with reconstituted geographically defined entities within a reasonable period of time. We also knew the other twelve annual conference organizations probably would not be able to transfer into regional organizations under circumstances that would preclude their indefinite existence as "racially" segregated entities. Thus, with respect to the other twelve *sub*units, we adopted a concept of "the Central Jurisdiction Organization in transition."

The four transferred annual conference organizations represented one-fourth of the Central Jurisdiction Organization's components. They comprised 650 plus local congregations with a combined membership of at least 120,300. The *Central Jurisdiction Organization in transition* was left with 2,214 local congregations, which had a total of approximately 252,725 members. This would be the "racially" segregated structure of The Methodist Church polity that the denomination would have to address in the future.

**The Committee of Five had established a framework of concepts, principles and procedures, and we had unleashed some dynamic forces that would be quite useful to the residual Central Jurisdiction Organization. For Methodists of good will who were committed to eliminating involuntary "racial" segregation from the polity of The Methodist Church, the examples and experiences of the transfer and consolidation of Delaware, Lexington and Washington Annual Conference Organizations could be very instructive.**

Subsequent to the episcopal election of Thomas, I was chosen as the chairman of the continuing Committee of Five. Dr. Major J. Jones was selected to replace me as secretary of the Committee.

We now had the added duty of serving in an executive capacity to the Central Jurisdiction Organization's Advisory Council. The Committee had good feelings regarding our accomplishments during the 1960-1964 quadrennium. With an overall policy and procedures framework established by delegates to the Central Jurisdiction Organization's 1964 meeting, and by The Methodist Church's legislative body, the Committee was ready to begin moving ahead with implementation actions.

However, before we could do so, the Southeastern Jurisdiction Organization posed an ominous challenge. As a sort of "pre-emptive strike," it sought a declaratory decision from the Judicial Council that would render invalid some major premises of our policy and procedures framework for the 1964-1968 quadrennium. The Committee of Five had to meet that challenge, which became our number one priority temporarily. Discussion of that issue follows in Chapter 10 of this book.

## Chapter Notes

1. The statement of Committee of Five Beliefs, modified to reflect the use of non-sexist language, is as follows:

**WE BELIEVE that an inclusive Methodist Church is a society of persons whose life and practice are based on the great Christian affirmation of unity and oneness of all believers in Christ.**

**WE BELIEVE with the Apostle Paul that "there is one God, the**

**Father, from whom are all things and for whom we exist; and one Lord Jesus Christ, through whom are all things and through whom we exist."**

**WE BELIEVE that persons who respond in love and obedience to the "call" of God in Christ necessarily comprise a "new creation," and that this new creation makes possible a fellowship that transcends all ethnic, racial, and class barriers.**

**WE BELIEVE that those who are "called into the fellowship of...Jesus Christ" are led to express that call by establishing concrete human associations, such as the society of individuals known as The Methodist Church.**

**WE BELIEVE that to be a genuine response to the "call" of God in Christ, the relationships among individuals who comprise an association must not be based on considerations of race, color, or anything else save obedience to the God and Father of Jesus Christ.**

**WE BELIEVE that in order to be true to its mission in the world, the historical church must not be governed solely by criteria regarded as relevant to non-church organizations; for Christians must regard no one solely from "a human point of view...If any one is in Christ [that person] is a new creation; the old has passed away, behold, the new has come."**

**WE BELIEVE that The Methodist Church must be completely uncircumscribed, at all levels of church life, by distinctions based on race and color.**

SOURCE: Committee of Five, *Bridges to Racial Equality in The Methodist Church Report to The Central Jurisdictional Conference* (1964), p.1.

2. At the 1964 quadrennial meeting of the Church's legislative body Dr. James S. Thomas proposed an amendment to the Report of the Commission of Thirty-Six. The amendment was adopted. It directed the regional organizations and the Central Jurisdiction Organization to establish Advisory Councils to the new denomination-wide Commission of Twenty-Four. These advisory councils would assist the Commission to achieve annual conference organization transfers under Amendment IX procedures.

3. The delegates to the 1964 session of the Central Jurisdiction Organization emphasized the crucial importance of Central Jurisdiction

*sub*units' taking the initiative in the whole process of implementing Amendment IX transfer procedures. Experience had shown that only through the exercise of such initiative could they be certain that the fundamental goal of a truly inclusive Methodist Church would be the primary consideration in the use of Amendment IX processes.

John T. King and W. Astor Kirk developed and presented to the Central Jurisdiction's West Texas Annual Conference Organization a resolution proposing a plan to transfer into the South Central Jurisdiction Organization. Meeting in Dallas, Texas at St. Paul Methodist Church, the west Texas Annual Conference Organization adopted the resolution. Thus the West Texas group became the first Central Jurisdiction Annual Conference Organization to adopt a transfer proposal following the 1964 session of the Church's legislative body. The delegates to the Central Jurisdiction Organization recommended the West Texas Plan as a model for other annual conference organizations.

# CHAPTER 10
# Committee of Five: Advocacy Before The Judicial Council

On July 10, 1964, delegates to the Southeastern Jurisdiction Organization (hereafter referred to in Chapter 10 as "*Southeastern*") duly adopted a resolution recommending

> **That each annual conference approve the transfer of such annual conferences of the Central Jurisdiction into the Southeastern Jurisdiction upon the condition that the merging of annual conferences within the jurisdiction will be a jurisdictional matter to be worked out when such merger is mutually agreeable to the conferences concerned, the boundaries of the transferring conferences to remain intact *until they may be changed by voluntary action of the Southeastern Jurisdictional Conference as provided in the Constitution of The Methodist Church*.** (*Daily Christian Advocate*, No. 5, pp. 4-5. *Emphases* added.)

> **JOHN C. SATTERFIELD (Mississippi): Mr. Chairman, Ladies and Gentleman of the Conference: I move that an appeal be taken to the Judicial Council to determine the constitutionality of the action of this Jurisdictional Conference which has just been taken recommending the transfer of the annual conferences of the Central Jurisdiction into the Southeastern Jurisdiction in accordance with the plan of action therein set forth, and *particularly the provision thereof that "the boundaries of the transferring conferences to remain intact until they may be changed by voluntary action of the Southeastern Jurisdictional Conference as provided in the Constitution of The Methodist Church*."** (*Ibid.* Emphases added.)

Southeastern adopted the Satterfield motion calling for an appeal to the Judicial Council of The Methodist Church. At a later date the Advisory Council on Interjurisdictional Affairs joined in the appeal pursuant to Memorandum Order 220 of the Judicial Council, which was issued October 30, 1964.

## Background

John C. Satterfield was, in many ways, a brilliant Mississippi lawyer. He was also a staunch defender of the involuntary "racial" segregation incorporated in the constitution of The Methodist Church. His motion to seek a Judicial Council ruling on the "constitutionality" of the *policy decision* of Southeastern was an adroit and surreptitious "pre-emptive" strike. It was aimed at preventing denominational legislative action similar to that the Committee of Five proposed in its Memorial #2 (the Mayes Amendment).

Satterfield knew that he would have the strong support not only of the conservative and powerful legal and political establishment of Southeastern but also of Charles C. Parlin and his Northeastern, North Central and Western cohorts. It was this "unholy alliance" that ambushed and derailed the Mayes Amendment at the 1964 session of the Church's legislative body. In the closing argument on the Mayes Amendment, after the previous question had been ordered, Parlin chose to express his *personal* opinion regarding the *constitutionality* of the Committee of Five's Memorial #2. Thus Parlin raised a constitutional issue at a time when his *personal* views could not be publicly challenged.

Shortly after the adjournment of Southeastern I received a telephone call from Winston Taylor of Methodist Information. He inquired whether I was aware that Southeastern had adopted a motion by Satterfield asking the Judicial Council for a decision **"on the General Conference [Organization's] power over racial discrimination in annual conferences.**" I responded that I was unaware of any such action. Taylor read a very brief news item that he had just received from Religious News Service.

Within a few days I was able to confirm that Southeastern had in fact supported Satterfield's call for a Judicial Council declaratory decision. Therefore, on July 22, 1964 I wrote the Secretary of the Judicial Council and requested that the Committee of Five be allowed to become an *Intervenor* in the Southeastern appeal.[1]

I filed this request on behalf of the Committee of Five because counsel for Southeastern intended to raise other important issues in addition to the question of the validity of the policy incorporated in the resolution Southeastern adopted July 10, 1964.

On October 26, 1964, two days prior to the date set for Judicial Council consideration of the case, we were notified that the Judicial Council had granted our request for permission to intervene in Southeastern's appeal. Because of the impossibility of preparing a brief and participating in oral argument upon such short notice, I asked the Central Jurisdiction Organization's College of Bishops to request a continuance of the case on the Judicial Council's docket. A continuance was granted in Judicial Council Memorandum Order 220. Because it illuminates the intentions of counsel for Southeastern, the Memorandum Order is included here.

### Judicial Council Memorandum Order 220

> **We have granted the request of the College of Bishops of the Central Jurisdiction for two reasons. First, the time interval between the receipt of the briefs for [Southeastern] and our annual meeting afforded no reasonable opportunity for representatives of the Central Jurisdiction to file reply briefs or to participate in oral argument with proper preparation. Secondly, [Southeastern's] briefs have placed new interpretations upon (a) the scope and purpose of the challenged "plan of action," (b) the legal issues sought to be raised, and (c) the grounds of our jurisdiction, with the result that there must be a clarification of these matters before we can properly determine this appeal.**
>
> **We are concerned by the fact that in [Southeastern's] brief, for the first time, expressly at least, we are asked to determine the important question whether the General Conference possesses any authority under the Constitution to determine, change or otherwise deal with the boundaries of Annual Conferences, particularly Annual Conferences of the Central Jurisdiction transferred pursuant to Amendment IX. We believe that a matter of this importance should not come before us indirectly, obliquely, or uncertainly or without full and complete opportunity for all concerned to participate by brief and argument in our determination of this question.**
>
> **We would welcome the filing of an appropriate petition under Par. 914 of the Discipline squarely and directly raising this or any other related question of constitutionality which either the Southeastern Jurisdiction or the Central Jurisdiction may deem to be involved in the above captioned appeal. Should any such petition for declaratory decision be filed we urge its submission to us at least 40 days prior to our scheduled meeting on April 22, 1965.**
>
> Dated: October 30, 1964.

In response to Memorandum Order 220, the Advisory Council on Interjurisdictional Affairs of the Southeastern Jurisdiction filed a Petition for a declaratory decision. That group asked the Judicial Council to decide four questions. From the perspective of the Committee of Five, only question No. 3 raised the critical issue. It asked:

> **Does the General Conference [Organization] have the power to enact legislation under Division Two, Section I, Article IV (Par. 8 of the 1964 Discipline) or any other provision of the Constitution requiring the elimination of racially segregated Annual Conferences transferred from the Central Jurisdictional Conference into regional Jurisdictional Conferences pursuant to Division Two, Section VIII, Article V of the Constitution (Amendment IX)?**

## Preparing A Petition for Declaratory Judgment and Supporting Brief

After receiving Memorandum Order 220, the Committee of Five had approximately three months to prepare and submit to the Judicial Council a petition for a declaratory judgment decision, supported by a well-reasoned brief. Southeastern had hired three prestigious law firms to prepare briefs and argument. Only $1,000 was allocated to the Committee for this purpose. Nevertheless, despite the enormous disparity in financial resources, we had to stand tall against Southeastern's legal giants.

Upon first reading of Southeastern's *appeal* and supporting brief, I discovered that Southeastern focused almost exclusively on the issue of "what body" in The Methodist Church polity had *boundary-changing authority*. That was never an issue with the Committee of Five. Only Question No. 3 of the four questions submitted to the Judicial Council by Southeastern's Advisory Council was phrased in *non-boundary-changing terminology*. I pointed this out to my Committee of Five colleagues and recommended that we, in effect, address the issue of *boundary-changing authority* simply by stipulation. That would free us to focus our energies and limited resources elsewhere.

Memorandum 220 set April 22, 1965 as the hearing date. Briefs were due not later than March 20, 1965. Hence we only had about four months of preparation time. To make matters worse, this time included the Thanksgiving, Christmas and New Year holiday periods. Faced with that critical situation, the Committee gave me, as its chairman, a completely free hand to develop our brief. We agreed that I would develop a "draft brief" and send it to each Committee member in time for him to offer comments and suggestions.

Although the time frame was quite limited and I had very little financial resources with which to work, I thought it would be helpful and strategic to get comments, suggestions and advice from as broad a segment of Methodists as possible. I developed a concise statement entitled:

> **Substantive Questions Before the Judicial Council of The Methodist Church in the Case of: "Appeal for Decision Determining the Meaning, application and Effect of Paragraphs 15 and 29 of the Discipline and the Constitutionality of Action by the Southeastern Jurisdictional Conference."**

On November 16, 1964, I sent the statement with a covering letter to over fifty Methodists throughout the United States. The letter and statement are included in the book as **Appendix 9.**

Most of the Methodists throughout the United States to whom I sent the letter and statement contacted me by telephone before the Christmas holidays that year. By February 15, 1965, I had received written comments and suggestions from the following sources:

A Faculty Group
Boston Univ. School of Theology
Boston, MA

A Faculty Group
Duke Univ. Divinity School
Durham, NC

Reverend James S. Chubb
Grand Island Methodist Parish
Grand Island, NE

Reverend Richard L. Clifford
District Superintendent
Alexandria, VA

Judge Floyd H. Coffman
District Judge
Ottawa, KS

Dr. Dwight W. Culver
Saint Olaf College
Northfield, MN

Dr. Georgia Harkness
Pacific School of Religion
Berkeley, CA

Bishop Willis J. King (Ret.)
The Methodist Church
New Orleans, LA

Edward H. Laylin, Esq.
Laylin, McConnaughey & Stradley
Columbus, OH

Dr. Franklin H. Littell
Chicago Theological Seminary
Chicago, IL

Judge Tom Reavley
District Judge
Austin, TX

Reverend J. Robert Regan, Jr.
Redeemer Methodist Church
Reston, VA

Charles S. Scott, Esq.
Scott, Scott, Scott & Jackson

Dr. Harvey Seifert
Claremont Sc. Of Theology

Topeka, KS

Claremont, CA

Dr. Willis M. Tate, President
Southern Methodist University
Dallas, TX

Herman Will, Esq.
Board of Christian Social Concerns
Washington, DC

Dr. Philip Wogaman
University of the Pacific
Stockton, CA

Dr. Daniel Wynn, Chaplain
Tuskegee Institute
Tuskegee, AL

Dr. Albert Outler of the Perkins School of Theology, Southern Methodist University, was in Rome attending the Third Session of the Vatican Council when my November 16, 1964 letter arrived at his Dallas, TX office. I had a lengthy telephone conversation with Dr. Outler upon his return to this country. I had many extensive discussions with Dr. A. Dudley Ward and Dr. Grover C. Bagby, staff executives at the Board of Christian Social Concerns.

The most productive "practice" exercises I had were the two afternoons I spent with Thelma Stevens of the Woman's Division of the Board of Missions. She played "the devil's advocate," actually the role of John C. Satterfield. Thelma Stevens was a native Mississippian—and a passionate advocate for social justice, human rights and reconciliation.

During the second week of January 1965 I gathered up all of my own research notes and all of the written comments and suggestions I had received. I spent the weekend alone at a church retreat center in order to systematically and thoroughly examine these materials. I also wanted to examine my own core values, thoughts and feelings with respect to the task of preparing a brief for the consideration of the Judicial Council.

And I needed to reflect not only intellectually but also prayerfully (1) on the fact that Charles C. Parlin had recently filed a "friend of the court" brief in support of Southeastern's position and (2) on the urgent "procedural" plea of Leonard Slutz, who had become chairman of the new 1964-1968 quadrennial Commission of Inter-Jurisdictional Relations *("Commission of Twenty-Four")*.

Leonard is a person for whom I then had, and still have, great respect for his sincerity, dedication and integrity—even when I disagree fundamentally with policy and program choices he might make. I could ill-afford to respond to his plea in the same manner that I might have reacted to a similar plea from Charles Parlin, former chairman of the 1960-1964 Commission of Thirty-Six.[2]

After, perhaps, an unnecessarily prolonged period of analysis and reflection, I decided against the procedural approach Leonard Slutz recommended. There were three main reasons: technical, political, and moral.

First, the *technical* reason. Now, almost forty years later, I have a slightly altered viewpoint. But in January 1965 I did not see how the Committee of Five could have standing to make an argument that the Judicial Council lacked jurisdiction to decide Southeastern's appeal. The Committee would already have a problem with respect to asserting standing to litigate its own petition for a declaratory judgment decision. Besides, for me to take the approach suggested by Leonard I would have to do additional research, which I had neither the time, nor the resources or the inclination to do.

Second, I had to take into account certain *political* realities. It was highly unlikely that I could have gotten the other persons in key leadership positions in the "Central Jurisdiction in transition" to agree to pursue Leonard's approach. The most bedrock of all matters on which Blacks were in agreement was that *indefinite* existence of "racially" segregated annual conference organizations in geographical jurisdiction organizations was unacceptable. Most of them would have been reluctant to even appear to concede that the Judicial Council, as one person said to me, "was without authority to determine the constitutionality of an extension of The Methodist Church's 'racial' segregation from the Central Jurisdiction to the regional jurisdictions." They would not have understood the procedural subtlety of Leonard's approach. It was my judgment then that opting for that approach would have seriously damaged the credibility of the Committee of Five.

Finally, it was profoundly troubling *morally* for me to use a procedural detour to "back" into the core issue involved in Southeastern's appeal rather than attack it directly. I was aware that lawyers often employ procedural tactics, *particularly when they sense some unusual vulnerability with respect to the merits of their case*. Nevertheless, it seemed to me then that the Committee and I had a moral obligation to directly and forcefully confront John Satterfield's "Trojan Horse."

As I viewed it, Southeastern sought judicial legitimacy for an ethically indefensible *policy decision* to institutionalize a future pattern of relations between Blacks and Whites within that regional organization of The Methodist Church. Specifically, the policy was that "racially" segregated annual conference organizations transferring into the Southeastern Jurisdiction Organization "*[shall] remain intact until they may be changed by the voluntary action of the Southeastern Jurisdictional Conference as provided in the Constitution of The Methodist Church.*" (Emphasis added.)

The policy was concealed in the form of a recommendation to Southeastern's annual conference organizations to vote to transfer Central Jurisdiction annual conference organizations into the Southeastern Jurisdiction Organization. I really believed the Judicial Council had authority to judicially scrutinize this policy decision. And I also believed I had a moral duty to say so up front in the Committee of Five's brief. Hence I chose not to opt for Leonard's procedural approach.

The weekend alone enabled me to develop the outline of a brief and to do a significant amount of text writing. By mid-February I had completed the brief in draft form and sent copies to the other members of the Committee of Five. I was able to finish the job and get the brief to the printer during the first week of March 1965. A week later copies of the printed document were delivered to me for signatures and transmission to the Judicial Council.

## Summary of Petition and Brief of Committee of Five

In accordance with our theory of the proceedings before the Judicial Council and the directives stated in Memorandum Order 220, the Committee's brief centered on two basic or primary themes:

1. **Serious damage to connectional interests of The Methodist Church would result if "racially" segregated annual conference organizations of the Central Jurisdiction became institutionalized in geographical jurisdiction organizations in the process of dissolving the Central Jurisdiction.**

2. **The constitutional grant to the Church's legislative body of "full legislative power over all matters distinctively connectional" and the provision of Section 4 of Amendment IX contain sufficient authority for the legislative body to enact appropriate legislation to prevent the institutionalizing of "racially" segregated annual conference organizations in geographical jurisdiction organizations.**

Consistent with these two themes, in the Petition section of our brief the Committee presented a single, albeit fundamental question, for Judicial Council consideration:

> **May the legislative body of The Methodist Church enact appropriate legislation, under the powers granted to it in Division Two, Section 1, Article IV (Par. 8 of the 1964 *Discipline*), to ensure the elimination of "racially" segregated *sub*units transferring from the Central Jurisdiction organization into regional organizations pursuant to Division Two, Section VIII, Article V of the Constitution (Amendment IX)?**

The Committee's brief was divided into six sections. Here I highlight only the most significant parts of the 41-page brief's **Argument**. In the interest of brevity and text simplification, citations and references are omitted. For more details the reader is encouraged to read the brief itself, which is entitled **Regional Segregation?** ***Before the Judicial Council of The Methodist Church*** (March 15, 1965).

## Boundary Issue

The issue before the Judicial Council in the proceeding was not who determines the boundaries of annual conference organizations in geographical jurisdiction organizations of The Methodist Church. The Committee of Five and Southeastern both agreed that geographical jurisdiction organizations determined such boundaries. The issue we asked the Judicial Council to decide was whether the Church's legislative body could preclude geographical jurisdiction organizations from making *"race" and color* the basis of their boundary-determination decisions. The Committee argued that the Church's legislative body had constitutional authority to prohibit geographical jurisdiction organizations from creating, or maintaining indefinitely, annual conference organizations based on "race" or color.

## Sources of Legislative Authority

1. The denomination's constitution granted The Methodist Church's legislative body "full legislative power over all matters distinctively connectional" in nature. From the time of Unification the Judicial Council had consistently ruled that the Church's legislative body had been specifically empowered to legislate on all matters *distinctively connectional.* The Council had affirmed, in numerous prior cases, that authority over distinctively connectional matters involves a "broad grant of power." Therefore, "unless there is found elsewhere in the constitution some modification of, or a limitation to this power," the Church's legislative body may enact such legislation as it deems necessary to protect or promote any connectional interest of The Methodist Church.

2. Historically, the Judicial Council had consistently viewed The Methodist Church's concept of "connectionalism" as a *dynamic* rather than a *static* concept. The Council had recognized that (a) historical evidence as to the intent of the drafters of Paragraph 8 of the *Discipline*, (b) textual analysis of the language of the constitution, and (c) application of the rules of logical thinking all have a useful place. *But neither alone nor in combination can they supply an exclusive key to the meaning of "matters distinctively connectional" in a particular case.* In ecclesiastical as well as in civil jurisprudence, the crucial factor of what Justice Holmes called "experience" must not be overlooked.[3] The Judicial Council had always followed the experiential approach in its search, within a given context of circumstances, for the existential meaning of the

phrase "all matters distinctively connectional." The Council had frankly recognized that interpretation of the concept embodied in that phrase must be approached in the light of present-day ethical, moral, and cultural values and by the sum total of Methodist experience. It was apparent from Methodist experience that *connectional* interests of the Church are involved wherever there exist *persistent circumstances, institutional practices, and structural relationships*—"anywhere in the connection"—that greatly enhance or seriously impede the life, work, witness and ministry of The Methodist Church.

### Involuntary "Racial" Segregation in The Methodist Church Had Become A *Connectional* Matter

1. For The Methodist Church, elimination of involuntary "racial" segregation and the achievement of "a racially inclusive fellowship at all levels of the church's life" had become a *distinctively connectional* matter.

2. In 1965, The Methodist Church existed and had to fulfill its ministries of witness and service in the midst of "a world in revolution." One dimension of the revolution was the determination of peoples throughout the world to secure their freedom from all forms of "racial" segregation and discrimination—ecclesiastical as well as secular. The Methodist Church was a worldwide Church, and involuntary "racial" segregation in its structures, processes, and programs had a serious adverse effect on the denomination's ministry, mission and witness.

3. The Committee of Five's brief strongly urged the judicial Council to make explicit in decisional law what was generally recognized as a practical fact: That the issue of whether or not regional and local structures of "racial" segregation would result from the dissolution of the Central Jurisdiction Organization (pursuant to the procedures of Amendment IX), was a "distinctively connectional" matter.

4. The challenge facing The Methodist Church was to prevent the institutionalizing of "racially" segregated Central Jurisdiction annual conference organizations once they were transferred into geographical jurisdiction organizations, and to achieve "a racially inclusive fellowship at all levels of the church's life." To meet this challenge the denomination's legislative body might be required to enact additional appropriate legislation. Southeastern's position regarding this issue ignored the vital currents of social forces, of ecclesiastical practices, and of ethical imperatives that had been operative during the past three quadrennia. Those forces had definitely impacted both the orientation and content of enactments of the Church's legislative body. Experience might indicate more clearly in the future than it had indicated in the past, that The Methodist Church would be unable to make a truly effective witness in the midst of "a world in revolution" so long as its polity included "racially" segregated administrative structures.

5. Southeastern was wrong, as a matter of church law, in contending that under no circumstances or conditions may the Church's legislative body constitutionally exercise its legislative powers to secure the dissolution of "racially" segregated Central Jurisdiction annual conference organizations that voluntarily transfer into geographical jurisdiction organizations pursuant to Amendment IX. In effect, Southeastern was asking the Judicial Council for a declaratory decision stating that no matter how seriously the development of regional structures of "racial" segregation may jeopardize vital "connectional" interests of The Methodist Church, the "supreme legislative body" of the denomination was barred by the Constitution from acting *legislatively* to forestall that development.

6. In its brief the Committee of Five reminded the Judicial Council that The Methodist Church had both urged and supported the exercise of legislative power by civil governments to eliminate "racially' segregated social structures from our secular society. It seemed incomprehensible, therefore, to argue, as Southeastern was doing, that the Judicial Council must necessarily so construe Paragraphs 15.4 and 29 of the *Discipline* as to preclude the legislative body of the Church from acting legislatively to eliminate involuntary "racial" segregation from the Church's own institutional life. The Committee of Five was unable to discern, in the comprehensive body of decisional law that had evolved since Unification in 1939, any compelling reasons for such a narrow construction of the Church's constitution.

7. The brief of the Committee of Five argued that where a judicial body has a *live option* of properly construing constitutional provisions so as to give "articulate expression" to moral imperatives and to the "social sense of justice," judicial wisdom required the judicial body to exercise that option. This principle had been recognized and applied by enlightened judicial bodies every since its articulation by Justice Benjamin Cardozo (1921) in *The Nature of the judicial Process.*

8. Judicial Council affirmation of the authority of the Church's legislative body to act legislatively, with respect to involuntary "racial" segregation in geographical jurisdiction organizations, would not negate the voluntary principle of Amendment IX. *Specifically, the Judicial Council may issue a declaratory decision holding that the Church's legislative body, through an appropriate exercise of its "full legislative power," has authority to enact legislation prohibiting the creation or indefinite maintenance of "racially" segregated structures in geographical jurisdiction organizations.*

9. The kind of declaratory decision the Committee of Five requested would not contravene the voluntary principle implicit in Amendment IX. It would simply mean that (a) when an annual conference organization voted *voluntarily* to transfer from the Central jurisdiction Organization; (b) when the other annual conference organizations of the Central Jurisdiction voted *voluntarily* to approve such transfer; and (c) when the annual conference

organizations in the geographical jurisdiction organization involved vote *voluntarily* to approve the transfer—all of these *voluntary* actions would be taken with the knowledge that the Church's legislative body, if it desired to do so, could enact appropriate legislation to protect and promote the "connectional" interests of The Methodist Church in achieving a polity that is completely free of structural "racial" separatism.

10. Judicial Council affirmation of the authority of the Church's legislative body to prohibit involuntary "racial" segregation in geographical jurisdiction organizations would be compatible with the **Plan of Action for the Elimination of the Central Jurisdiction** adopted by the legislative body in 1964. In adopting this plan, it was the hope of the Church's legislative body that the Central Jurisdiction Organization, including the institutional appurtenances thereof, might be eliminated during the 1964-1968 quadrennium. The plan was based on the judgment that strategic and influential leadership groups in the Church—bishops, district superintendents, members and executives of denominational boards and agencies, official boards and pastors—should be given an opportunity to make a real effort to eliminate the Central Jurisdiction Organization and achieve "a racially inclusive fellowship at all levels of the church's life" (*Plan of Action, Recommendation* 7, p. 3). In the event that the hopes of the legislative body should not be realized, the Commission of Twenty-Four was directed to draft a new plan of action to achieve *both of these objectives*, and to recommend the new plan to the legislative body for consideration in 1968.

11. The declaratory decision sought by the Committee of Five would not only be compatible with the objectives of the Church's legislative body, but it would also facilitate achievement of these objectives. On the other hand, the decision Southeastern sought would be inherently incompatible with the objectives of the legislative body. The judicial decree Southeastern desired would effectively foreclose the possibility of legislative action by the Church's legislative body, should such action become necessary or advisable to remove "racially" segregated structures from geographical jurisdiction organizations. Apparently, the intent of Southeastern was to effectively insulate such structures against any exercise of the "full legislative power" of the Church's legislative body over this "distinctively connectional" matter.

12. The Committee of Five's brief strongly challenged the view of Southeastern that, with respect to Central Jurisdiction annual conference organizations transferred under Amendment IX, Section 4 of Amendment IX did not render inapplicable the limitations of Paragraphs 15.4 and 29 of the *Discipline*. The Committee of Five argued that the Judicial Council must construe Section 4 as rendering inoperative all restrictions upon the authority of the legislative body "to enact such...legislation as may be necessary" to resolve all issues arising from the transfer of Central Jurisdiction annual conference organizations under Section 2 of Amendment IX.

## CONCLUSIONS

From its analysis of the issues in the proceeding before the Judicial Council, the Committee of Five concluded that the answer to the question presented in its Petition for a declaratory decision should properly be as follows:

**First,** the Church's legislative body possessed legislative authority under the constitution (Paragraphs 8, 8.14 of the *Discipline*) to prohibit a geographical jurisdiction organization from exercising its *boundary-determination powers* in any manner that jeopardizes a legitimate "connectional" interest of the Methodist Church.

**Second,** the Church's legislative body may properly find that annual conference organizations (or other structures) and programs in geographical organizations that are based on "race" or color thwart or frustrate the achievement of "a racially inclusive fellowship at all levels of the church's life," which is a legitimate "connectional" interest of The Methodist Church.

**Third,** If the Church's legislative body deems such action necessary or desirable to protect or promote any "connectional" interests of The Methodist Church, it may enact appropriate legislation prohibiting a geographical jurisdiction organization from applying "racial" criteria in the exercise of its *boundary-determination* authority.

**Fourth,** the elimination of involuntary "racial" segregation and the achievement of *de facto* "racial" inclusiveness at all levels of church life are legitimate "connectional" ends of The Methodist Church. All legislative means adopted by the legislative body that are appropriate, that are plainly adapted to those ends, and are not *expressly* prohibited, but are in accord with the letter and spirit of Amendment IX interpreted as a whole, are within the constitutional authority of the Church's legislative body.

**Fifth,** the action of Southeastern is invalid—to the extent that it seeks to appropriate sole authority to determine under what circumstances and for what period of time annual conference organizations transferred to it from the Central Jurisdiction Organization under Amendment IX, shall remain "racially" segregated "connectional" units of The Methodist Church.

> The goal of eliminating involuntary "racial" segregation was not only an ethically or morally legitimate one, but its practical achievement was also necessary for The Methodist Church to be one of God's main instruments for mediating the gospel in "a world in revolution."

## Brief Sent To Judicial Council

The Secretary of the Committee of Five, Major J. Jones, and I signed the Committee's brief and delivered it in March 1965 to the Judicial Council in a timely manner. Both of us were thankful that what had seemed an impossible task three months earlier had been accomplished in a professional manner. We were confident that even with severely limited financial resources and a very short time frame, we had in fact "stood tall" against the three prestigious law firms representing Southeastern. And we had a strong intuitive feeling that the brief's moral and legal argument would have a positive impact on the Judicial Council. Major Jones and I would now begin to marshal our energies and thoughts for the oral presentation scheduled for April 22, 1965 in Evanston, Illinois.

## Church-Wide Concerns Aroused

On March 22, 1965, as chairman of the Committee of Five, I sent identical letters to Bishops Willis J. King (Retired), Edgar A. love (Retired), M. L. Harris, Charles F. Golden, Noah W. Moore, Jr., James S. Thomas, and Prince A. Taylor, Jr. (The last two bishops had been recently transferred from the Central Jurisdiction organization under Amendment IX.)[4]

Methodist Information and Religious News Services disseminated throughout the Church information regarding the basic propositions asserted in the Committee of Five's brief. It soon became apparent that this case had the potential of generating throughout The Methodist Church the same kinds of diverse and intense passions that *Brown v. Board of Education* had generated in the civil society ten years earlier.

In various "leadership circles" in the Church efforts were made to resolve the issues outside the litigation process. Leonard Slutz's letter to me dated January 9, 1965 (included as **Note 2** at the end of this chapter) indicates that the Commission of Twenty-Four initiated some of the efforts. Two months earlier, on November 4, 1964, Leonard had forwarded to me copies of letters he had written to Messrs. Welliver and Witwer of the Judicial Council, with information copies to Charles Parlin and Theodore M. Berry (a member of the Judicial Council). There were ex parte communications between Lester A. Welliver of the Judicial Council and Charles Parlin, including a letter from Welliver to Parlin dated October 19, 1964. There is also a letter dated February 16, 1965 from W. Astor Kirk to Bishop Noah W. Moore, Jr.

When the parties arrived in Evanston, Illinois on the eve of the hearing, each side received an identical telegram from the Council of Bishops requesting "postponement of the imminent presentation before the Judicial Council." In response to the telegram, the parties filed with the Judicial Council a **Joint Statement and Motion.**[5]

The Judicial Council granted the joint motion of the parties requesting continuance of the proceeding until the October 1965 session of the Council. And in Evanston, Illinois on April 22, 1965, the Committee of Five issued the following **Press Release** through Methodist Information

> **"The basic goal which we have long sought and which we still seek is the elimination of all forms of racial segregation from the organizational structures, processes and programs of The Methodist Church, at all levels of church life.**
>
> **Since the efforts of the General Conference to achieve this goal through encouragement of discussions and negotiations have not been fully successful thus far, we have urged the enactment of specific legislation by the General Conference.**
>
> **The Southeastern Jurisdiction has contended that the General Conference has no constitutional power to enact the legislation recommended. Through this proceeding it seeks a Judicial Council ruling to that effect.**
>
> **We interpret the telegram from the Council of Bishops to mean that the bishops themselves will undertake immediate, specific, and positive actions throughout the church to achieve the goal we seek, hoping thereby that litigation and further General Conference legislation will not be necessary. Therefore, we have acceded to the request of the Council of Bishops that we postpone our presentation before the Judicial Council.**

**W. ASTOR KIRK, Chairman Committee of Five**
**M. J. JONES, Secretary Committee of Five"**

Subsequent to getting the telegram from Bishops Wicke and Short, I received no further communication from them. I was not privy to any information regarding the initiatives of the Council of Bishops aimed at rendering unnecessary any further judicial proceedings. Therefore, the Committee of Five went forward with its preparation for an oral presentation before the Judicial Council at its October 25, 1965 session.

## A Collateral Case

Both as Chairman of the Committee of Five and as a lay member of the West Texas Annual Conference Organization of the Central Jurisdiction Organization, I participated in the meetings of the Central Jurisdiction Advisory Council established under the 1964 Thomas Amendment to the Commission of Thirty-Six's Plan of Action.

At the February 8, 1965 joint meeting of the Advisory Councils from the Central Jurisdiction Organization and South Central Jurisdiction Organization, a fascinating question was raised several times. **The question was whether it would be possible for plans involving the Central Jurisdiction's Central West Annual Conference Organization and the South Central Jurisdiction Organization's Missouri East and Missouri West Annual Conference Organizations to "merge" without permissive action from the South Central Jurisdiction Organization.**

The chairman and secretary of the South Central Advisory Council asked me to examine the possibility of getting this issue before the Judicial Council. I agreed to do so, particularly in view of the fact that the delegates to the 1964 meeting of the Central Jurisdiction Organization had already approved a recommendation strongly urging Central West to adopt an appropriate resolution to transfer into the South Central Jurisdiction Organization as soon as possible.

The Central West Annual Conference Organization was in the Episcopal Area supervised by Bishop Noah W. Moore. On February 16, 1965 I wrote to Bishop Moore advising him of my views on the question raised at the joint meeting of the two Advisory Councils.[6]

At the 1964 meeting of the Central Jurisdiction Organization the delegates recommended that Central West call a special meeting to consider transfer matters. When Bishop Moore and the cabinet decided to convene a special session of Central West on May 20, 1965, that decision prompted me to think about an entirely different approach to getting a petition to the Judicial Council.

The Committee of Five had recommended and the delegates to the Central Jurisdiction Organization had adopted a "transfer contract" strategy That strategy was specifically designed to make a geographical jurisdiction organization part of a transfer agreement in order to ensure the dissolution of "racially" segregated transferring units. Now where the only annual conference organizations *directly affected* by a proposed transfer desire to amalgamate, why not use the "transfer contract" principle to obviate an otherwise need to obtain permission from the geographical jurisdiction organization?

In accordance with this line of reasoning, I helped the leaders of Central West, Missouri East and Missouri West develop a mutually agreeable "transfer contract" containing the following paragraph:

> **"3. The Central West Annual Conference, the Missouri West Annual Conference and the Missouri East Annual Conference, by the adoption of this resolution agree that the Central West Annual Conference, after it shall have been transferred to the South Central Jurisdiction, shall no longer continue to exist as a racially segregated conference; and the**

**said Conferences further agree to proceed with the merger of the Central West, the Missouri West, and the Missouri East Annual Conferences pursuant to Section 4 of...Amendment IX."**

Central West Annual Conference Organization adopted the "transfer contract," which included the foregoing Paragraph 3. More than two-thirds of the members present and voting cast an affirmative vote for the proposal. The body then adopted the following resolution:

> **"BE IT RESOLVED, therefore, that the Central West Annual Conference hereby petitions the Judicial Council of The Methodist Church, pursuant to Paragraph 914 of the 1964 *Discipline*, for a declaratory decision with respect to the following question:**
>
>> 'May the Central West Annual Conference, after it shall have been transferred from the Central Jurisdiction to the South Central Jurisdiction pursuant to Section 2 of Amendment IX, legally merge with the Missouri East Annual Conference and the Missouri West Annual Conference, under the authority of Section 4 of Amendment IX, to form racially inclusive conferences in the State of Missouri?'"

Central West requested that I represent it before the Judicial Council "in all matters pertaining to the adjudication of [its] petition for a declaratory decision." In order to control the process of presenting this petition to the Judicial Council, I agreed to the request of Central West. In that connection, on July 12, 1965 I sent an identical **Memorandum Letter** to the College of Bishops of the Central Jurisdiction and the College of Bishops of the South Central Jurisdiction, in which I stated, inter alia:

> **"It is now apparent that the 'RESOLUTION FOR THE TRANSFER AND MERGER OF THE CENTRAL WEST CONFERENCE TO THE SOUTH CENTRAL JURISDICTION AND GEOGRAPHIC CONFERENCES' has been adopted by both the Central Jurisdiction and the South Central Jurisdiction, in accordance with Section 2 of Amendment IX of the Constitution of The Methodist Church.**
>
> **"Your attention is directed to the fact that Paragraph 3 of the transfer and merger resolution state...**
>
> **"Upon adoption of the transfer and merger resolution... the Central West Annual Conference, by vote of the confer-**

**ence members present, petitioned the Judicial Council for a declaratory decision, pursuant to Paragraph 914 of the 1964 *Discipline*, with respect to the legality of the above-mentioned third paragraph...**

**"I was requested by the Central West Annual Conference to represent it before the Judicial Council 'in all matters pertaining to the adjudication of [its] petition for a declaratory decision.' Please be advised that I have acceded to the request of the Central West Annual Conference.**

**"I shall prepare and file with the Judicial Council for consideration at its fall meeting a brief based upon the following premise, to wit:**

> "In order to eliminate racial segregation at the Annual Conference level, a plan to merge two or more conferences may be made an integral part of a transfer agreement between the Central Jurisdiction and the South Central Jurisdiction, pursuant to Section 2 of Amendment IX of the Constitution of The Methodist Church. Where such a plan of merger, for that specific purpose, is made an essential part of such an agreement, legal authority to consummate that particular merger derives from Section 4 of Amendment IX, notwithstanding the provisions of Paragraphs 15.4 and 29 of the 1964 discipline."

I was more than simply pleased by this development. Regardless of the outcome of the Committee of Five's petition, I felt that, *procedurally*, the Judicial Council could not avoid taking jurisdiction of the Central West petition. Moreover, I had a strong intuitive feeling that the rule of Methodist Church law enunciated by the Judicial Council in Decision No. 169 would be controlling in the Central West case. At least that would be my principal legal argument, both orally before the judicial Council and in a written Central West memorandum brief. (See Chapter 5, Section B for a discussion of Judicial Decision No. 169.)

Ethically and morally, it was very important that the fundamental goal of the "transfer and merger" resolution was *"to form racially inclusive conferences in the State of Missouri."* The goal of a "racially" non-segregated conference entity is neither expressed nor implied in Charles Parlin's October 27, 1964 letter to Judicial Council member Lester A. Welliver, which was in response to Welliver's letter dated October 19, 1964. Nor is it affirmed anywhere in Parlin's brief Amicus curiae filed in support of Southeastern.

Strategically, the Central West petition would afford another opportunity to emphasize that for Blacks with major leadership responsibilities in

The Methodist Church, **indefinite existence of "racially" segregated annual conference organizations in geographical jurisdiction organizations was a totally unacceptable outcome of the dissolution of the Central Jurisdiction Organization.**

In that connection, I should mention a bizarre incident. At his personal request, John C. Satterfield was given the courtesy of leave to argue orally before the Judicial Council against the Central West petition. In my view, the Central West *transfer and merger* resolution represented "voluntarism" at its finest hour. For one of the most vocal proponents of *voluntary action* to oppose implementation of voluntarism by Methodists in Missouri was "an enigma wrapped in a mystery," to use another Winston Churchill phrase.

### Oral Argument Before the Judicial Council

The fall docket of the Judicial Council included both (a) the Southeastern/Committee of Five petitions and (b) Central West's petition. During the summer of 1965 no developments occurred that obviated the need for Judicial Council adjudication of the issues involved in these cases. Consequently, at the October 21, 1965 session of the Judicial Council I presented oral arguments in both cases—on behalf of the Committee of Five's petition in the morning and in support of Central West's petition in the afternoon.

***Committee of Five's Petition.*** My five-part oral presentation covered seven typed pages. It was a summary review of the 41-page printed brief, including restatements of (1) the fundamental issue in our petition, (2) the premises and principles of law, morality and ethics on which we relied, (3) the applicable judicial precedents, and (4) the positive impact that a favorable decision would have on the mission, witness and services of The Methodist Church in a "world in revolution."

Because of space constraints, I include here only the first half of Part I, and all of Part V, which comprises a single closing paragraph.

**Honorable Gentlemen of the Judicial Council:**

> **I appear before you this morning at a most significant period in human history to present the humble views of Negroes in The Methodist Church, on a most vital issue, one that has arisen at a most critical moment in the life of our beloved church. I come before you hoping and praying, in the words of that great hymn, that God will grant each of us courage for the facing of this hour and for the living of these days.**
>
> **The appeal ordered by the Southeastern Jurisdictional Conference, the petition of the Central Jurisdiction**

**Committee of Five, and the petition of the Advisory Council of the Southeastern Jurisdiction all present only one fundamental issue for adjudication by the Judicial Council.**

**That issue involves a single question: Does the General Conference possess any constitutional authority to act legislatively with respect to racially segregated Annual Conferences that may be established by or transferred to regional jurisdictions of The Methodist Church?**

**The fundamental issue, therefore, is not a question of who determines boundaries of Annual Conferences. Both the Central Jurisdiction and the Southeastern Jurisdiction acknowledge that Jurisdictional Conferences have authority to determine boundaries of Annual Conferences, subject to the limitations of the Constitution of The Methodist Church.**

**The disagreement between the parties is confined to a narrow but basic question...do...regional Jurisdictional Conferences have unlimited discretion under the Constitution to establish or maintain indefinitely Annual Conferences that are based on race?**

******

**V**

**We plead for an affirmative answer to the question presented in our petition for a declaratory decision in this proceeding. But above all, with respect to the crucial issue now before the Council, we plead for one thing—a clear and worthy view of the Constitution of our great Church. That Constitution must continue to be a constant source of life-giving spiritual and ethical perceptions. For we believe with all our hearts and souls, gentlemen of the Council, that the God of our Fathers, who guides us with his Almighty Hand, earnestly hopes that The Methodist Church will not cease to be an instrument for mediating the gospel to a world that is characterized by indescribable complexity and by precipitous and immeasurable revolutionary changes. THANK YOU, AND MAY GOD BLESS YOU!**

### Central West's Petition

The oral argument in support of Central West's petition required very little time. That was because it did not involve a multi-faceted issue, as was the situation in the Southeastern/Committee of Five case. And the brief itself was relatively short.

I simply explained to the Judicial Council that through mutually agreeable *voluntary action* a Central Jurisdiction annual conference organization and two annual conference organizations of the South Central Jurisdiction Organization, all in Missouri, had developed a plan **"to form racially inclusive conferences in the State of Missouri"** (1) by effecting the transfer under Amendment IX of the Central West Annual Conference into the South Central Jurisdiction Organization and (2) by amalgamating or consolidating the transferring entity with the Missouri East and Missouri West Annual Conference Organizations.

All that Central West desired from the Judicial Council was a decision that would remove any doubt as to whether Missouri East and Missouri West had legal authority, under Section 4 of Amendment IX, to go forward with implementation of the plan, without having to get the prior approval of the South Central Jurisdiction Organization. Central West, Missouri East and Missouri West affirmed that their "transfer and merger" plan was consistent with the policy of The Methodist Church "to achieve a racially inclusive fellowship at all levels of the church's life."

I experienced a big surprise at the session of the Judicial Council set aside for oral argument on the Central West petition. It was the fact that John C. Satterfield, co-counsel for *Southeastern*, appeared and presented a passionate argument against the Central West petition. I was not apprised in advance of the "courtesy" that the judicial Council had extended to him. I suspect, but I have been unable to verify, that Satterfield's appearance was associated with some tactic of the law firms retained by Southeastern. At least Satterfield's oral argument appeared to betray a fear that a Judicial Council decision in favor of Central West would seriously damage one of the foundation stones of Southeastern's case. The possibility of such fear was known.

## Judicial Council Decisions

On December 10, 1965 the Judicial Council rendered a decision in the ***Southeastern/Committee of Five*** case. It is codified as Decision No. 232. The Judicial Council's decision in the ***Central West*** case was rendered on December 11, 1965. It is codified as Decision No. 233.

### Decision No. 232

The Judicial Council's decision in the Southeastern/Committee of Five case really consists of two parts. The first part addresses the "distinctively connectional" issues raised by the Committee of Five's petition. The second part deals with the question whether or not the petitions of the parties presented any "justiciable" issues. Here I will comment briefly on both parts of Decision No. 232.

***"Distinctively Connectional" Matters***—The Committee of Five's brief in support of the Committee's petition for a declaratory decision explicitly asserted that in the 1960s "world in revolution," involuntary "racial" segregation in The Methodist Church had become a "distinctively connectional" matter.[7]

In Decision No. 232 the Judicial Council said, "Whether a matter is 'distinctively connectional' is a question of fact which can only be determined in the light of the facts and circumstances of each particular situation." However, the members of the Council unanimously agreed to the following finding:

> **We have no doubt that the creation of a racially inclusive church is now a matter "distinctively connectional." ...The importance of interracial relationships in both national and world affairs further emphasizes the connectional concern of the church with this matter.** ***The church cannot be effective under today's conditions if it sponsors or permits contradictory policies on race in different section of the church.*** **Racial inclusiveness is clearly a connectional matter and, consequently, an appropriate subject of General Conference legislation.** (Emphasis added.)

There is hardly any room for reasonable doubt that Decision No. 232 provided unequivocal judicial support for the following proposition of the Committee of Five: **Whether or not "racially" segregated annual conference organizations of The Methodist Church would be institutionalized in geographical jurisdiction organizations, after dissolution of the Central Jurisdiction Organization, constituted a "matter distinctively connectional."**

Moreover, Decision No. 232 definitely put limits on a *disguised policy* of the Southeastern Jurisdiction Organization. The policy said Central Jurisdiction annual conference organizations transferring into the Southeastern Jurisdiction Organization would remain "racially" segregated "*until they may be changed by voluntary action of the Southeastern Jurisdictional Conference*" (Southeastern's Brief, p. 2). (Emphasis in the original.)

***"Justiciable" Issues***—Ecclesiastical courts, like their civil counterparts, try to avoid dealing with "non-justiciable" issues. These are issues that do not present a real and substantial controversy that is appropriate for judicial determination, but primarily involve a hypothetical, contingent, or abstract dispute.

While affirming that "interracial relationships," presumably including the institutionalizing of involuntary "racial" segregation in geographical jurisdiction organizations, are appropriate subjects for legislation by the Church's legislative body, the Judicial Council refused "to pass upon purely hypothetical questions without the benefit of facts," which might well be decisive of its answer.

The actual *decision* of the Judicial Council, as distinguished from the *analysis* or *reasoning* presented above, is included here.

**Judicial Decision No. 232**

**DECISION**

**The subject of racial inclusiveness in The Methodist Church is a matter that is distinctively connectional, and therefore a subject within the legislative competence of the General Conference. However, this power must be exercised within the context and limitations of the various provisions of the Constitution. Paragraphs 15.4 and 29 of the *Discipline* relate to the right of a Jurisdictional Conference to determine Annual Conference boundaries, as well as their names and number. Amendment IX has established procedures by which churches may transfer from one Annual Conference to another, and by which Annual Conferences may transfer from one jurisdiction to another. The petitions now under consideration present no justiciable issue or conflict between Paragraphs 15.4 or 29 and Amendment IX, although we conclude from the petitions before us that there is some apprehension such a conflict may arise. If in the future conflict arises between these or other portions of the Constitution, and legislation adopted by the General Conference pursuant to Paragraph 8 of the *Discipline*, it will be appropriately reviewed and dealt with by the Judicial Council when such issue arises.**

December 10, 1965.

**Decision 233**

The Central West case turned out to be more contentious, judicially, than the Southeastern/Committee of Five matter. I had thought the situation would be the other way around.

The Judicial Council, by a 5 to 4 majority, rendered a favorable decision in the Central West case. The majority included a concurring opinion signed by two Judicial Council members. The minority included two dissenting opinions—one signed by a single member of the Council and one signed by three Council members.

The core matter that caused this division in the Council was the fundamental issue of whether Section 2 of Amendment IX should be interpreted broadly or narrowly.[8] A narrow interpretation of this section would mean (1) viewing "transferring" an annual conference organization from the Central Jurisdiction Organization into a geographical jurisdiction organization as one *separate and independent* act and (2) regarding the "amalgamation," "consolidation" or "dissolution" of the transferred annual conference organization as a second *separate and independent* act.

A narrow interpretation of Section 2 would also mean that the two separate and independent acts involved in the Central West petition could not be *conjoined* in a single "transfer contract" so as to obviate the need for prior approval of the South Central Jurisdiction Organization. A broad interpretation of Section 2 would allow the Central West, Missouri East and Missouri West annual conference organizations to conjoin the two acts in what the majority characterized as "the contract of transfer."

A broad interpretation of Section 2 of Amendment IX was wise and prudent, the majority reasoned, because

> **"To adopt a contrary interpretation of Section 2 would suggest that it might be the policy of The Methodist Church merely to terminate the Central Jurisdiction, as such, while distributing and maintaining intact its racially segregated Annual Conferences among the regional jurisdiction. We believe this was not the objective sought by Methodists in changing the Constitution of their church. The objective was most recently expressed by the 1964 General Conference when it affirmed a policy "to achieve a racially inclusive fellowship at all levels of the Church's life."** ***Discipline*** **Par. 1813.5."**

Several important related matters should be pointed out here. **First**, in his October 22, 1964 letter to Judicial Member Lester A. Welliver and in his "friend of the court" brief in the Southeastern/Committee of Five case, Charles Parlin argued for a very narrow interpretation of Section 2 of Amendment IX. Presumably that interpretative philosophy was the basis of his characterizing the Mayes Amendment (i.e., Committee of Five's Memorial #2) as unconstitutional. Welliver was one of the dissenters in the Central West case.

**Second,** in his oral argument in the Central West case, John Satterfield, co-counsel in the Southeastern/Committee of Five case strongly urged the Judicial Council to adhere to a strict and "technical" interpretation of Section 2 of Amendment IX. His position was that there is a "sharp, technical differentiation" between the words "transfer" and "merger." The Council majority rejected Satterfield's contention, holding that since the Central West plan "is integrally related to and conditioned upon [an] effective merger," it was not a "transfer" under Section 2 of Amendment IX.

**Third,** the Council majority adopted the interpretative theory and line of reasoning that I applied to the questions raised in the February and March 1965 joint meetings of the Central Jurisdiction and South Central

Jurisdiction Advisory Councils. (See Chapter **Note 6** for text of my February 16, 1965 letter to Bishop Noah W. Moore, Jr.) I operated within the context of a broad interpretation of Section 2 of Amendment IX in writing a brief to support Central West's petition to the Judicial Council. Some of the language in my brief was incorporated in the reasoning of the majority.

**Finally,** from my perspective the root cause of the problem, judicially speaking, goes back at least to the Judicial Council's unfortunate adoption in 1952 of a constitutional theory of "racial boundaries," in Judicial Decision No. 85. (See **Appendix 1.**) In Chapter 3, I drew attention to "the managerial rigidities, apart from the doubtful morality, of weaving into the constitutional fabric of The Methodist Church organizational definitions solely in terms of 'race.'"

Judicial Decision No. 85 was The Methodist Church's equivalent of *Plessy v. Ferguson.* It linked all congregational and other institutional developments *involving only or mostly Blacks* to a dysfunctional "separate but equal" constitutional framework.

During the 1948-1952 quadrennium, new inter-organizational configurations were being developed, mostly in large urban areas, for strategic planning, coordinated administration, and program management purposes. The Judicial Council viewed these initiatives *constitutionally* as actual or potential boundary changes. In doing so, it created the constitutional myth of "racial boundaries." This myth became the source of intellectually indefensible notions such as those stated in Southeastern's brief, and in John Satterfield's oral argument against the Central West-Missouri East-Missouri West transfer and merger plan.[9]

In 1965, the amalgamation or consolidation of three corporate entities of The Methodist Church "to form racially inclusive conferences in the State of Missouri" did not have to be viewed in terms of boundary changes. As I noted earlier, they could have been seen as voluntarism at its finest hour.

### Appraisal of Committee of Five's Litigation Strategy

The Committee of Five did not proactively initiate a litigation strategy. It embraced litigation from a reactive posture. We had to respond to the preemptive strike of Southeastern. But once we were forced to seek Judicial Council intervention, my Committee colleagues and I were determined to use the litigation machine as creatively as possible and to put it in *proactive overdrive.*

We wanted not only to "checkmate" Southeastern, but also to evolve some legal concepts that could be applied legislatively to prevent institutionalizing "racially" segregated annual conference organizations of the Central Jurisdiction Organization within the geographical organizations of The Methodist Church.

**As for me personally, I had a burning desire to bring to the discussion *such a degree of thoroughness, integrity and forthrightness* that the Judicial Council would have to consider the constitution in the light of current realities of The Methodist Church and the challenges to the Church's ministries "in a world in revolution." I wanted to make it as *intellectually and spiritual uncomfortable* as possible for the members of the Judicial Council to simply regard as controlling the conditions and understandings that existed in 1939, when the Plan of Union was adopted.**

How did we do with our litigation strategy? What were the outcomes of that strategy?

The major outcomes of the Committee's litigation intervention include at least the following five results:

- The constitutional concepts, the legal framework and the ethical flavor of Judicial Decision No. 232 would have been quite different if the Committee of Five had not filed a petition for a declaratory decision in the Southeastern appeal. The reasoning of the Judicial Council would not have favored so substantially the legislative competence of the Church's legislative body to prevent **"contradictory policies on race in different sections of the Church."** (Emphasis added.)

- By filing a carefully researched and well-reasoned brief, we were able to clearly establish a nexus between "matters distinctively connectional" and our ultimate goal of blocking the establishment of "racially" segregated annual conference organizations of geographical jurisdiction organizations of The Methodist Church.

- In the research for and the writing of the Committee of Five's brief, we were able to draw upon sources of intellectual, moral and spiritual support in ways that otherwise would not have been possible.

- By actively participating in the development of the Central West petition and brief, and by controlling the process of presenting the issues to the Judicial Council, we were able to establish a legal context for creative use of Amendment IX to achieve the goal of "racial inclusiveness at all levels of the Church's life."

- Our brief in the Southeastern/Committee of Five case and our oral argument before the Judicial Council encouraged an executive of the Evangelical United Brethren Church, who later became a bishop, to strongly oppose including The Methodist Church's apartheid system in the plan of union with his denomination, which was aimed at forming the United Methodist Church.

I worked around the clock on the Committee's litigation strategy for a period of over six months. In doing so, I had the benefit of similar past experiences in working with legal-advocacy strategies for the NAACP in the 1940s and 1950s.

In 1965, I occupied a full-time staff position at the denominational Board of Christian Social Concerns (now Board of Church and Society). I was director of the Board's church/governmental relations department. The staff executive to whom I reported, Dr. Grover C. Bagby, had a keen interest in the Committee of Five's litigation strategy. He allowed me to "put Board staff work on hold" in order to do the research and brief-writing work the litigation effort required.

The give-and-take negotiation experience I gained, and the "talent for consensus and a tolerance for ambiguity" (Cleveland 1972, 77) I developed in the process of designing and implementing a litigation strategy, proved to be quite useful with respect to the next phase of the Committee's work. That phase—**preventing the institutionalization of involuntary "racial" segregation in the proposed new United Methodist Church**—is the subject of Chapter 11.

## Chapter Notes

1. On July 22, 1964 I wrote Dr. John D. Humphrey the following letter.

**Dr. John D. Humphrey**
**Secretary, The Judicial Council**
**P. O. Box 721**
**Grenada, Mississippi**

**Dear Mr. Humphrey:**

**It is my understanding that the Southeastern Jurisdictional Conference has requested a declaratory decision from the Judicial Council regarding certain actions taken by that Jurisdictional Conference under the Constitution of The Methodist Church.**

**By action of the Central Jurisdictional Conference its Committee of Five is directed to "give guidance and assistance to Annual Conferences and local churches of the Central Jurisdiction as they develop and implement plans to transfer into regional jurisdictions."**

**Therefore, I am writing on behalf of the Committee of Five to request that in accordance with Paragraph 915 of the 1960 *Discipline* the Committee of Five of the Central Jurisdictional Conference be made a party to the petition for a declaratory decision. Further, it is requested that the Committee of Five be furnished a copy of the position of the Southeastern Jurisdictional Conference.**

**Sincerely yours,**

**/s/ W. Astor Kirk, Secretary**
**Committee of Five**

**cc: Mr. Paul R. Ervin**

2. Dated January 9, 1965, Leonard had written me the following letter:

**Dear Bill:**

**I have given a great deal of thought to the Judicial Council problem and I am even more strongly of the opinion that any decision either way as to the relative powers of the General and Jurisdictional Conferences may cause very serious trouble.**

**Just yesterday I heard from a member of the Judicial Council sending me a copy of the memorandum, which invited the direct presentation of the issue. He said, "Since this memorandum was issued, there has developed some concern regarding the wisdom of a showdown on the issue any sooner than need be."**

**I would very much like to see your Committee file a brief arguing just as vigorously as possible that the Judicial Council does not have jurisdiction to consider whether some action the General Conference has not yet taken, and may never take, and the form of which no one can now know, would be constitutional. Then I would hope your brief would go on to say that while you believe there is no jurisdiction, in the event the Judicial Council should decide otherwise, they should hold that properly drawn General Conference action would be valid for the reasons you outlined so ably in the recent draft.**

**I am trying to obtain authority from our Commission to file a brief on the jurisdictional question. In addition to those I have already consulted, I am writing to others, for I feel we can very properly oppose jurisdiction and at the same time point out to the Judicial Council how much damage any decision might cause if they were to assume jurisdiction we do not believe they now have.**

**I really believe, Bill, this approach is best and still gives you just as good a chance of a favorable decision in the event the judicial council goes beyond the jurisdictional question. I do hope your Committee will not file a petition, which might very possibly give the Council the jurisdiction it now lacks.**

**I will very much appreciate your keeping me informed as to developments. I am very anxious to know about both the atmosphere and the substance of discussions between the Central and South Central Advisory Councils.**

**With best regards,**

**/s/ Leonard D. Slutz**

3. The Committee of Five's brief directed the attention of the Judicial Council to one of the most famous passages in Justice Holmes' lectures on *The Common Law*. The passage states:

> **"The life of the law has not been logic: it has been experience. The felt necessities of the time, the prevalent moral and political theories, intuitions of public policy, avowed or unconscious, even the prejudices which judges share with their fellowmen, have had a good deal more to do than the syllogism in determining the rules by which men should be governed."** Quoted in Pritchett, *The American Constitution* (1959), at p. 46.

4. As the Committee of Five's chairman, I sent the Bishops the following letter.

**General Board of Christian Social Concerns**
**The Methodist Church * The Methodist Building**
**100 Maryland Avenue, NE * Washington, DC 20002**

**March 22, 1965**

**Dear-**

**Enclosed herewith is a copy of the Committee of Five's Brief in the Southeastern Jurisdiction case. Also enclosed is a copy of the new petition filed by the Southeastern Jurisdiction Advisory Council.**

**You will note that we anticipated the filing of this new petition, and hence we made sure that our Brief covered the questions raised by the Advisory Council.**

**The Committee of Five has sought in its Brief to put before the Judicial Council, supported by sound scholarship, three basic propositions, as follows:**

***First,* The Constitution of The Methodist Church confers upon the General Conference "full legislative power" over all "distinctively connectional" matters, and that the General Conference may exercise that power to promote and protect *all* connectional interests of the church.**

***Second,* the issue whether or not racially segregated "connectional" units of The Methodist Church, heretofore confined exclusively to the Central Jurisdiction, shall now become established in regional jurisdictions, is a "distinctively connectional" matter.**

***Third,* with respect to this particular matter, as with all other classes of such matter, the Jurisdictional Conference does not have authority to exercise its constitutional powers in such manner as to *nullify or render inapplicable* the power of the General Conference to promote and protect "distinctively connectional" interest of The Methodist Church.**

**The Committee of Five wishes to thank you for your counsel and support in connection with the tremendous work that went into the preparation of its Brief. No one can predict what any judicial body will decide. However, I do not hesitate to say that we believe, on the basis of our research and study, that there is solid merit in the basic propositions of the Committee of Five.**

**With best personal regards, I am**
**Sincerely yours,**

**W. Astor Kirk, Chairman**
**Committee of Five**

5. The parties filed with the Judicial Council the following joint **Statement and Motion:**

## STATEMENT AND MOTION

In view of the fact that the following telegram has been received, to wit

:

**"The Council of Bishops, sharing your concern for the general welfare of our Church, respectfully request a postponement of the imminent presentation before the Judicial Council. We trust a Committee established by this Council will set itself to the task immediately. Your cooperation will be greatly appreciated.**
**Lloyd C. Wicke, Chairman**
**Roy Short, Secretary."**

**"It appearing that the Council of Bishops has thus expressed interest in the substantive issues raised in this proceeding,**

**Accordingly, the Advisory Council of the Southeastern Jurisdiction and the Central Jurisdiction Committee of Five, parties hereto, respectfully move for a continuance of the hearing of this proceeding until the next succeeding session of the Judicial Council without prejudice to the rights and privileges of either of said parties hereto, and without any indication of pre-judgment by the Judicial Council upon questions of jurisdiction, status of the parties or any other procedural or substantive matter.**

**/s/ Reber Boult** ______________________________
**Attorney for the Advisory Council of the Southeastern Jurisdiction**

**/s/ W. Astor Kirk** ______________________________
**Chairman**

**/s/ M. J. Jones** ______________________________
**Secretary**

**For the Central Jurisdiction Committee of Five"**

6. In my letter to Bishop Moore, which is dated February 16, 1965, I stated:

> **As I have reflected on the meeting, it seems to me that we need to treat the Central West Annual Conference separately from the other Conferences of the Southwestern [Episcopal] Area. We need to insist that the movement of Central West into South Central Jurisdiction be on the basis of the criteria established at our Central Jurisdictional Conference. *This would mean the establishment of a precedent in the South Central Jurisdiction, and would serve as a frame of reference as we work with other situations.* (Emphasis added.)**
>
> **After giving some thought to the matter of seeking a Judicial Council ruling, I have put my ideas on the attached confidential draft. May I ask that you and the other Bishops of the Jurisdiction, in your own way and as you deem expedient, seek the reaction of your South Central Jurisdiction Colleagues on the Council of Bishops.**
>
> **It does seem to me that some such petition to the Judicial Council might add another dimension to the Southeastern Jurisdiction Case in which the Committee of Five is involved. In our brief we argue that Section 4 of Amendment IX renders inapplicable the limitations implicit or explicit in Paragraphs 15.4 and 29. A petition such as the one contained in the attached draft copy would present the Judicial Council with another aspect of this issue in a less abstract way.**
>
> ***If it would be your judgment that such a petition to the Judicial Council has merit, I would believe that we should control the process of its presentation to the Council.* If the approach has merit and members of the South Central Jurisdiction College of Bishops show some hesitation about being involved, the alternative is to explore at our March 30 meeting the possibility of having the two Advisory Councils of the two Jurisdictions file the petition. This would still give about two weeks before the Judicial Council meets April 22. However, an earlier filing would be preferable, should such a filing be considered expedient.** (Emphasis added.)

**Sincerely yours,**

**/s/ W. ASTOR KIRK, Chairman**
**Committee of Five**

**Enclosure**

**cc: Bishop M. L. Harris**
**Bishop C. F. Golden**

7. Southern, in its Reply Brief complained, "Beginning on page 18 of Central's brief, and extending to the end thereof on page 41, the key words 'distinctively connectional' or 'connectional' taken from [Paragraph 8 of the *Discipline*] appear directly or argumentatively on each and every page thereof, excepting only pages 32 and 33." *Southeastern's Reply Brief*, at p. 7.

8. Section 2 of Amendment IX provides, "An Annual Conference may be transferred from one Jurisdictional Conference to another upon approval by: (a) The annual Conference desiring transfer, by a two-thirds majority of those present and voting. ... (b) The remainder of the Jurisdiction from which transfer is to be made, by a two-thirds majority of the total Annual Conference members present and voting. ... (c) The Jurisdiction to which transfer is to be made, by a two-thirds majority of the total Annual Conference members present and voting.

9. The brief Southeastern submitted to the Judicial Council contained the following statement:

> **"...When there have existed in the past or may exist in the future Annual Conferences within a Jurisdictional Conference based upon race, whether it be Negro, German, Swedish, Norwegian, Danish or Spanish, the fixing or changing of the boundaries of such Conferences is a power vested exclusively in the Jurisdictional Conference of which the Annual Conference is a part."** *Brief in Behalf of the Southeastern Jurisdictional Conference* (1965), p. 12.

# CHAPTER 11
# A *New* United Methodist Church Without *Involuntary* "Racial" Segregation

## Part I. Preparing for Methodist-EUB Church Union

The ultimate goal of the Committee of Five, particularly, and of the leaders of the Central Jurisdiction Organization generally, was an inclusive fellowship at all levels of The Methodist Church. The immediate objective was to eliminate *structures of involuntary "racial" segregation* in the Church's polity. By constitutional definition, the Central Jurisdiction Organization represented highly visible involuntary "racial" segregation, and possibly "racial" *discrimination* as well.

During the 1960-1964 quadrennium I was preoccupied with the work of the Committee of Five of the Central Jurisdiction Organization. Our mandate did not require us to interact with The Methodist Church's Commission on Church Union. Hence it was at the 1964 quadrennial session of the denominational legislative body that I first became aware of that Commission's proposed Plan of Union of The Methodist Church and The Evangelical United Brethren Church.

On the morning of May 5, 1964, the pending business of the legislative body was consideration of the report of the Commission on Church Union. The most important part of the Commission's report was a "Working Document" that contained a draft of a proposed **Plan of Union of The Methodist Church and The Evangelical United Brethren Church.**

The document stated, "Conversations concerning union between the two churches and their constituent members have taken place over a long period of years and the churches have a long and impressive history of fellowship and cooperation." It acknowledged that the two churches "are essentially one in origin, in belief, in spirit, and in purpose." Therefore, the Commissioners of the two churches, "desiring that this essential unity be made actual in organization and administration in the United States of America and throughout the world," proposed and transmitted to their respective legislative bodies the Plan of Union, and recommended its adoption by the processes that they respectively required.

Early in the discussion of the Working Document's proposed Plan of Union Robert Burtner (a delegate from Oregon) moved "that in the new Constitution the Central Jurisdiction **not** be included." *Daily Christian Advocate* **("DCA")**, 5/7/64, p. 482.

The Burtner motion was strongly supported by Dean Richardson (a delegate from New York). The position of the Commission on Church Union, as stated by Charles C. Parlin, its secretary, was ambiguous and equivocal. Following general debate, the Burtner motion was lost on a vote by show of hands. (*DCA*, 5/7/64, p. 485.)

Later in the session the Commission proposed an amendment of its report, with specific reference to the Plan of Union. The substance of the Commission's amendment was as follows:

> **That union with the Evangelical United Brethren Church be approved *in principle*, and that a Special Session of the legislative body be called in October 1966 to vote on the Plan of Union.** (The text of the Commission amendment appears in *DCA*, 5/4/64, p. 319.)

I was a reserve delegate from the West Texas Annual Conference Organization of the Central Jurisdiction Organization. Fortunately I was seated during the morning session on May 5, 1964. I was quite disturbed that the Burtner motion was defeated. When the Commission proposed the amendment to its report, I got recognition from the presiding officer and offered the following motion:

> **"That The Methodist Church record its judgment that the Central Jurisdiction *structure* of The Methodist Church not be made a part of the Plan of Merger with the Evangelical United Brethren Church."** (1964 General Conference *Journal*, Vol. I, p. 529.)

Among other things, I told the delegates "There is neither rhyme nor reason for carrying over into a new Church, a merged Church, a racially segregated organization and hope to try to get rid of it." (Chapter **Note No. 1** at the end of this chapter includes the full text of my statement.)

In my statement I alluded to the "leadership" that had brought the "racially" segregated Plan of Union to the 1964 meeting of the Church's legislative body. The key individual in that leadership group was Charles C. Parlin—referred to by some as "Mr. Methodist Layman." He was the chairman of the Commission on Inter-Jurisdictional Relations, and had sought to get rid of the Central Jurisdiction in 1961 by distributing its "racially" segregated annual conference organizations among the five geographical jurisdiction organizations of The Methodist Church. (See Chapter 6 of this book.) As secretary of the Commission on Church Union, Parlin was its principal spokesperson with respect to the proposed Plan of Union with the Evangelical United Brethren Church.

In the discussion of it at the meeting of the legislative body, and elsewhere, my motion was generally referred to as the **"Kirk Amendment."**

The following comments from Charles Parlin will indicate his reaction to the Kirk Amendment.

> **"I think it is clearly my sentiment personally about getting rid of the Central Jurisdiction and getting rid of it as fast as we can. As I say, in the enabling act it is automatically provided that if the Central Jurisdiction has been abolished in the quadrennium, as we hope, it will automatically come out of the Constitution. The only question is if we have not for any reason succeeded, *are we going to hold up the ecumenical movement because of this? This is the question. I would say not.* I would say we should move in 1966 and 1968 in connection with the ecumenical movement in this movement forward for church unity."** (1964 *General Conference Journal*, Vol. I, p. 530. Emphasis added.)

I will return to the Parlin position a little later in this discussion, after explaining the outcome of the Kirk Amendment. Robert M. Thorp (a delegate from the Pacific Northwest Annual Conference Organization of the Western Jurisdiction Organization) supported the Kirk Amendment. He told his fellow delegates:

> **"I am one of those who have opposed the fixing of a hard date for the elimination of the Central Jurisdiction. Until a few hours ago I would have opposed this Amendment. I support it now because we hear and gain insight into this matter and I realize...those of us who have tried to be moderates, who have tried to be a bridge of understanding, must at some time come out of the bushes and state what we believe is the right order of preference in this Church. And, I think that the elimination of the segregated Church and a new fundamental document, our new Constitution for another half century, is more important than the delay for perhaps a year or two of the merger. "** (*Ibid.* p. 531.)

Later in the proceeding on the morning of May 5, 1964, delegate John R. Van Sickle *(Rock River—NC)* offered a substitute motion for the Commission's amendment and the Kirk Amendment thereto. The Van Sickle substitute would have sent all of these matters back to the Commission on Church Union. The Van Sickle substitute was defeated.

After disposing of a number of "parliamentary inquiries," the presiding officer put the Kirk Amendment to a count vote. After the count, the Secretary of the legislative body announced that the Kirk Amendment was **adopted by 464 affirmative votes to 362 negative votes.** (1964 *General conference Journal*, Vol. I, p. 537.)

**There can be no doubt that in May 1964, a clear majority of the 826 delegates who voted on the Kirk Amendment did not want the "racially" segregated system, which was included in the 1939 Constitution of The Methodist Church, to be incorporated in the Constitution of the proposed United Methodist Church.** Their strong preference for a new United Methodist Church that would be free of involuntary "racial" segregation was a factor that the Commission on Church Union had to deal with up front.

The Kirk Amendment exposed the duplicitous conduct of Charles C. Parlin, who would publicly express *anti-segregationist* views but more often than not opt for *pro-segregationist* policy choices. The fact that *involuntary "racial" segregation* was morally and ethically wrong per se did not invariably control his policy choices—where he had available and feasible "anti-segregation" alternatives. For example, in his comments on the Kirk Amendment he posed a clearly *fictitious dilemma* of "holding up the ecumenical movement because of [involuntary 'racial' segregation] **or** accepting such segregation in order to proceed "with the ecumenical movement...forward for church unity." It is inconceivable to me that Parlin did not know the world in which The Methodist Church and The Evangelical United Brethren Church *("EUB Church")* performed their ministries in 1964 was totally different from the world of 1939.

> The Methodist Church of 1964 was an entirely different ecclesiastical and social institution than the Methodist Episcopal Church (North) was in 1939, when it had to deal with the issue of "the status and role of Blacks" in connection with the 1939 Plan of Union.

A writer in a EUB Church publication quoted Parlin as stating, "The Methodist Church must not be split, and to view the Kirk Amendment as anything but advisory threatens to split the church." (*Behold Magazine*, February 1965, p. 7.)

As a political scientist, it appeared to me at the time that Parlin never established any real connections with the emerging leaders of the "New South." He was closely allied with the "old guard" conservative Methodist laymen and laywomen for whom John Satterfield, Edwin Jones, and Trigg James spoke. Apparently, Parlin never ventured beyond the bounds of the conservative southern legal, business and religious establishment when he sought "to take the pulse" of the Southeastern Jurisdiction Organization of The Methodist Church. It was this cabal that provided resources and leadership for the notorious White Citizens Councils in the early years of the civil rights movement in the south.

## Establishing Linkages with the Joint Commission on Methodist-EUB Union

As noted in the previous chapter of the book, I became chairman of the continuing Committee of Five upon the election of James S. Thomas to the episcopacy. My new responsibilities included interacting with the Joint Commission on Methodist and Evangelical United Brethren (EUB) Union. I wrote letters to several individuals who were key actors in this ecumenical endeavor. Three such letters, and one *response* letter, are included in the Chapter **Notes** in order to provide context and perspective for the reader's own appraisal of the efforts of the Committee of Five to prevent exporting "racially" segregated annual conference organizations from the Central Jurisdiction organization of The Methodist Church to the new United Methodist Church.[2]

In my letter to Mr. Parlin I tried to express my real feelings as Christianly and also as candidly as possible. I really wanted, but never had, an opportunity for a one-on-one frank discussion of "racial" segregation with Parlin.

At the time of our meeting in Chicago, Dr. Paul Washburn was pastor of the First Evangelical United Brethren Church in Naperville, Illinois. He was also the Executive Director of the Commission on Church Union of the Evangelical United Brethren Church, and he played a very important role in the Committee of Five's efforts to prevent the institutionalization of "racially" segregated structures in the polity of the new United Methodist Church. Dr. Washburn was later elected to the episcopacy. Subsequent to our Chicago meeting I wrote him an informational letter. [2]

Dr. Washburn wasted no time in arranging a date, place and time for the Committee of Five to meet with a subcommittee of the Joint Methodist-EUB Commission. Within a few days I received a letter from him containing a schedule for the meeting with a subcommittee of the Joint Methodist-EUB Commission.

The August joint meeting of the Committee of Five and a subcommittee of the Joint Methodist-EUB Commission was very helpful. It provided an opportunity for open and candid discussion of issues, viewpoints and approaches with respect to involuntary "racial" separation and the proposed new United Methodist Church. I was advised in advance that I would be expected to explain the rationale of the Kirk Amendment. Consequently, I had prepared some notes to help me be both brief and focused.

I reminded the group that in 1939, when the Plan of Union was adopted creating The Methodist Church, in a large part of the American civil community institutionalized inter-"racial" relationships were based on *"separate and presumed equal"* norms and principles. At the end of the Nineteenth Century those norms and principles were given constitutional legitimacy by the United States Supreme Court in the infamous *Plessy v. Ferguson* decision.

Notwithstanding the fact that involuntary "racial" separatism was ethically and morally wrong, Whites incorporated "separate and presumed equal" norms and principles in the constitutional fabric of The Methodist Church. And they did so over the strong opposition of Blacks. In 1939, prominent church leaders consciously and willingly compromised fundamental New Testament standards of "Christian" human relationships in order to achieve a Plan of Union. Creation of a new church took precedence over *Christian universalism*.

I also reminded the group that in 1954 the United States Supreme Court had renounced the notorious *Plessy v. Ferguson* "separate and presumed equal" doctrine as a constitutional norm for the American civil community. Governmental policies of involuntary "racial" separatism could no longer claim constitutional protection. Moreover, many public and private sector leaders were courageously calling upon the entire Nation to eliminate racism and discrimination in all sectors of the American commonwealth. And through the perseverance, untiring efforts, and moral leadership of an amazing American woman, Eleanor Roosevelt, the international community now had a Universal Declaration of Human Rights.

In light of all these progressive developments within the human family, I concluded, the fundamental message and the universal meaning of the Kirk Amendment were simple. **They proclaimed that a tragic moral and ethical mistake would be made if The Methodist Church and The Evangelical United Brethren Church incorporated any principles, processes, and structures of involuntary "racial" separatism in the constitutional foundation of the new United Methodist Church.**

Lively give-and-take discussion followed the explanation of my rationale for the Kirk Amendment. Individually and collectively, members of the Committee of Five emphasized two basic points. ***First***, The Methodist Church and not the EUB Church was responsible for removing "racially" defined structures from The Methodist Church.

***Second***, indefinite existence in geographical jurisdiction organizations of "racially" defined annual conference entities transferred from the Central Jurisdiction Organization would be totally unacceptable to Blacks with leadership roles and responsibilities in The Methodist Church.

All participants in the meeting agreed that it was highly desirable for The Methodist Church "to put its house in order 'racially'" before any merger with the EUB Church. The problem was to find the best way to accomplish this goal. Some Committee of Five members lamented the absence of credible evidence that *all key lay and clergy leaders of all geographical jurisdiction organizations* of The Methodist Church were committed to including all Central Jurisdiction local churches in the annual conference organizations in which they would be located once they were in geographical jurisdiction organizations. They alluded to the Southeastern case pending before the Judicial Council as expressive of an intent of the Southeastern Jurisdiction Organization to ensure that it may not be compelled to abandon "racially" defined annual conference organizations within a reasonable period of time.

Some Committee of Five members also strongly expressed their disappointment that many of the top leaders in The Methodist Church seemed not to recognize that "termination of the Central Jurisdiction Organization" and "elimination of 'racial' segregation" actually were two different things. Thus the delegates to the 1964 meeting of the Church's legislative body stated rather simplistically, **"There appears to be no valid reasons for further delaying this step"** (i.e. transferring *"racially" defined* annual conference organizations from the Central Jurisdiction organization into geographical jurisdiction organizations). [3] (Emphasis added.)

Apparently, a genuine desire to know up front if the leaders of a geographical jurisdiction organization were firmly committed to a policy of eliminating involuntary "racial" segregation, within a specified time frame, was not considered to be a "valid" concern. Yet it was possible to dissolve the Central Jurisdiction Organization by such transfers without eliminating involuntary "racial" separation in The Methodist Church. Our meeting resulted in an understanding by the Methodist-EUB commissioners that achieving the latter outcome of the transfer process was a primary objective of the Committee of Five.

I shared with the group my perception that the Commission on Inter-Jurisdictional Relations had really created a lot of unnecessary confusion by its ambiguous use of the terms "merger" and "steps" when discussing the transfer process. The Committee of Five, on the other hand, was quite clear and explicit about the transfer process.

- **We wanted Central Jurisdiction annual conference organizations to be transferred into geographical jurisdiction organizations. Thereafter, we wanted the local churches comprising the**

**transferred annual conference organizations to become part of the geographical jurisdiction organizations in which they were located.**

At the end of the meeting each participant pledged his best efforts to assist in resolving major issues that impacted planning for the union of The Evangelical United Brethren Church and The Methodist Church. The Committee of Five also agreed to recommend some specific language that might be incorporated in the Plan of Union—in the event that the twelve remaining annual conference organizations had not been successfully transferred into the Southeastern and South Central Jurisdiction Organizations by the time of the adjournment of the special session of The Methodist Church's legislative body in November 1966.

Upon my return to Washington, DC following the Chicago meeting of the Committee of Five with the subcommittee of the Methodist-EUB Joint Commission, I wrote Bishop Mueller a letter with a suggestion of language in the Plan of Union to accomplish the dissolution of an annual conference organization formerly of the Central Jurisdiction Organization.[2]

### Methodist-EUB Merger Negotiations & Involuntary "Racial" Segregation

The delegates to the meeting of the 1964 Central Jurisdiction Organization outlined a program of action for the Committee of Five. Our mandate included cooperating with the Methodist Commission on Ecumenical Affairs with respect to planning for the merger of The Methodist Church and The Evangelical United Brethren Church. With respect to promoting the merger of the two denominations to create a new United Methodist Church, we were expected to work within the spirit of the Kirk Amendment.

Within fifteen months of the meeting between the Committee of Five and the subcommittee of the Joint Commission there would be a special session of The Methodist Church's legislative body. The special session was authorized for November 1966, to consider the proposed merger of The Evangelical United Brethren Church and The Methodist Church.

As the date for the special session approached, one could discern the existence of four groupings of Methodists, each with a different primary objective. *First*, there was a group of Methodists whose major concern was to get the Church's legislative body to approve the Plan of Union, which would establish a new United Methodist Church. This group was driven by a strong interest in and an attachment to the ecumenical and church union movement within mainline Protestantism.

*Secondly*, there was an influential group of Methodists, which included both the laity and the clergy, whose principal immediate objective was to remove from the Church's polity a highly visible and very embarrassing *symbol* of involuntary "racial" separatism. They wanted to dissolve the Central Jurisdiction Organization by immediately effecting transfers of its remaining twelve annual conference organizations into the South Central and Southeastern Jurisdiction Organizations. Thereafter, there would be no **centralized** Central Jurisdiction Organization. The Methodist Church's system of involuntary "racial" separatism would then be Balkanized and hidden.

*Thirdly*, there was a group of Methodists whose immediate primary goal was to eliminate from The Methodist Church all forms of involuntary "racial" separatism. They were unwilling to support transfers of the twelve remaining Central Jurisdiction annual conference organizations without some genuine commitment that these entities would not continue to exist indefinitely as "racially" defined ecclesiastical bodies of The Methodist Church.

*Fourthly*, a relatively small but very powerful group of Methodists had as their primary objective ensuring that geographical jurisdiction organizations maintained the power to determine **if, when and under what circumstances** "racially" defined annual conference organizations transferring from the Central Jurisdiction Organization would be eliminated. Most, but not all, of the Methodists who comprised this group were in the South Central and Southeastern Jurisdiction Organizations.

The preferences for the proposed new United Methodist Church were so strong among many individuals in the first group that they appeared willing to sacrifice the principles and values associated with a denomination free of involuntary "racial" separation. Practically speaking, they would vote for a Methodist-EUB Plan of Union that included involuntary "racial" segregation, if that act were required to achieve a new United Methodist Church. The fact that such an arrangement would be morally and ethically wrong under New Testament standards was of secondary concern to this group. Moreover, they seemed unmoved by the argument that the effectiveness of the ministry and witness of a worldwide United Methodist Church would be impaired by manifestations of involuntary "racial" separation. However, if the EUB leaders took a stand in favor of the Kirk Amendment, this group would do likewise.

## Special Session Acts To Resolve Central Jurisdiction Issue

As noted earlier in this chapter, the 1964 quadrennial session of The Methodist Church's legislative body authorized a special session for November 1966. The purpose of that special meeting was to vote on the Plan of Union of The Evangelical United Brethren Church and The Methodist Church. In the discussion of the Kirk Amendment, the legislative body also directed the continuing Commission on Inter-Jurisdictional Relations *(Commission of Twenty-Four)* to make a progress report on "the Central Jurisdiction issue" at the 1966 special session.

The Commission of Twenty-Four prepared a progress report. The report included an explanation of the transfers and dissolution of the Central West, Delaware, Lexington and Washington Annual Conference Organizations of the Central Jurisdiction Organization. These transfers left a "Central Jurisdiction in transition" consisting of twelve remaining annual conference organizations—four within the South Central Jurisdiction Organization and eight within the Southeastern Jurisdiction Organization. The Central Jurisdiction Organization had been reduced to three episcopal areas.

With respect to the elimination of this residual Central Jurisdiction Organization, the Advisory Councils had held several meetings. However, they had failed to agree upon a resolution to recommend to their respective annual conference organizations. There was an impasse over the issue of incorporating local churches transferred from the Central Jurisdiction Organization into geographical jurisdiction organizations.

The "deadlocking" issue may be explained by way of a specific example, using the Central Jurisdiction Organization's North Carolina-Virginia Annual Conference Organization. Transferring that entity into the Southeastern Jurisdiction Organization would include its 225 local churches. Each of these local churches would have a membership comprised primarily if not exclusively of Blacks. Also each of these local churches would be located in one of three annual conference organizations of the Southeastern Jurisdiction Organization. The issue that deadlocked negotiations among the Advisory Councils was **whether, when, and under what circumstances** any given local church would become part of the annual conference organization in which it was located.

The Southeastern Advisory Council believed that (1) transferring the North Carolina-Virginia Annual Conference Organization into the Southeastern Jurisdiction Organization and (2) making a decision about incorporating its 225 local churches into annual conference organizations *were two separate and independent acts*. It was opposed to addressing the "local church" matter prior to the transfer of the North Carolina-Virginia Annual Conference Organization into the Southeastern Jurisdiction Organization.

In contrast, the Central Jurisdiction Advisory Council and the Committee of Five operated from a different premise. They insisted that in the *transfer decision-making process*, some consideration had to be given to when and under what circumstances the 225 local churches of the North Carolina-Virginia Annual Conference Organization would be incorporated into the structures of the annual conference organizations in which they were located.

The Central Jurisdiction Organization needed assurance that the 225 local churches would not continue indefinitely to constitute a "racially" defined ecclesiastical body of The Methodist Church. The Central Jurisdiction Advisory Council and its executive agent, the Committee of Five, had no evidence to warrant a conclusion that the key leaders of the

Southeastern Jurisdiction Organization were really committed to the discontinuance of "racially" defined structures, once such structures were transferred from the Central Jurisdiction Organization. It was reasonable to interpret the Southeastern Jurisdiction Organization's pleadings before the Judicial Council as evidence of an absence of this kind of commitment. Consider the following statement in the brief Southeastern submitted to the Judicial Council:

> **"...an Annual Conference may exist with racial boundaries outside of the geographical Jurisdiction of which it may become a part. Certainly it may thus exist within the geographical boundaries of the Jurisdiction to which it transfers, just as it theretofore existed as a Conference of the Central Jurisdiction. The five Annual Conferences embracing the German, Swedish, Norwegian, Danish and Spanish work, which were set up by the Uniting Conference, occupied a similar status.**
>
> **"...When there have existed in the past or may exist in the future Annual Conferences within a Jurisdictional Conference based upon race, whether it be Negro, German, Swedish, Norwegian, Danish or Spanish, the fixing or changing of the boundaries of such Conferences is a power vested exclusively in the Jurisdictional Conference of which the Annual Conference is a part."** *Brief in Behalf of the Southeastern Jurisdictional Conference* (1965), p. 12.

When the Commission of Twenty-Four was established, it was given a directive regarding elimination of the Central Jurisdiction Organization. The mandate was to present to the 1968 quadrennial session of the legislative body "a plan for the termination of the Central Jurisdiction" if, for any reason, it had not been dissolved by September 1, 1967. As part of its progress report to the 1966 special meeting of the legislative body, the Commission developed a comprehensive set of procedures and an Omnibus Resolution "for further implementation of Amendment IX and the Plan of Action adopted by the 1964 [meeting of the legislative body]."

The Commission asked the legislative body to adopt its proposed procedures and Omnibus Resolution, and to recommend their adoption by (1) each geographical jurisdiction organization (2) the Central Jurisdiction organization (3) each College of Bishops and (4) the Council of Bishops.

The Commission said that if the Omnibus Resolution were adopted by all of these bodies of The Methodist Church, then "the Central Jurisdiction issue" would be nominally resolved. There would be no such issue to be addressed in the proposed Plan of Union of The Evangelical United Brethren Church and The Methodist Church.

The Commission's Omnibus Resolution was entitled **RESOLUTION FOR THE ELIMINATION OF RACIAL STRUCTURE AND THE DEVELOPMENT OF GREATER UNDERSTANDING AND BROTHERHOOD IN THE METHODIST CHURCH** ***("Resolution").***

It was the belief of the Commission that the deadlock between the Central Jurisdiction Advisory Council and the Southeastern and South Central Advisory Councils could be broken if the entire denomination, at all levels, made certain explicit commitments to move forward toward the elimination of all involuntary "racial" separation in The Methodist Church. The Commission presumed that by adopting the Resolution, each of these bodies would have a stake in eliminating all manifestations of involuntary "racial" separation in The Methodist Church. Articles Two and Ten of the Resolution contained a pledge and an expression of a determination "to do everything possible to develop greater understanding and brotherhood in Methodism as well as in the world."

With respect to the Central Jurisdiction Organization, the Omnibus Resolution was to be adopted in identical form, in accordance with the voting requirements of Amendment IX, (1) by each annual conference organization of the Central Jurisdiction Organization, (2) by each annual conference organization of the South Central Jurisdiction Organization and (3) by each annual conference organization of the Southeastern Jurisdiction Organization Such adoption by these entities would result in:

**(A) The transfer into the South Central Jurisdiction Organization the Louisiana, Southwest, Texas, and West Texas Annual Conference Organizations of the Central Jurisdiction Organization, effective upon the close of the special sessions of the Central Jurisdiction Organization and the South Central Jurisdiction Organization.**

**(B) The transfer into the Southeastern Jurisdiction Organization and the dissolution of the North Carolina-Virginia Annual Conference Organization of the Central Jurisdiction Organization, effective following the close of the special sessions of the Central Jurisdiction Organization and the Southeastern Jurisdiction Organization. Each local church formerly a part of the North Carolina-Virginia Annual Conference Organization would be incorporated in the annual conference organization of the Southeastern Jurisdiction Organization within whose geographic bounds it would then be located.**

**(C) The transfer into the Southeastern Jurisdiction Organization and the dissolution of the Tennessee-Kentucky Annual**

**Conference Organization of the Central Jurisdiction Organization, effective following the close of the special sessions of the Central Jurisdiction Organization and the Southeastern Jurisdiction Organization. Each local church formerly a part of the Tennessee-Kentucky Annual Conference Organization would be incorporated in the annual conference organization of the Southeastern Jurisdiction Organization within whose geographic bounds it would then be located.**

**(D) The transfer into the Southeastern Jurisdiction Organization the Central Alabama, Florida, Georgia, Mississippi, Upper Mississippi, and South Carolina Annual Conference Organizations of the Central Jurisdiction Organization, effective following the close of special sessions of the Central Jurisdiction Organization and the Southeastern Jurisdiction Organization.**

**(E) The transfer into the South Central Jurisdiction Organization for residential and presidential assignment the Bishop serving the Southwest Episcopal Area of the Central Jurisdiction Organization.**

**(F) The transfers into the Southeastern Jurisdiction Organization for residential and presidential assignment the Bishops serving the Atlantic Coast and the Nashville-Carolina Episcopal Areas of the Central Jurisdiction Organization.**

**(G) The dissolution of the Central Jurisdiction Organization following the close of special sessions of the South Central Jurisdiction Organization, the Southeastern Jurisdiction Organization, and the Central Jurisdiction Organization.**

The proposed Omnibus Resolution represented a bold and daring step by the Commission. The recommended plan of action did not command the unanimous support of all twenty-four members of the Commission. Edwin L. Jones and John C. Satterfield, lay members from the Southeastern Jurisdiction Organization, wrote an 11-page minority report. In their minority report they charged that the majority, among other things, (a) had drafted procedures and a Resolution that went beyond the mandate the 1964 legislative body gave the Commission, (b) presented a report with recommendations that were contrary to the 1964 actions of the Church's legislative body, and (c) formulated for the consideration of "Annual Conferences" a Resolution that was inconsistent with the letter and spirit of Amendment IX. The minority report strongly criticized the Commission's majority for developing a Resolution that required pledges from the Colleges of Bishops and the Council of Bishops "to do everything possible to bring about the merger of Annual Conferences not later than the close of the Jurisdictional Conferences of 1972."

## Legislative Decisions Regarding Omnibus Resolution

The special session of the Church's legislative body met in Chicago November 8-12, 1966. It was authorized for the purpose of voting on the plan of union with The Evangelical United Brethren (EUB) Church. Nevertheless, it had to deal with the proposed Omnibus Resolution of the Commission of Twenty-Four.

The first issue that the legislative body considered was the concern of many delegates regarding the failure of the Omnibus Resolution to establish a definitive date for the discontinuance of all "racially" defined annual conference organizations. If the Omnibus Resolution were adopted in the form proposed by the Commission, all twelve "racially" defined Central Jurisdiction annual conference organizations would be transferred into regional organizations. However, only in the cases of the North Carolina-Virginia and Tennessee-Kentucky Annual Conference Organizations was a time frame specified for their local churches to be incorporated into the annual conference organizations within whose geographic bounds they would be located.

With respect to the other ten "racially" defined Central Jurisdiction annual conference organizations, the proposed Omnibus Resolution only provided for the following course of action: Each geographical jurisdiction organization, each annual conference organization of the two geographical jurisdiction organizations directly involved, the Colleges of Bishops, the Council of Bishops, and the Church's legislative body would take **"all necessary steps...to eliminate any structural organization in The Methodist Church based on race at the earliest possible date and no later than three (3) months prior to the 1972 General Conference."** (Emphasis added.)

For many delegates, this provision of the Omnibus Resolution was unsatisfactory. It only established 1972 as a *target date* for the incorporation of all Central Jurisdiction local churches into the annual conference organizations within whose geographic bounds they would be located. Many delegates felt strongly that "racially" defined organizations should not exist indefinitely in the new United Methodist Church

During the legislative body's consideration of the report of the Commission of Twenty-Four, the proposed Omnibus Resolution was subjected to a dual attack. It was opposed by a relatively small number of delegates who favored the John Satterfield-Edwin Jones Commission minority report.

They argued that the Commission's Omnibus Resolution violated the spirit of voluntarism by going too far in the direction of establishing a mandatory date for terminating "racially" defined organizations in The Methodist Church. The efforts of this group to substitute the minority report and resolution for the Omnibus Resolution were overwhelmingly defeated.

On the other hand, a significant number of delegates believed that merely setting a "target date" was insufficient. They supported the position of the Commission members from the Central Jurisdiction; namely, that a *definite date* should be established for ending "racially" defined annual conference organizations transferring into geographical jurisdiction organizations. Several delegates offered amendments aimed at converting the 1972 target date into a *definite date*. The chairman and other officers of the Commission of Twenty-Four opposed those proposed amendments. Each was defeated in plenary sessions of the legislative body. However, the target date was changed from *"no later than three (3) months prior to the 1972 General Conference"* to ***"not later than the close of the Jurisdictional Conferences of 1972."*** (Emphasis added.)

The delegates from the Central Jurisdiction Organization who served on the Commission of Twenty-Four, and those who were members of the Advisory Council of the Central Jurisdiction Organization, stated publicly that they could not, in good conscience, vote for the Omnibus Resolution. They needed assurance that involuntary "racial" separation would not exist indefinitely in the geographical jurisdiction organizations of the contemplated new United Methodist Church. In the plenary session of the legislative body in which the vote on the Omnibus Resolution was taken, the voting was by show of hands. The presiding bishop announced that the Resolution had passed. Later interviews with delegates from the Central Jurisdiction Organization indicated that virtually all of them voted against the Omnibus Resolution.[4]

The Omnibus Resolution was sent to the bodies of The Methodist Church designated in the document for a vote at their meetings in 1967. The votes of the annual conference organizations of the Central Jurisdiction Organization and annual conference organizations of the South Central and Southeastern Jurisdiction Organizations would be critical. These bodies needed to approve the Omnibus Resolution by the required number of votes in order to effectuate the transfers specified in the Resolution.

- **In the aggregate, Central Jurisdiction annual conference organizations voted 1,145 for and 360 against the Resolution. Annual conference organizations of the South Central Jurisdiction Organization voted 4,717 for and 323 against the Resolution. Annual conference organizations of the Southeastern Jurisdiction Organization voted 5,712 for and 2,719 against the Resolution.**

In terms of impact on the Central Jurisdiction Organization, what outcomes did these votes accomplish? It was apparent from the reported votes cast by all the annual conference organizations of the Central Jurisdiction Organization and of the South Central and Southeastern Jurisdiction Organizations:

1. **That the Louisiana, Southwest, Texas, and West Texas Annual Conference Organizations of the Central Jurisdiction Organization could be transferred into the South Central Jurisdiction Organization.**

2. **That the Central Alabama, Florida, Mississippi, North Carolina-Virginia, and Upper Mississippi Annual Conference Organizations of the Central Jurisdiction Organization could be transferred into the Southeastern Jurisdiction Organization.**

3. **That the Central Jurisdiction's Georgia Annual conference Organization had approved the Omnibus Resolution but not by the requisite percentage, and that the South Carolina and Tennessee-Kentucky Annual Conference Organizations rejected it.**

4. **It also appeared that authority had been granted for the incorporation of each local church of the North Carolina-Virginia Annual Conference Organization into the particular annual conference organization of the Southeastern Jurisdiction Organization within whose geographic bounds the local church was located.**

Before any of these changes were implemented, certain legal issues were raised regarding the validity of the Omnibus Resolution and presumed authority it conferred. That development prompted (a) the Committee on Interjurisdictional Affairs of the North Carolina-Virginia Annual conference Organization, (b) the Central Jurisdiction Organization, (c) the College of Bishops of the Central Jurisdiction, and (d) the Commission of Twenty-Four to each petition the Judicial Council for a declaratory decision on separate but related legal issues. The Judicial Council consolidated the petitions and rendered a declaratory decision in February 1968—in **Judicial Decision No. 253**. In that decision the Judicial Council:

- **Affirmed the validity of the Omnibus Resolution as submitted to designated bodies of The Methodist Church.**

- **Held that the votes necessary to transfer the Louisiana, Southwest, Texas and West Texas Annual Conference Organizations into the South Central Jurisdiction Organization had been properly taken.**

- **Held that the requisite votes had been taken for transferring the Central Jurisdiction Organization's Central Alabama, Florida, Mississippi, North Carolina-Virginia, and Upper Mississippi Annual Conference Organizations into the Southeast Jurisdiction Organization.**

- **Found that authority had been granted for the incorporation of the North Carolina-Virginia local churches into the annual conference organizations within whose geographic bounds they were geographically located.**

- **Stated, "The Georgia, South Carolina and Tennessee-Kentucky Annual Conferences remain in the Central jurisdiction by reason of their failure to approve [the] Omnibus Resolution...by the required majority. All other Annual Conferences of the Central and Southeastern Jurisdiction have given the required consents to their transfer into the Southeastern Jurisdiction. Hence, if any of the three Annual Conferences were to reconsider their vote on the Omnibus Resolutions, they could do so at any time before the United Methodist Church replaces [The Methodist Church]."**

It should be noted here that 76% (1,145 out of a total of 1,505) of all votes cast by voters in the Central Jurisdiction Organization voted to approve the Omnibus Resolution. Only two of the twelve annual conference organizations of the Central Jurisdiction Organization voted disapproval of the Resolution. This voting behavior occurred in the spring of 1967, approximately six months after the adjournment of the November 1966 special meeting of the legislative body.

In the 1967 meetings of the ten Central Jurisdiction annual conference organizations voting to approve the Omnibus Resolution, there was evidence of some disappointment. There was concern over the failure of the Church's legislative body to establish a definite date to end "racially" defined organizations in the Methodist Church. **However, lay and clergy leaders of these annual conference organizations manifested a remarkable degree of sophistication in their analysis of the situational dynamics of 1967.**

They knew that the special meeting of the Church's legislative body had approved the proposed Plan of Union with the EUB Church. In the new United Methodist Church, there would be only five geographical jurisdiction organizations. There would be no Central Jurisdiction Organization. The constitution of the new United Methodist Church would have a specific Article on *"Inclusiveness of the Church,"* which would expressly prohibit involuntary "racial" separatism. Furthermore, they sensed that the sympathies of the EUB Church leaders were on their side. Finally, in the spring of 1967, the lay and clergy leaders of the Central Jurisdiction annual conference organizations felt that they would be in a better bargaining position, at the 1968 quadrennial meeting of the Church's legislative body, operating within the regional organizations.[3] They would be able to work more closely with leaders of the "New South."

## Part II. A United Methodist Church Is Created

As the year 1968 began most Blacks in The Methodist Church wanted to eliminate the *structural* (i.e. involuntary) "racial" separatism in their denomination before the new United Methodist Church was formally created. Throughout the denomination a significant number of Whites with strong "anti-segregationist" values shared the same desire. These Methodists realized, however, that the delay in carrying out changes authorized in the Omnibus Resolution, caused by challenges of its validity before the Judicial Council, would prevent the realization of their dream. Hence they began to consider the prospects of getting the Uniting Conference to set a definite date for removing involuntary "racial" separatism from the new United Methodist Church.

In 1966, Methodist and EUB Church leaders agreed that the Uniting Conference to establish the new United Methodist Church would be held in April 1968. Dallas, Texas was the city chosen for this historic event.

**On April 23, 1968, when the United Methodist Church was formally launched, the *Central Jurisdiction Organization* of the former The Methodist Church disappeared.**

But the new United Methodist Church included twelve "racially" defined ecclesiastical bodies. They were located in two of its geographical jurisdiction organizations within the United States of America—four in the South Central and eight in the Southeastern. The recent ruling of the Judicial Council of the former The Methodist Church, in Decision No. 253, had paved the way for implementing a mutually agreed upon dissolution plan, with respect to the North Carolina-Virginia Annual Conference Organization. However, the process of incorporating its local churches into geographical annual conference organizations of the Southeastern Jurisdiction Organization had not been completed before the new United

Methodist Church came into existence. Nevertheless, there was hardly any reasonable doubt that the process would be completed in a timely manner under the auspices of the United Methodist Church.

As noted earlier in this chapter, nine of the twelve "racially" defined ecclesiastical bodies were components of geographical jurisdiction organizations by virtue of having been transferred from the former Central Jurisdiction Organization, through approval of the Omnibus Resolution. On April 4, 1968 the Tennessee-Kentucky Annual Conference Organization, one of the three that voted against the Omnibus Resolution, held a special session, pursuant to a holding in Judicial Decision No. 253. At that special session it reconsidered its 1967 action, this time voting overwhelmingly to transfer into the Southeastern Jurisdiction Organization.

All bodies of The Methodist Church that adopted the Omnibus Resolution had expressed

> **their determination to do everything possible to bring about the elimination of any structural organization in The Methodist Church based on race at the earliest possible date and not later than the close of the Jurisdictional Conferences of 1972.**

The EUB and Methodist members of the Joint Commission that drafted the Plan of Union agreed to include this pledge in the Enabling Legislation for the new United Methodist Church. Thus the Enabling Legislation placed a responsibility upon all bodies involved in the adoption of the Omnibus Resolution to implement their commitments as soon as possible, *but "not later than the close of the Jurisdictional Conferences of 1972."*

During the proceedings of the Uniting Conference of the United Methodist Church, several efforts were made to convert the 1972 "target date" into a "mandatory date." Some of the efforts involved legislation only, while others involved a proposed constitutional amendment. The delegates to the Uniting Conference voted down all such attempts to change the nature of the United Methodist Church's 1972 commitments with respect to eliminating *structural* "racial" separatism from the polity of the new denomination.

Blacks, of course, preferred a different outcome. But they were not discouraged. They perceived a significant metamorphosis in the inter-"racial" attitudes and values of key lay and clergy leaders of the South Central and Southeastern Jurisdiction Organizations. The discussions and debates in the proceedings of the Uniting Conference were informative. They provided credible evidence that these key leaders were actually committed to the incorporation of each former Central Jurisdiction local church into the annual conference organization within whose geographic bounds the church was located. Additionally, the Uniting Conference had created a new

**Commission on Religion and Race**. This new organization was given the responsibility of facilitating and monitoring implementation of the commitment of the United Methodist Church with respect to the Omnibus Resolution. Specifically, this Commission would have "general church responsibility" for such matters as the inclusion of former Central Jurisdiction local churches in geographically defined annual conference organizations of geographical jurisdiction organizations

.

## 1972 Legislative Actions

The first quadrennial session of the new United Methodist Church's legislative body met in Atlanta, Georgia in April 1972. When the legislature convened there were still in existence five "racially" defined annual conference organizations of the former Central Jurisdiction Organization. One—the Southwest—was located in the South Central Jurisdiction Organization. Four—the South Carolina, the Central Alabama, the Mississippi, and the Upper Mississippi—existed as entities of the Southeastern Jurisdiction Organization. There was also a "racially" defined district in the Southeastern Jurisdiction Organization's North Georgia Annual Conference Organization. (See Report of the Commission on Religion and Race, *Journal of the 1972 General Conference*, Vol. II, p. 1881.)

In January 1972 a plan was approved under which all local churches of the former Central Jurisdiction's South Carolina Annual Conference Organization would become a part of the annual conference organization within whose geographical bounds they were located. The plan was scheduled to become effective in June 1972. Consequently, the legislative body faced the issue of what to do about the remaining "racially" defined vestiges of the old Central Jurisdiction Organization.

It is important to note here that the Enabling Legislation, adopted in 1968 at the Uniting Conference, set "the close of the Jurisdictional Conferences of 1972" as the *target date* for the elimination of all structures of the United Methodist Church that were defined in terms of "race." The Commission on Religion and Race reminded the legislative body that

> **Now it is 1972...The elimination of the remaining vestiges of racial structure through the merger of the last four Negro annual conferences with the overlapping geographic conferences will be opposed by some, but we are convinced it will be approved by the overwhelming majority of United Methodists. What is more important, it is something that should be and must be done with no further delay. *Journal of the 1972 General Conference*, Vol. II, p.1882,**

The Church's legislative body sought and got Judicial Council clarification of its constitutional authority to enact the specific legislation the Commission on Religion and Race recommended. (See Judicial Council Decision No. 357, in *Journal of the 1972 General Conference*, Vol. I pp. 708-714.)

On April 27, 1972 the Church's legislative body adopted Report No. 88 of its Legislative Committee on Conferences, which stated, inter alia, that

> **The Plan of Union included Enabling Legislation which contemplated a transitional period during which merger of the ten then remaining racially structured Annual Conferences with overlapping Conferences would be accomplished, and that any structural organization based on race would be eliminated at the earliest possible date, and not later than the close of the Jurisdictional conferences of 1972.**
>
> **The General Conference now hereby decides that the transitional period for voluntary mergers is over and the prohibition of racial structures in Paragraph 4 [of the Constitution] is now made effective. Pursuant to the authority of the General Conference to legislate in matters distinctively connectional, we hereby direct all Annual Conferences and other units of the church to comply with Paragraph 4 of the Constitution.**
>
> **The General Conference hereby directs the Jurisdictional Conferences at their 1972 meetings to determine the number, names and boundaries of their constituent Annual Conferences without regard to race.**
>
> **The General Conference hereby directs the remaining four racially structured Annual Conferences and the seven Annual Conferences with which they overlap to take all steps necessary to consummate mergers at the earliest possible date, the initial action to be taken in their sessions of 1972 and to be concluded not later than their regular session of 1973, and in any event not later than July 1, 1973. *Ibid.* pp. 1197-1198**

This directive action of the United Methodist Church's legislative body affected eleven annual conference organizations, including four formerly of the Central Jurisdiction Organization. Three of the affected structures were entities of the South Central Jurisdiction Organization; eight were entities of the Southeastern Jurisdiction Organization.

The legislative body established "a Board of Arbitration with power to make binding decisions" in the event of a deadlock between the parties directly involved in any particular amalgamation or consolidation of annual conference organizations. The Board of Arbitration consisted of "the Presidents of the five Colleges of Bishops." It was urged, "to determine the procedures they will follow in the event arbitration should become necessary and promptly inform the eleven Annual Conferences involved." *Ibid.* p. 1198.

The legislatively mandated elimination of the last vestiges of structural organization based on "race" was carried out according to schedule. The former Central Jurisdiction's Georgia, South Carolina and Southwest Annual Conference Organizations were dissolved in 1972; and dissolution of the Central Alabama, Mississippi and Upper Mississippi Annual Conference Organizations occurred in 1973.

These actions resulted in a United Methodist Church whose polity was free of "racially" defined *governance* institutions. They also prevented indefinite existence in geographical jurisdiction organizations of annual conference organizations transferred from the Central Jurisdiction Organization.

**The United Methodist Church had ended what I have referred to in this book as *involuntary "racial" separatism.***

In many ways, however, a more difficult task confronted the denomination. It was to achieve the elusive goal of genuine "inclusiveness at all levels of the church's life," which is the goal that Blacks in the denomination had explicitly articulated two generations earlier.

We have entered the 21st Century. United Methodists of the present generation need to understand that "inclusiveness at all levels of the church's life" is the state of affairs that the Central Jurisdiction's **Cincinnati Study Conference** clearly articulated four decades ago. That "new breed" of Blacks said quite eloquently:

> **We are confident that we articulate the genuine aspirations, desires, and concerns of a great majority of Negroes who are members of The Methodist Church when we affirm our dedication to the principles of the achievement of an inclusive Methodist Church. Lest there be some misunderstanding, we must indicate here what we mean by an inclusive Methodist Church.**
>
> **For us an inclusive Methodist Church is one whose life and practice are based upon the Christian affirmation of unity. It is a church composed of persons who respond to the call of Christ in love and obedience and who are, therefore, members of a new kind of fellowship, which transcends all ethnic, racial, and class barriers...**
>
> **We believe that all Methodists must be led to understand that the ultimate and fundamental objective to which we are committed in seeking to abolish the Central Jurisdiction is the achievement of an inclusive Methodist Church. (See Appendix 4.)**

## CONCLUDING SUMMARY

This chapter began with a discussion of my efforts, in May 1964, to prevent the inclusion in the new United Methodist Church of the system of involuntary "racial" separatism that had existed in The Methodist Church for twenty-five years. The Church's legislative body adopted my resolution expressing a judgment that the "Central Jurisdiction *structure* of The Methodist Church [should] not be made a part of the Plan of Merger with the Evangelical United Brethren Church."

Unfortunately, when the United Methodist Church was officially launched in 1968 it included vestiges of a *Central Jurisdiction in transition.* However, with strong support from EUB church leaders the Uniting Conference took three very important favorable decisions.

**First**, a Plan of Action for dissolving the twelve remaining "racially" defined entities that came from the former Central Jurisdiction Organization was included in the Enabling Legislation. Based on the principle of "voluntarism," the plan set a non-binding target date of 1972 for the removal of the twelve former Central Jurisdiction annual conference organizations.

**Second**, an article on "Inclusiveness of the Church" was incorporated in the *Constitution of the United Methodist Church*. Among other things, **Division One, Article IV** states, "In the United Methodist Church no conference or other organizational unit of the Church shall be structured so as to exclude any member or any constituent body of the Church because of race, color, national origin, or economic condition."

**Third,** a denomination-wide Commission on Religion and Race was established to review and monitor **"the practices of the entire church so as to further ensure racial inclusiveness."**

When 1972 arrived, the Commission on Religion and Race reported to the Church's lawmakers that four structural organizations based on "race" still remained, and that *"directive legislation"* was needed to ensure their elimination. The legislative body responded with legislation mandating the termination of the four organizational entities on or before July 1, 1973. Hence it was in 1973 that the "racially" defined Central Alabama, Mississippi and Upper Mississippi Annual Conference Organizations of the Southeastern Jurisdiction Organization of the United Methodist Church were dissolved.

For more than a decade prior to 1973, thousands of Methodists throughout the United States actively participated, in many different ways, in the *"racial" desegregation reform movement* within their denomination.

**In 1962, at the Cincinnati Study Conference, Blacks in The Methodist Church decided to shape their own religious destiny by taking charge of that reform movement.**

They defined the ultimate goal of the movement and adopted basic strategies to achieve it. The Article on ***"Inclusiveness of the Church"*** in the constitution of the new United Methodist Church, and the 1973 Legislative Directive of the Church's legislative body were outcomes of their efforts during the decade following the Cincinnati Study Conference.

As discussions throughout this book have indicated, the author played critical and principal roles in the reform movement directed at eliminating involuntary "racial segregation" from The Methodist/United Methodist Church. And I always made a clear distinction between my ideas of ""racial" **desegregation** and "racial" **integration**.

In my view, the two concepts do not have identical meanings. Desegregation is the absence of involuntary "racial" separation. It is a necessary step toward integration.

Thirty years have passed since the last vestiges of *involuntary* "racial" separatism in the United Methodist Church were eliminated. There needs to be a thorough and systematic study of the Church's accomplishments in ensuring that its programs, services, ministries, fellowships, and official decision making are not *negatively* influenced by considerations of "race," color, gender, or economic status. Today it would be appropriate to add "sexual orientation" to this list of factors.

In the final chapter of this book I make a feeble attempt to highlight some critical *performance indicators* that must be included in a comprehensive and systematic study of the Church's progress, or lack thereof, toward integration. I hope that the very brief discussion presented in Chapter 12 will encourage scholars more capable than I to undertake the task mentioned here.For any scholars who may dare to take on this challenge, I offer the following small bit of advice. You will do well to use language and terminology that do not feed the misconceptions, myths and stereotypes so many United Methodists already have.

In the **Preface** to this book I briefly discussed the need to avoid any language usage that "reinforces and legitimizes the pernicious notions of racial differences that we say we want to get rid of."*

In Chapter 12, I will continue to try, as I have attempted throughout the preceding chapters, to avoid language usages that reinforce existing myths and stereotypes about "race" and religion.

***NOTE: Since this Chapter was written, I discovered and read an insightful book written by Martha McNeil Hamilton and Warren Brown. The book is entitled *BLACK AND WHITE AND RED ALL OVER*. The authors allude to some of the types of misconceptions, myths and stereotypes I mentioned in the Preface to this book. Hamilton is a female who happens to be White, and Brown is a male who happens to be Black. They are not only colleagues at *The Washington Post*; they are also close friends. Hamilton gives Brown a kidney to save his life. The story, as told by the authors, really describes**

**not just an indication of "'racial' desegregation" at *The Washington Post* but a particular case of "integration," as I view it.**

## Chapter Notes

1. The full text of statement by W. Astor Kirk on the Kirk Amendment is as follows:

   **Mr. Chairman, I think the time has come for some of us to do some plain talking at this point. I am very concerned about a proposition to take over the Central Jurisdiction structure into the Evangelical United Brethren Church merger at a time when you are asking those of us who have leadership responsibility in the Central Jurisdiction to do everything that we can to get rid of this structure,**

   **I think that we are here proposing to make the same kind of mistake that was made in 1939, when this kind of structure was created.**

   ***There is neither rhyme nor reason for carrying over into a new Church, a merged Church, a racially segregated organization and hope to try to get rid of it.***

   **Secondly, I fear that some of this [legislative body], some delegates here, might misunderstand the kind of intellectual commitment that we, who have responsibility in the Central Jurisdiction, have to try to move toward this inclusive church. And already, people across our jurisdiction, whom we have to persuade to go along with the kind of program we have indicated, have raised this kind of question: Is this [denominational legislative body], or are these Methodists really sincere?**

   ***The same leadership that has brought this proposal to us is the same leadership that has been telling us to get rid of the Central Jurisdiction, and throughout the Jurisdiction the question is being raised as to whether or not this leadership is really sincere about this problem. If it were sincere, then why does it bring over into this proposition the same kind of proposal for a racially segregated structure?***

   **Finally, Mr. Chairman, I think that a great number of delegates here misunderstand the kind of responsibility and the determination to discharge that responsibility on the part of those who have it in the Central Jurisdiction.**

   **In 1939, you gave us a choice. The Central Jurisdiction was voted into creation against the opposition of the annual**

**Conferences composed of Negroes. We had three choices. We had the choice then of not accepting the plan, establishing a segregated denomination. We had the second choice of not accepting the plan, merging with C.M.E., A.M.E., or A.M.E. Zion. And, we had the third choice of accepting the organization and hoping to persuade the Church, as the Bishops said in the Episcopal Sermon of 1940, to find a more Christian way.**

**If you force this kind of choice in 1964-66, you are going to get a different kind of response, because no self-respecting Negro in this day and time is going to carry this kind of structure over into the new Church, and it is going to be resisted all out. I think this [legislative body] needs to realize that. (*General Conference Journal*, Vol. I, p. 529.)**

2. Letters W. Astor Kirk wrote to Charles C. Parlin, Dr. Paul Washburn, and Bishop Ruben H. Mueller:

**General Board of Christian Social Concerns of The Methodist Church**
**The Methodist Building – 100 Maryland Avenue, NE**
**Washington, DC 20002**

**March 25, 1965**

**Mr. Charles C. Parlin, Esq.**
**20 Exchange Place**
**New York, New York 10005**

**Dear Mr. Parlin:**

**This is to express my appreciation of your sharing with me on yesterday the information that the Joint Commission on Methodist-EUB Union voted to appoint a committee to meet with the Committee of Five for a sharing of concerns and viewpoints with respect to avoiding the establishment of racially segregated structures in the New United Methodist Church.**

**I am sure the Committee of Five will welcome this opportunity to meet with a committee of the Joint Commission. Dr. Paul Washburn talked with me about such a meeting just before I left Chicago, and we agreed to explore available dates via correspondence.**

I would like very much to have the opportunity in the near future to become more familiar in depth with your approach to the complex problem of racial segregation in The Methodist Church. I may be wrong, and frankly I hope I am, but it appears to me that wherever there are choices of policies in decision-making, the alternatives you have selected to support have in effect aided the cause of those who wish to maintain racial segregation in the organization, programs and processes of The Methodist Church.

I have tried hard and sincerely, regretfully without success thus far, not to find a basis for interpreting in this light your policy choices during the last quadrennium as chairman of the Inter-Jurisdictional Relations Commission and as secretary of the Commission on Church Union, as well as your choices at General Conference and in the Amicus curiae brief filed in the Southeastern case. Thus I do hope that in the near future we may have the opportunity to discuss frankly these and related matters of racial segregation in The Methodist Church.

Sincerely yours,

/s/ W. ASTOR KIRK, Chairman
Committee of Five

General Board of Christian Social Concerns of The Methodist Church
The Methodist Building – 100 Maryland Avenue, NE
Washington, DC 20002

March 25, 1965

Dr. Paul Washburn, Executive Director
Commission on EUB Church Union
601 West Riverview Avenue
Dayton, Ohio 45406

Dear Dr. Washburn:

I am delighted to have had the opportunity of meeting you. I also appreciate very much the information you gave me relative to the decision of the Joint Methodist-EUB Commission to have the Committee of Five meet with a subcommittee of the Joint Commission.

As you requested, I am enclosing herewith the names and addresses of the members of the Central Jurisdiction Committee of Five. I shall await information from you with respect to the result of your effort to determine a meeting date for the subcommittee of the Joint Commission and the Committee of Five to meet for sharing of viewpoints.

I am pleased to enclose herewith a copy of the Committee of Five's Brief in the case now pending before the Methodist Judicial Council. If I can be of any assistance in interpreting our position to the members of your EUB Commission on Church Union, please do not hesitate to call on me.

Sincerely yours,

/s/ W. ASTOR KIRK, Chairman
Committee of Five

Commission on Church Union
The Evangelical United Brethren Church
1961-1966

March 30, 1965

Dr. W. Astor Kirk
100 Maryland Avenue, NE
Washington, DC 20002

Dear Dr. Kirk:

I was happy that I had an opportunity to meet you last week. It has been my desire to meet you and have conversation with you for many months. At last, it appears that my desires will be fulfilled.

**Yesterday here in Dayton I had an opportunity to have Bishop Wicke, Bishop Mueller, Dr. Tracey Jones and myself together to seek a date when we can meet with the Committee of Five. All of us will be in Chicago on August 3, 1965. We were not able to find a date in July when all four of us could meet with your committee. We are proposing, therefore, that we meet with you at the O'Hare Inn in Chicago on August 4 at 9 a.m. Can you clear this date, and can you take responsibility for calling your Committee of Five to the meeting on that day and Hour?**

**Your letter indicated that you would enclose a copy of the "Committee of Five Brief". It may be that your secretary failed to do so because I have not received that brief, and I would appreciate having it.**

**Please be assured that my personal commitment makes it necessary for me to stand on the side of the Spirit of the amendment which you presented to the General Conference in Pittsburgh, and that you can expect me to work on that side of the proposal. However, I have at times thought that perhaps it was not altogether appropriate to make a complete wedding of the issues of church union and the Central Jurisdiction. I am confident that you will have an opportunity to talk these issues out when we meet, and that we can talk out in a brotherly spirit.**

**It is my prayer that your journey through Good Friday and Easter may have profound significance and satisfaction for you in these days.**

**Sincerely yours.**

**/s/ Paul W. Washburn**

**General Board of Christian Social Concerns of The Methodist Church**
**The Methodist Building – 100 Maryland Avenue, NE**
**Washington, DC 20002**

**August 6, 1965**

**Bishop Ruben H. Mueller**
**1401 Castle Avenue**

**Indianapolis, IN 46227**

**Dear Bishop Mueller:**

**On behalf of the Committee of Five of the Central Jurisdiction of The Methodist Church, I am writing this letter to express our appreciation for the opportunity to meet with the special committee of the Joint Commission on merger of The Evangelical United Brethren and The Methodist Churches.**

**We believe the discussions of August 4 were of mutual benefit to both the Committee of Five and the special committee of the Joint Commission. The meeting afforded a useful opportunity for a frank exchange of viewpoints and a sharing of mutual concerns about a common problem.**

**We sincerely trust that the members of the special committee of the Joint Commission will continue to share our deep conviction that there is no moral justification, especially at this crucial period in human history, for any institutionalizing of structures of racial segregation in the Household of God.**

**It does not appear to the Committee of Five that the exciting new church we all hope for, in the merger of the two denominations, will be an effective instrument of God's purposes in the world, if that church gives expressions in any of its institutional forms to un_hases_a_ attitudes and ideologies of racism.**

**In order to meet the problems of a practical nature, which are involved in eliminating existing racially segregated structures within The Methodist Church, we strongly urge inclusion, at an appropriate place in the Constitution of the new church, the following provision:**

> **"An Annual Conference formerly of the Central Jurisdiction of The Methodist Church may be maintained for a period not exceeding one year following adjournment of the Uniting Conference. Thereafter each local church of any such Annual Conference shall become a part of the other Annual Conference in which that local church is geographically located."**

**Please be advised of our willingness and readiness to be of further service to both the special committee and the Joint Commission itself at the request of either group.**

**Sincerely yours,**

**W. ASTOR KIRK, Chairman,**
**Committee of Five**

**cc: Bishop Lloyd C. Wicke**
**Dr. Paul Washburn**
**Dr. Tracey K. Jones, Jr.**
**Dr. M. J. Jones**
**Reverend W. H. Handy**
**Reverend J. D. Grier, Jr.**
**Attorney Richard C. Erwin**

3. See *Plan of Action for the Elimination of the Central Jurisdiction* (1964 General Conference), p. 4.

4. The author did not attend the November 1966 special meeting of the legislative body. In March of that year I resigned my staff position at the denominational Board of Christian Social Concerns and accepted an appointment to the senior executive position of a Deputy Regional Director of the U. S. Office of Economic Opportunity in the Johnson Administration.

5. In the previous chapter I alluded to a July 6, 1962 letter from Dean Richardson to Charles Parlin. At the time Richardson was a District Superintendent in upstate New York and a member of the Commission on Interjurisdictional Relations. He had been an observer at the Cincinnati Study Conference. In his letter to Charles Parlin, Richardson described the effectiveness and sophistication displayed by the "new leaders" who directed and coordinated the activities of the Cincinnati Study Conference. He opined that through their leadership Blacks in the Central Jurisdiction organization were in a position to "bargain collectively" and ensure that their annual conference organizations and local churches would "not enter into a merger in disorder and disarray."

# CHAPTER 12
# From Desegregation to *Integration*

In the previous chapters of this book our principal focus was on eliminating involuntary "racial" segregation from The Methodist Church and its successor denomination—the United Methodist Church.

We viewed segregation on the basis of "race" as *involuntary* where it is induced by prescriptions—both formal and informal in nature—in the structures, processes, policies, programs and services of an organization. Thus involuntary "racial" segregation involves elements of collective pressure.

The Central Jurisdiction Organization of The Methodist and of the United Methodist Churches was clearly a manifestation of involuntary "racial" segregation. It existed as a *constitutionally mandated* structure of the denomination. While the organization participated equally with the five geographical entities at the denominational level, Blacks were **officially segregated.** They could elect their own Bishops, but these episcopal leaders could only administer and preside over Central Jurisdiction annual conference organizations

Whatever resource for self-identity and self-achievement the Central Jurisdiction Organization presented for Blacks, it, nevertheless, represented a glaring contradiction of the radical *Christian universalism*—the "oneness in Christ" ideals—that the Church affirmed so devoutly.

To "desegregate" the Church meant, in its most basic sense, removing from the Church the formal and informal instruments of collective pressures and sanctions that caused or influenced Methodists to interact with one another on the basis of "race" alone.

Our focus in this chapter is on that human and corporate entity known as the United Methodist Church, which is supposed to be a divine worldwide instrument through which God may act redemptively in human history.

In the context of the United Methodist Church, I regard "racial" *integration* as involving more than merely the absence of involuntary "racial" separatism.

- **For me, integration also involves an ongoing state of affairs within the denomination where the *moral stance*, the *institutional structures*, and the *prevailing culture* of the United Methodist Church create, nurture and sustain an atmosphere in which "racial," "ethnic" and "gender" identities of Methodist communicants play no significant role in determining how they associate with one another, how they support one another, how they care for and share with one another, and how they nurture one another *spiritually*.**

I want to highlight this particular concept of "racial" *integration*—as it applies to the United Methodist Church in this first decade of the 21st Century. Therefore, henceforth when the concept is referred to or involved in the discussion in this chapter, I will capitalize the word "Integration."

In a previous chapter of the book I articulated my concept of a "*community of Christian believers*." In that regard, my faith affirmation is as follows:

> **With respect to any *authentic* Christian believer—i.e., any Son and Daughter of Christ—there is a level of being that transcends "race," color, gender and caste. When two or more Sons and Daughters of Christ establish institutions, organizations, or other structures to communicate with one another as *Christians*, they may not appropriate and apply secular categories of "race," color, gender and caste without diminishing the *distinctly Christian elements* of the established collective.**

For me, this concept of a *community of Christian believers* epitomizes an ideal state of Integration within the United Methodist Church. Presumably, United Methodists "desegregated," and eliminated *involuntary* "racial" separatism from the Church, over three decades ago.

**The subject of Chapter 12 of this book is From Desegregation To *Integration*. Its crucial questions include the following:**

- **What evidence can we present to show that the United Methodist Church is formally and officially committed to the ideal of Integration?**

- **"Having achieved desegregation, what progress have we, as a denomination, made since 1968 in moving toward Integration?"**

- **Is that progress equally manifest at all hierarchical levels throughout the denomination?**

- **What entities within the United Methodist Church are responsible for constantly monitoring the progress of the denomination toward Integration?**

## Local Churches

United Methodists have a unique form of polity known as "connectionalism." As a connectional body, each local congregation maintains its separate identity, yet is accountable to external denominational entities. No local church is an entity unto itself, but rather is "connected" at various levels to other units and offices of the United Methodist Church. Thus the extent of Integration at the level of the local congregation is quite important.

Let me begin the discussion by referring to some commonly recognized and acknowledged phenomena. The United Methodist Church, along with other mainline denominations, helps to create the phenomenon described as "the most 'racially' segregated hour in America."

At 11:00 A.M. on any given Sunday morning United Methodist Blacks worship in congregations composed primarily of Blacks.

Similarly, on any given Sunday morning at 11:00 A.M. United Methodist Whites worship in congregations consisting primarily of Whites.

**In other words, most United Methodist Blacks are not members of nor do they regularly attend local churches in which non-Blacks constitute a numerical majority of the membership!**

**And most United Methodist Whites are not members of, and they do not regularly attend local churches in which non-Whites constitute a numerical majority of the membership!**

- **Why do these patterns of "worship and church-related fellowship" exist among United Methodist Sons and Daughters of Christ?**

- **If, by definition, the factor of *involuntary* "racial" separatism is ruled out, then what are the causative factors?**

- **What compelling or reasonable explanation can we give for existing membership and attendance patterns in United Methodist congregations?**

- **Are these patterns of worship inherently inconsistent with the fundamental principle of *Christian Community* that affirms: "By one Spirit we were all baptized into one body, whether Jew or**

Greek, whether slave or free, and we were all made to drink of one Spirit"?

- Is achieving and maintaining a "racially" diverse membership a goal that United Methodist congregations pursue proactively?

- Do existing patterns of worship and membership of United Methodist congregations have a negative impact on the denomination's ministries of witness and service within our "global community?"

- Is the *consciousness* of "race," "color" and "cast" so deeply embedded in the psyche of United Methodist communicants that authentic communities of Christian believers are virtually impossible to build and sustain in American society?

- How important is it that we come up with credible answers to these questions?

## Pastoral Service

The actual outcomes of governing and managerial decision-making, at all levels within the United Methodist Church, are indicators of progress or the lack of progress in moving toward the ideal standard of Integration affirmed in this book.

The Bishop of each episcopal area is ultimately responsible for managerial decision-making involving pastoral service at the level of the local congregation. Ordinary or routine *cross-"racial"* pastoral service within the denomination is one indicator of progress toward Integration.

This indicator brings to the forefront, for example, appointments of Blacks as pastors of congregations with numerical majorities of members who are non-Black. And similarly it highlights the appointments of Whites as pastors of congregations with numerical majorities of members who are non-White.

It was the "new breed" of Blacks in the denomination who raised a vision of *inclusiveness* that encompassed cross-"racial" pastoral service. I like the way they stated the Integration principle involved here. In their Joint Declaration (see Appendix 5) they said:

> We seek a fellowship in which all Methodists may enjoy the responsibility, privilege and opportunity of making their contributions to our Church's ministries of preaching, teaching, witnessing, and serving solely on the basis of their ability,

competence, and depth of understanding of the Christian faith and our Methodist heritage.

During the quadrennium 1960-1964 many Blacks serving as pastors of large urban churches within the Central Jurisdiction Organization expressed to the Committee of Five their concerns regarding open itineracy. A study of itineracy trends, using this book's "Integration" indicators, should yield useful information for assessing how much progress has been made since 1968.

The United Methodist Church has had thirty-six years of development without the Central Jurisdiction Organization. I believe it is very important for lay and clerical leaders of the denomination to objectively and systematically examine the Church's track record during the past three decades with respect to cross-"racial" appointments of clergy persons for pastoral service in local congregations.

## Service Beyond the Local Church

The same indicators of progress or lack thereof toward Integration are applicable to governing and managerial decision-making involving appointments to the office of district superintendent, and staff to appointments and assignments to annual conference and jurisdiction organizations. They also apply similarly to appointments and assignments to denominational boards and agencies.

As Chapter 11 noted, an organized movement was begun in 1964, at the General Conference Organization's quadrennial meeting in Pittsburgh, to block institutionalizing "racially" segregated annual conference organizations in the United Methodist Church.

In 2004, forty years later, a quadrennial session of the Church's legislative body convened again in Pittsburgh, Pennsylvania. It would have been very useful if the delegates had been presented at that meeting with the results of a study of progress toward Integration, with respect to appointments to service beyond the local church. The degree of diversity achieved in appointments and staff positions beyond the local church is likely to have a positive impact on open itineracy for all United Methodist clergy persons.

## Episcopal Elections

Bishops are top leaders of the United Methodist Church. In the United States they are chosen through a process of election in the Northeastern, Southeastern, North Central, South Central and Western Jurisdiction Organizations.

The Committee of Five had to deal with a lot of anxieties, some grounded in reality and some irrational, regarding episcopal elections. One of our objectives in 1964 was an attempt to respond to some of these anxieties. We sought to ensure that the Central Jurisdiction Organization elected to the episcopacy not only a most capable Black but also a person young enough for two decades of episcopal service.

I can recall quite vividly the fears many Blacks expressed in 1968 that geographical jurisdiction organizations would not elect Blacks to the episcopacy. Personally, I did not share much of the fear expressed then.

I sensed, intuitively perhaps, that (1) when the omnibus Resolution was adopted and (2) when an article on "Inclusiveness" was added to the constitution of the new United Methodist Church, some healthy seeds of *Integration-values* were sown. I believed these seeds would germinate and produce good fruit within the episcopal election processes of the United Methodist Church. I felt that the emerging younger generation of lay and clergy leaders (both Blacks and Whites) would creatively nurture Integration-values in the contexts of episcopal elections in all five of the geographical jurisdiction organizations.

In conducting a limited research undertaking for this chapter, I found some revealing data on episcopal elections since the dissolution of the Central Jurisdiction Organization.

- 3 Blacks were elected Bishop in 2004 (3 males)
- 7 Blacks were elected Bishops in 2000 (3 females and 4 males).
- 12 of the 50 Bishops in active service (not retired) are Black.
- 30 Blacks (26 males and 4 females) have been elected Bishops since the 1968 Uniting Conference of The Methodist Church and the Evangelical United Brethren Church.

Since the establishment of the United Methodist Church in 1968, each of the five geographical jurisdiction organizations has elected Blacks to the episcopacy of the Church. The numbers are as follows:

| | |
|---|---|
| Northeastern Jurisdiction Organization | 9 |
| North Central Jurisdiction Organization | 6 |
| Southeastern Jurisdiction Organization | 5 |
| South Central Jurisdiction Organization | 6 |
| Western Jurisdiction Organization | 4 |
| Total for All Jurisdiction Organizations | 30 |

As noted, 12 of the 50 (24%) Bishops in the United States in active service currently are Black. This statistic certainly does not signify that full Integration has been achieved in the episcopal electoral processes within the United Methodist Church. But it does clearly suggest that some of the dire predictions of 1968—i.e., that once the Central Jurisdiction Organization was abolished Blacks would not achieve significant leadership positions through episcopal elections—have been dramatically proven untrue.

Involved here is an indicator of a degree of progress that deserves more than a passing glance or "sound bite" reporting. Obviously, *all* of the facts and factors behind each episcopal election are not likely to be known. But the impact of the known and reportable *Integration-values* involved should be carefully examined.

> Episcopal election outcomes no one in 1968 would have believed possible have been achieved!

- How were these episcopal election outcomes achieved in the Southeastern and South Central Jurisdiction Organizations?
- What lessons can the Church as a whole learn from these unexpected episcopal election outcomes?

## CODA

In the United States of America, the term "race," according to Nikhil Singh (2004, p. 230, n. 38), "is a signifying practice whose effects are registered across central aspects of our common social life and social relations (i.e., economic class, gender, sexuality, and political participation) that might otherwise appear neutral with respect to race." If Singh's premise is affirmed, then when the term "race" is used, with reference to some individual or group, it is critical to know the specific identifying traits the user of the term is *signifying*.

Historically, in common practice the term "race" has been used to signify a presumed set of unchanging biological characteristics or essences. No matter what these putative biological attributes may or may not be, they are almost universally assumed to have important social and behavioral consequences in the secular realms of society.

The fundamental normative principle I have articulated in this chapter explicitly rejects the *"signifying practice"* alluded to here, at least with respect to authentic communities of Christian believers. It is my faith affirmation that to the extent United Methodist communicants are

**_authentic_ Christian believers, they can establish and maintain institutions and structures in which the secular categories of "race," "color," "gender," and "sexuality" are neutral if not totally irrelevant**

**When we included an article on "inclusiveness" in the constitution of the United Methodist Church, we United Methodists committed our denomination –_presumptively an authentic community of Christian believers_—to principles and values of Integration.**

**United Methodists made that commitment thirty-six years ago. We have entered a new century since that time.**

**I believe we are now at a "time out" moment in the history of the United Methodist Church!**

- **We should pause and reflect prayerfully on the road we have traveled over the last three decades.**

- **We should comprehensively and systematically assess our "Integration" accomplishments and failures.**

- **We should clearly identify the challenges that we face in this first decade of the 21st Century.**

- **We should follow the 1962 example of the "new breed" of Blacks—we should develop and implement strategies to ensure that Integration-values have a strong impact on all of the ministries of the United Methodist Church in a world of 21st Century revolutions.**

- **We need to identify and intentionally confront those instances and places in our United Methodist _community of Christian believers_ where our practices and our interactions with one another are "antithetical to the agenda of God's realm." (Spong, 2001, 226.)**

# APPENDICES

## Appendix 1

### EXERCPTS FROM JUDICIAL COUNCIL DECISION NO. 85

The character of the proposed legislation indicated by the Report involves the question of changing boundaries of Jurisdictions....

The proposed legislation indicated by the Report under consideration is based upon an interpretive theory that [the] Constitutional provision for the changing of the "number, names, and boundaries of Jurisdictional Conferences" authorizes such change in *racial boundaries* as well as in geographical boundaries [emphasis added].

With this interpretation of [the] Constitutional provision the Judicial Council is in accord. Otherwise it would have no meaning for the Central Jurisdiction...

The Report under consideration indicates that the legislation to be proposed is to deal with *individual local churches*, and that in addition to the Constitutional provisions by which the boundaries of Jurisdictions may be changed, the legislation will also require the approval of the local church or churches involved and the consent of the particular Annual Conference affected in each Jurisdiction concerned [emphasis added].

Under...the Constitution the General Conference has "full legislative power over all matters distinctively connectional." It appears, therefore, that it does have the power to throw around the matter of such changes in the boundaries of Jurisdictions other safeguards to arbitrary action of Jurisdictional and Annual Conferences contrary to the wishes of the local church or churches involved.

Under the Constitution, however..., it appears that each change must rest upon its merits, and must be proposed by a specific act of the

**General Conference and approved by a majority of the Annual Conferences in each Jurisdiction involved; but that the General Conference, under its broad legislative powers, may enact a general act to apply to all such proposed changes in the boundaries of Jurisdictions requiring that before such changes can be effected, consent thereof must be had from the local church or churches involved and from the particular annual Conferences concerned.**

**It is the decision of the Judicial Council that no blanket enactment may be made by the General Conference for changes in the "number, names, and boundaries of the Jurisdictional Conferences...it appearing from the Constitution that specific action on each case is required.**

**It is the decision of the Judicial Council, however, that the General Conference may pass legislation applicable to all such proposed changes, requiring the consent of the local church or churches involved and the consent of the particular Annual Conferences concerned, and may prescribe the method in which such consent shall be obtained—either by petitions or memorials to the General Conference in advance of action by the General Conference, or by ratification or consent after the action of the General Conference. In all cases, however, there must be an act of the General Conference making the particular change in the boundaries of the Jurisdictions desired.**

**Since the inclusion of a local church of the Central Jurisdiction in an Annual Conference of another Jurisdiction would be, *from a racial standpoint*, the changing of the boundaries of an Annual Conference, it appears...that the Jurisdictional Conferences of the two Jurisdictions involved would also have to take appropriate action [emphasis added].**

***It is argued by some that such a complicated procedure for such changes is not in keeping with the trend of the thinking in our Church, and therefore should not be held to be necessary. Regardless of such changes in sentiment and thought it must be held in mind that this Constitution was prepared with a view of getting adopted by all three of the Uniting Churches, and such procedural restrictions were inserted as seemed necessary to bring about the desired result—Unification. Along with these restrictions, however, were inserted provisions for the amendment of the Constitution. It is not the province of the Judicial Council to effect by judicial interpretation changes in the procedure set out in the Constitution. It is the decision of the Judicial Council that the Constitutional provisions for the transfer of work from the Central Jurisdiction to under the Constitution* [emphasis added].**

**May 1, 1952**

# SIXTH JURISDICTIONAL CONFERENCE OF THE CENTRAL JURISDICTION OF THE METHODIST CHURCH

**RESOLVED:**

1. That a Central Jurisdiction Study Committee of two (2) ministers and three (3) laymen shall be elected, upon nomination of the College of Bishops of the Central Jurisdiction, to:

    (a) Study the administrative structure of the Central Jurisdiction.

    (b) Examine and analyze the socio-economic forces and factors that affect significantly the local churches, agencies, and institutions of the Central Jurisdiction.

    (c) Take an inventory of the amount and value of real and personal property of churches, organizations, agencies, and institutions (excluding institutions of higher education) of the Central Jurisdiction.

    (d) Analyze the proposals, recommendations, and actions of the Commission on Inter-Jurisdictional Relations as they relate to or involve the Central Jurisdiction.

    (e) Study any other matters that, in the judgment of the Committee, have or may be expected to have a significant bearing on the status of the Central Jurisdiction.

2. The Committee, after consultation with the College of Bishops of the Central Jurisdiction, may seek financial or other support of its work from such organizations, agencies, boards, and individuals of The Methodist Church that may be interested in such work, and from interested philanthropic foundations.

3. The Committee shall make interim reports annually to the College of Bishops of the Central Jurisdiction. It shall submit a final report with such recommendations, as it deems appropriate, to the 1964 Jurisdictional Conference of the Central Jurisdiction.

W. Astor Kirk—July 14, 1960, Cory Methodist Church, Cleveland, Ohio

**Appendix 3**

## DUTIES OF THE COMMISSION OF THIRTY-SIX

1. The continuing program of The Methodist Church to abolish the Central Jurisdiction, promote interracial brotherhood through Christian love, and achieve a more inclusive church shall be entrusted to a quadrennial Commission on Interjurisdictional Relations. The General Conference of 1960 shall elect on nomination of the College of Bishops of each Jurisdiction a commission composed of the following representatives of each Jurisdiction: one bishop, two ministers, and three laymen. Officers shall be elected from the ministerial or lay membership.

2. The responsibilities and authority of this commission shall be as follows:

   (a) To study and recommend courses of action which shall implement the use of Amendment IX on all levels of church structure.

   (b) To study the possibilities and problems inherent in the transfer of local churches, districts, Annual Conferences, and areas as provided in Amendment IX, and to give such information, guidance, and other assistance as may be possible and proper to those considering such transfer.

   (c) To make an immediate study of the reasons for reluctance to make use of Amendment IX, where such reluctance exists, and to bring together responsible churchmen, ministerial and lay, to expedite action.

   (d) Where such transfers cannot be made in either direction at present, to recommend the immediate development of a long-range program designed to create better understanding of mutual problems.

   (e) To give special attention and study to such matters as may impede the speedy implementation of Amendment IX, including the adjustment of ministerial requirements, pension and apportionment differentials, minimum support, church extension, and ministerial itinerancy.

(f) To make progress reports to the Council of Bishops, and to the church through the church press.

(g) To present an inclusive report to the General Conference of 1964 containing findings and recommendations which shall be printed and distributed to the delegates at least three months prior to the convening of the conference.

(h) To work closely with the General, Jurisdictional, and Annual Conference Boards of Christian Social Concerns, with the Department of Christian Social Relations of the Woman's Division of Christian Service, and with all other agencies having information and facilities for expediting the use of Amendment IX and for promoting interracial brotherhood and Christian love.

3. The Commission shall consider the duly elected representatives of each jurisdiction on its membership as jurisdictional commissions, and delegate them such responsibilities as may properly and expeditiously be fulfilled by them.

4. The general commission shall make specific delegation of responsibilities wherever possible, on local, district, conference, and area levels of church structure:

(a) In cooperation with existing agencies to formulate and promote programs of education and courses of action to develop greater interracial understanding and brotherhood on all levels of church life.

(b) To study the policies, programs, and activities of the church, its agencies, and related institutions with respect to the practices of interracial brotherhood.

(c) To assist church extension through the establishment, wherever possible, of preaching places, and the organization of new congregations characterized by interracial brotherhood.

5. The Commission shall be given adequate financing to carry out fully and efficiently the responsibilities assigned to it.

6. The Commission shall meet before the conclusion of the 1960 General Conference.

**Appendix 4**

## STATEMENTS AND RECOMMENDATIONS OF THE CENTRAL JURISDICTION STUDY CONFERENCE

### Introduction

THIS STUDY CONFERENCE WAS CALLED BY THE COLLEGE OF BISHOPS of the Central Jurisdiction upon the request of the Central Jurisdiction Study Committee (Committee of Five), which was established by the 1960 Central Jurisdictional Conference. The participants attending the conference consist of a representative group of lay and clerical leaders of the annual conferences of the Central Jurisdiction.

The purpose of the conference is to counsel with and assist the Committee of Five in its efforts to (1) determine where The Methodist Church is today in the matter of readjusting the jurisdictional structure of the church so as to abolish the racially segregated Central Jurisdiction; (2) identify possible alternatives that are available to The Methodist Church in general and the Central Jurisdiction in particular; and (3) explore the procedures for seeking consensus within the Central Jurisdiction with respect to achieving the goal of an inclusive Methodist church at all levels of church life.

We, the participants in this conference, having been requested by the Committee of Five to give our counsel and prayerful reflections on the important matters with which the committee is concerned, respectfully make the following statements of conviction and recommendations:

### Statement of Purpose

WE ENDORSE THE STATEMENT OF THE 1960 CENTRAL JURISDICTIONAL CONFERENCE recognizing "the inevitability of the abolition of the Central Jurisdiction as a racial unit in the structure of The Methodist Church." Similarly, we endorse the Jurisdictional Conference's expression of a "willingness and intention to help develop satisfactory plans and procedures to abolish the Central Jurisdiction with as much speed as sound and satisfactory planning may permit."

We believe that progressive movement toward the goal of the abolition of the Central Jurisdiction should proceed in an atmosphere of prayerful concern that is free from any pressures except those exerted by the imperatives of our Christian faith.

We regard the Central Jurisdiction as both a fact and a symbol of racial segregation in The Methodist Church. But it is also obvious to us that the racially segregated administrative structure is only one of a number of unmistakable manifestations of racialism within the fellowship and policy of The Methodist Church.

We are confident that we articulate the genuine aspirations, desires, and concerns of a great majority of Negroes who are members of The Methodist Church when we affirm our dedication to the principle of the achievement of an inclusive Methodist Church. Lest there be some misunderstanding, we must indicate here what we mean by an inclusive Methodist Church.

For us an inclusive Methodist Church is one whose life and practice are based upon the Christian affirmation of unity. It is a church composed of persons who respond to the call of Christ in love and obedience and who are, therefore, members of a new kind of fellowship, which transcends all ethnic, racial, and class barriers.

We believe that all Methodists ought to be reminded continuously that this conception of inclusiveness is both implicit and explicit in the 1956 and 1960 pronouncements of the General Conference on "The Methodist Church and Race."

We believe that all Methodists must be led to understand that the ultimate and fundamental objective to which we are committed in seeking to abolish the Central Jurisdiction is the achievement of an inclusive Methodist Church.

We believe that it is of decisive importance that abolition of the Central Jurisdiction must be sought by The Methodist Church as a whole within a framework of over-all planning, procedures, programs and Christian understanding designed to promote in demonstrable and concrete ways ultimate achievement of an inclusive Methodist Church.

We are agreed in principle on the realignment of annual conferences of the Central Jurisdiction in order to facilitate transference to geographical jurisdictions.

There is not agreement, however on the transfer of the North Carolina Conference to the Northeastern Jurisdiction, on the grounds that the North Carolina Conference is outside the geographical boundary of the Northeastern Jurisdiction. This would cause the

**Northeastern Jurisdiction, which is geographical, to overlap the Southeastern Jurisdiction, which is also geographical. It is also the feeling of this Study Conference that the North Carolina Conference should remain within the Central Jurisdiction until such time as it might transfer with other Central Jurisdiction Conferences into the Southeastern Jurisdiction.**

**It is the feeling of this conference that the *First Report* of the Commission on Interjurisdictional Relations, dated April 29, 1961, did not allow sufficient time for appropriate action by the several annual conferences of the Central Jurisdiction. This has resulted in some unfortunate criticism of the Jurisdiction. We believe that the Commission on Interjurisdictional Relations will recognize that the letter accompanying its *First Report* was embarrassing to the Central Jurisdiction. We are all involved in the total program of the church and should be treated accordingly. It is our conviction that the principle of voluntarism should be operative in the case of the Central Jurisdiction as in all other jurisdictions.**

**Recommendations**

**We recommend that:**

1. **With regard to the matter of transfers of annual conferences under Amendment IX, no annual conferences of the Central Jurisdiction be transferred into a regional jurisdiction in which it is not located geographically.**

2. **The period between now and the 1964 General Conference be one of intensive study and preparation to create a suitable climate for the transfer of local churches and annual conferences from the Central Jurisdiction to the five regional jurisdictions. This should include:**

    (a) **The sponsoring of preparatory inter-conference and inter-area meetings to study and make specific recommendations regarding the problems that may be involved in the transferring of local churches and annual conferences.**

    (b) **The further implementation of the Quadrennial Emphases on Race through the 39 Regional Consultative Committees.**

- **The development of a definite plan of action for presentation to the 1964 Central Jurisdictional Conference by the Committee of Five in consultation with the Commission on Interjurisdictional Relations. This plan of action will take into account the decisions reached by this Study Conference. Further, this plan of action will involve the preparation of proposals for General Conference legislation.**

**1. The 1964 Central Jurisdictional Conference realign the boundaries of its annual conferences so that each conference will be located within the boundary of not more than one regional jurisdiction. In preparation for this action the Committee of Five, in consultation with the College of Bishops and selected leaders of the Central Jurisdiction, should develop a proposal for presentation to the 1964 Jurisdictional Conference.**

**2. Following the 1964 Central Jurisdictional Conference, the realigned annual conferences and remaining local churches of the Central Jurisdiction be transferred to the Northeastern, North Central, South Central, Southeastern and Western Jurisdictions with all deliberate speed; and wherever possible, the transfer of Central Jurisdiction churches, conferences, institutions, etc., be consummated in terms of merger with existing geographic units.**

**3. Each annual conference be requested to designate the Conference Board of Christian Social Concerns, or a special committee, as the conference agency to:**

   **1. Set up the standards or criteria for the transfer of all churches under Amendment IX;**

   **2. Receive, study and make recommendations to the conference on all matters relating to local church transfers on which the conference must act;**

   **3. Serve as the agency of the conference to engage in joint enterprises of study, discussion and planning with conference agencies in other jurisdictions in preparation for the local church transfer contemplated.**

**4. The Committee of Five be urged to work out criteria for the guidance of the respective conferences of the Central**

**Jurisdiction, with a view to establishing some degree of uniformity in the transfer of local churches under Amendment IX; and that such criteria or standards be made available to the agency of each annual conference charged with responsibility for its information and guidance.**

5. **The 1964 General Conference be memorialized to declare in unequivocal terms that the entire Methodist Church and all of the institutions related to it, such as educational institutions, homes, hospitals, assembly grounds, etc., should be desegregated and that no person should be denied admission or employment because of color or racial identity.**

6. **The 1964 General Conference raise an Interjurisdictional Commission for the 1964-1968 quadrennium to:**

    **(a) Encourage further integration on conference and local church levels.**
    **(b) Develop programs for communication, understanding, and co-operation.**
    **(c) Indicate specifics to protect minority right.**

**The Study Conference presents this report with full awareness that the magnitude and complexity of the problems faced have not been fully explored. These explorations and confrontations must be continued in order to progressively move toward our goal of an inclusive church.**

**Findings-Steering Committee**

**L. S. Allen, *Chairman***
**J. P. Brawley**
**Thomas W. Cole**
**Ernest T. Dixon, Jr.**
**Dennis Fletcher**
**W. D. Lester**
**Richard V. Moore**
**J. S. Thomas**
**M. J. Wynn**
**W. Astor Kirk, *Secretary***
**George W. Carter, Jr.**
**C. Anderson Davis**
**Thurman L. Dodson**
**Mrs. Anita Fields**
**Mrs. C. T. Griffin**
**John T. King**
**J. E. Lowery**
**John M. Sawyer**

**SOURCE: *Central Jurisdiction Speaks* (1962), pp. 6-10.**

**Appendix 5**

# JOINT DECLARATION

With regard to the polity, administrative organization, programs, and procedures of The Methodist Church, The College of Bishops of the Central Jurisdiction and the Central Jurisdiction Study Committee *(Committee of Five)* are committed to the fundamental objective of a Christian fellowship completely uncircumscribed, at all levels of church life, by distinctions based on race or color.

As followers of Jesus Christ and as loyal members of The Methodist Church, the goal we seek is a fellowship in which all Methodists may enjoy the responsibility, privilege, and opportunity of making their contributions to our church's ministries of preaching, teaching, witnessing, and serving solely on the basis of their ability, competence, and depth of understanding of the Christian faith and our Methodist heritage. We believe this basic principle of equality within Methodism must apply also to all institutions affiliated with or supported by The Methodist Church, such as colleges and universities, hospitals and homes, and camping and recreational facilities.

The racially segregated administrative structure represented by the Central Jurisdiction is both a fact and a symbol of racialism within The Methodist Church. It is incompatible with the basic principle of equality and hence it must be abolished by the Methodist Church.

The College of Bishops of the Central Jurisdiction and the Committee of Five hold the firm conviction that no premise is of more crucial importance than that the Central Jurisdiction must be abolished *within a framework of overall planning and programming* which will facilitate rather than impede achievement of the goal of equality within The Methodist Church.

The only existing procedural machinery for abolishing the Central Jurisdiction is Amendment IX of the Constitution of The Methodist Church. This amendment is inherently limited in scope. Nevertheless, it may be used creatively to achieve the pattern of abolition of the Central Jurisdiction to which we are committed, provided Methodists in all jurisdictions are willing to use it for that purpose.

The decisions of the Cincinnati Study Conference, held March 26-28, 1962, provide a basis for both the clerical and lay leadership of the Central Jurisdiction to support the use of Amendment IX to abolish the Central Jurisdiction in an orderly fashion.

## Time Table on Annual Conference Transfers

The first step to be taken, in order to utilize the annual conference transfer provision of Amend IX, is to realign the boundaries of annual conferences in the Central Jurisdiction so that no conference will overlap territory of two or more regional jurisdictions. We believe it is essential that the integrity of the boundaries of the regional jurisdictions be protected in the process of dissolving the Central Jurisdiction.

The Committee of Five has been requested to submit a proposed plan of realignment of the conferences of the Central Jurisdiction to the College of Bishops by November 1, 1962. It is expected that a recommended realignment plan shall be approved *for purposes of general study* by the end of the 1962 calendar year. It will be the desire of the College of Bishops of the Central Jurisdiction and the Committee of Five that during the calendar year 1963 the recommended realignment plan shall be discussed thoroughly by all parties and groups within the Methodist Church who may be affected directly or indirectly by the final adoption of the plan at the 1964 Central Jurisdictional Conference.

We note that jurisdictional conferences of regional jurisdictions are scheduled to begin during the last week of June 1964. Consequently, we shall recommend to the appropriate committee of the Central Jurisdiction that the convening of the 1964 Central Jurisdictional Conference be scheduled at the earliest possible date in June of 1964 consistent with paragraph 520 of the *Discipline*. This will provide an opportunity for the regional jurisdictions, in regular session, to take any action they may desire regarding the realignment plan adopted by the Central Jurisdictional Conference.

### Basic Standards

With a view to programming the abolition of the Central Jurisdiction, we believe that the Central Jurisdictional Conference should adopt basic standards relating to the transfer of annual conferences to regional jurisdictions under Amendment IX. The Committee of Five has been requested to develop a set of recommended standards for the consideration of the 1964 Central Jurisdictional Conference. We shall encourage the "realigned" conferences of the Central Jurisdiction to initiate immediate action under Amendment IX, in accordance with such standards as may be adopted by the 1964 Jurisdictional Conference, for transference to the regional jurisdictions in which they will then be located geographically.

## Local Church Transfers

Local churches may be transferred, under Amendment IX, from a Central Jurisdiction annual conference to a regional jurisdiction annual conference in which they are located geographically. Such a transfer does not give rise to a boundary problem. But in considered relation to the basic goal of racial equality within The Methodist Church, broad policy questions are inescapably involved in the transferring of local churches from the Central Jurisdiction to annual conferences in the regional jurisdictions.

There is nothing to prevent local churches from transferring to annual conferences in the regional jurisdictions during the current (1960-64) quadrennium. Where properly planned and executed, we not only look with favor on but [also] recommend such transfers. We strongly urge, however, that where transfers of local churches are involved careful consideration be given, at all stages of the transfer process, to the following factors:

a. The relative advantage of transferring a group of local churches in a given geographical area rather than a single church in that area.

b. The future conference status (including opportunity for itineracy) of the minister involved.

c. The obligations and responsibilities that the new conference relationship will entail.

d. The opportunities for spiritual and intellectual growth and Christian service through full participation, without regard to race or color, in all aspects of the program of the new conference.

## Annual Conference Agency

All transfers under Amendment IX require action by the annual conference. Experience indicates that intelligent and responsible conference action on transfer proposals can be expected only where some agency of the conference has the responsibility of studying the proposals and making recommendations to the conference regarding them. Therefore, we urge each annual conference to establish or designate a conference agency to study and make recommendations to the conference on all matters of local church or annual conference transfers under Amendment IX.

We further recommend that the established or designated conference agency assume responsibility, on behalf of the conference, for promoting joint programs, projects, and plans with annual conferences of the regional jurisdictions. Such cooperative enterprises should have as a major objective the creation of a climate of understanding that will facilitate the utilization of Amendment IX to achieve a *programmed* abolition of the Central Jurisdiction.

## Conclusion

Both the College of Bishops and the Committee of Five hereby reaffirm their expressed willingness and readiness to cooperate with all agencies of The Methodist Church that have a genuine interest in working creatively to achieve a racially undifferentiated Methodist fellowship. For we truly believe:

> "The Church is the instrument of God's purpose. This is his Church. It is ours only as stewards under his lordship. The requirements for its membership and the nature of its mission are set by God. The House of God must be open to the whole family of God. If we discriminate against any person, we deny the essential nature of the Church as a fellowship in Christ."

Adopted by the College of Bishops of the Central Jurisdiction and the Committee of Five September 1, 1962.

SOURCE: *Central Jurisdiction Speaks* (1962), pp. 11-14.

**Appendix 6**

## QUALIFICATION STATEMENT FOR 1964 MEMORIALS DOCUMENT

## AUTHORITY

The signers of this document are individually members of The Methodist Church as follows: James S. Thomas is a minister and a member in full connection of the South Carolina Conference, Central Jurisdiction; he is appointed to the staff of the General Board of Education of The Methodist Church. John H. Graham is a minister and a member in full connection of the Upper Mississippi Conference, Central Jurisdiction; he is appointed to the staff of the General Board of Missions of The Methodist Church. John H. Hicks is a minister and a member in full connection of the Central West Conference, Central Jurisdiction; he is appointed to the pastorate of Union Memorial Methodist Church in St. Louis, Missouri. W. Astor Kirk is a lay member of Wesley Methodist Church in Austin, Texas, West Texas Conference, Central Jurisdiction. Richard C. Erwin is a lay member of St. Paul Methodist Church in Winston-Salem, North Carolina, North Carolina Conference, Central Jurisdiction.

Collectively, the signers of this document comprise an organization of The Methodist Church, to wit: the Central Jurisdiction Study Committee (hereafter called the "Committee of Five"). The Committee of Five was created and given its mandate by the 1960 Central Jurisdictional Conference.

### MEMORIALS

The Methodist Church has now arrived at a point in its history, and in the history of the world, when our Church must become a prominent witness, within its own institutional life, to the principles of equality, brotherhood and "oneness of all Christians in Christ," which have been affirmed as essential elements of the Christian faith.

To achieve this goal, it seems urgently necessary that the General Conference enact fundamental additions to the main body of law of The Methodist Church. We respectfully memorialize, therefore, the General Conference to amend and otherwise add to the provisions of the *Discipline* of the Methodist Church as follow:

- **Add a new Paragraph #106 to Part II (The Local Church), Chapter II (Church membership) to read as follows:**

1. **Any person, without regard to race, color or nationality shall have the right to attend any of the worship services and enroll in any of the church school programs of The Methodist Church.**

2. **Any person, without regard to race, color or nationality shall be admitted into membership of a Methodist church by the pastor on profession of his faith, transfer from some other church, or by restoration. Likewise, he shall have the right be enrolled as an affiliate member of a Methodist Church.**

**REASONS**

Nowhere in the existing main body of law is of The Methodist Church there a provision clearly establishing the right of an individual not to be barred from worshiping at, or admission into the membership of a Methodist church because of the person's race, color or nationality. Consequently, in a number of communities church officials have refused to admit persons into membership in the church, or have denied them the privilege of worshiping in the church, because of their race, color or nationality. These actions have resulted in serious injury and embarrassment to the Methodist "world fellowship." They contribute to the climate of reluctance in some sections of the church to the use of the processes of Amendment IX.

- **Amend Part IV (The Conferences), Chapter II (The Jurisdictional Conference) by placing a semicolon at the end of the first sentence of Paragraph #527, and adding the following words thereto:**

**"provided that in the exercise of these powers and duties [a regional organization] shall take only such action or authorize and sanction only such activities, programs and practices as are in harmony with the policy of The Methodist Church to eliminate racial segregation and discrimination."**

**REASONS**

Adoption of this proposed amendment of Paragraph #527 of the *Discipline* would clearly establish the rule that a regional organization of The Methodist Church shall be expected to exercise all of its powers and duties in ways and for purposes that are clearly in harmony with the policy of the church to eliminate segregation and discrimination from its internal life.

Incorporation of this provision into the main body of church law would prevent the lawful establishment or maintenance of racially segregated *sub*units by regional organizations. This would facilitate the use of Amendment IX to dissolve the Central Jurisdiction organization by transferring its *sub*units into regional organizations. It would mean that once a Central jurisdiction *sub*-unit is transferred into a regional organization, the receiving organization would be required to reconstitute all of its *sub*units.

The signers of this document cannot emphasize too firmly their unwillingness to accept or support the indefinite existence of racially segregated *sub*units in regional organizations as a consequence of the dissolution of the Central Jurisdiction organization nationally. At this point in its history and in the history of the world, The Methodist Church must not revert to the organizational pattern that prevailed in the Northern ME Church prior to 1939.

- **Amend Part IV (The Conferences), Chapter VIII (The Annual Conference) by placing a semicolon at the end of the first sentence of Paragraph #634, and adding the following words thereto:**

  **"provided, further, that no Annual Conference shall take any action or authorize or sanction any activities, programs and practices of conference agencies that involves racial segregation or discrimination."**

**REASONS**

Adoption of this proposed amendment of Paragraph #634 of the *Discipline* would establish a rule in the main body of church law that a *sub*unit of a regional organization may not take any action, engage in any activities, promote any programs, sanction any practices, or support any projects that involve racial segregation or discrimination.

Under the Constitution of The Methodist Church *sub*units of the Central Jurisdiction organization and of regional organizations are "basic" bodies of the church (***Discipline*, 1960 Edition, Par. #22**). If the term "inclusive church" is to be more than a pious but empty phrase, all racial segregation and discrimination must be eliminated from such bodies. Elimination of racial segregation and discrimination in the processes, programs, activities and institutions of these bodies will help to create a climate of opinion favorable to a more expeditious use of Amendment IX. Therefore, we plead for the enactment of our proposed amendment of Paragraph #634.

- **Amend Part VII (Administrative Agencies), Chapter I (General Provisions) by adding a new Paragraph #1109, to read as follows:**

  **"Paragraph #1109. It is the policy of The Methodist Church that all of its administrative agencies shall (a) recruit, employ, utilize**

**and promote their professional staff and other agency personnel without regard to race or color, and (b) fulfill their duties and responsibilities in a manner that does not involve racial segregation or discrimination."**

**REASONS**

To the signers of this document one thing seems crystal clear: The Methodist Church cannot be an effective instrument for mediating the gospel of our Lord Jesus Christ to the secular structures of our society if it continues to permit its administrative agencies to engage in or support activities that involve racial segregation and discrimination.

We respectfully urge the adoption of our proposed Paragraph #1109, thereby establishing in the main body of church law a policy banning racial segregation and discrimination on the part of all administrative agencies of the church. Adoption of this rule would establish definite standards to govern decision-making with respect to (a) agency personnel policies and programs and (b) the formulation and implementation of service programs by all administrative agencies.

We take this opportunity to point out that this nation has arrived at a point in history when government and private secular organizations and institutions recognize the urgent necessity of eliminating racial segregation and discrimination from their services, programs, practices, and employment policies. They have taken concrete, practical steps, including the adoption of specific policies, designed to achieve the goal of equality and human brotherhood, which historically has been verbalized as the American Creed. In this connection, it is worthy of note that the Roman Catholic Church, the United Church of Christ, the United Presbyterian Church, USA, and the Protestant Episcopal Church have adopted specific policies to end racial segregation and discrimination in the institutional life of their denominations.

The decade of the Sixties is a time of "rising expectations" on the part of disadvantaged and disprivileged people in America and around the world. The prophetic voice of The Methodist Church will have little meaning for the civil and other social structures around us unless our church manifests more willingness in the future than it has shown in the past with respect to becoming a prominent witness, within its own institutional life, to its avowed value system regarding the irrelevance of race and color in Christ Jesus. Adoption of our proposed Paragraph #1109 would be a solid, concrete demonstration of such willingness.

- **Amend Part V (Temporal Economy), Chapter II (Church Finance) by adding a new subparagraph to Paragraph #737, to read as follows:**

**"14. It shall withhold approval of the entire budget of any agency for inclusion in the budget or budgets receiving general church funds until such agency certifies to the Council in writing that it has established and follows a policy of (a) recruiting, employing, utilizing and promoting its professional staff and other agency personnel without regard to race or color, and (b) fulfilling its duties and responsibilities in a manner which does not involve racial segregation or discrimination."**

**REASONS**

The proposed addition to Paragraph #737 is designed to implement the forgoing equal employment policy that the signers to this document recommended. Enactment of this addition to Paragraph #737 would require the Council on World Service and Finance to withhold general church funds from any administrative agency of The Methodist Church until it certified to the Council in writing that it has adopted and is actually carrying out a policy designed to eliminate all forms of racial segregation and discrimination from its programs, practices and activities.

We call attention to the fact that leadership groups within The Methodist Church, at various times and in various places, have recommended that Federal funds be withheld from States and local communities that practice racial segregation and discrimination in their services and employment policies. Surely the church is willing to apply this same social technique to its own agencies and institutions. The best test of any church's commitment to a principle or a procedure is its willingness to implement that principle or apply that procedure in its own institutional life.

- **Amend Part IV (The Conferences), Chapter VIII (The Annual Conference) by adding a new Paragraph #681, to read as follows:**

**"Paragraph #681. 1. With respect to the dissolution of an Annual Conference transferred from one Jurisdiction to another under the Constitutional provisions of Division Two, Article V, Section VII (Amendment IX), the following rule shall prevail:**

**2. The ministerial members in full connection of an Annual Conference that transfers from one Jurisdiction to another under Amendment IX shall be eligible for membership in full connection in any Annual Conference of the other Jurisdiction involved."**

**REASONS**

Requirements for membership in full connection vary considerably among the *sub*units of all regional organizations. Consequently, there will be uncertainty regarding the membership status of ministers in full connection with Central Jurisdiction *sub*units transferred into regional organizations under Amendment IX and thereafter dissolved as racially segregated bodies. Since the denominational legislature has established minimum requirements for full membership in any *sub*unit of The Methodist Church, we believe it would be fair to all concerned if the minimum standards of the general church governed all adjustments resulting from transfers under Amendment IX. Therefore, we urge the adoption of our proposed Paragraph #681.

## Appendix 7

### LEGISLATIVE DEBATE ON MAYES AMENDMENT
*(Committee of Five's Memorial #2)*

ALLEN MAYES: Mr. Chairman, I move to amend Section I, of the report, page 24, by adding the following, after Recommendation 2-A:

> *"The Jurisdictional Conference shall have powers as described in the constitution, Paragraph 15, and such others as may be conferred by the General Conference; provided that in the exercise of these powers and duties, it shall take only such action, including creation and maintenance of annual conferences, and authorize or sanction only such activities, programs and practices as are consistent with the policy of The Methodist Church to eliminate from its organizational structure all patterns of racial discrimination and segregation."* (1964 General Conference *Journal*, Vol. I, p. 309.)

MAYES: The [Jurisdictional] Conference would be expected to exercise all of its duties in ways and purposes clearly in harmony with the policy of The Methodist Church to eliminate segregation and discrimination from the Methodist fellowship. With the adoption of this amendment, any further steps can be taken for the elimination of the Central Jurisdiction on a voluntary and mutually satisfactory basis...

I believe we must do everything in our power to keep from reverting to a pattern that prevailed in the Methodist Episcopal Church prior to 1939, and *without the direction which this proposed amendment would give to The Methodist Church, we could conceivably still end up in 4 years, 8, or even 25 years with racially segregated Annual Conferences, in regional jurisdictions as a consequence of the dissolution of the Central Jurisdiction...*

We believe this General Conference should be able to say that the people called Methodists, by the Grace of God, have moved forward toward removing segregation.

I believe that this 1964 General Conference would be taking a forward step toward the achievement of this ultimate end by its adoption of this proposed amendment.

I ask that it be supported. (*Ibid.* pp. 309-310. Emphasis added.)

**Statement Opposing Amendment**

GEORGE H. ATKINSON: *(California-Nevada—W)*: Members of the General Conference, this is one of the touchy places where the

**[Commission] of Thirty-Six is not able to go as far as some of our Central Jurisdiction brethren would like to take us, and *they are going too fast.***

**The effect of this motion, this amendment, if carried, would be to simply ruin and cut right across the whole theory of the report of the [Commission] of Thirty-Six. This is a main issue and you might as well understand it.**

**This, as amended, is item No. 2 of this pamphlet *Creative Pursuit of an Inclusive Church*, put out by the Committee of Five of the Central Jurisdiction. This pamphlet—at the bottom of page 4, most of it on page 5—[contains] the motion made by the previous speaker, Dr. Mayes. [It] is an exact copy except that in the wording, he changed from "in harmony" to "consistent with."**

******

**May I digress for just a minute to report to you or recall to you the theory on which the [Commission] of Thirty-Six has been going, *which is a theory of volunteerism....we propose a step-by-step basis to go as rapidly as you can—as the individual jurisdictions can go...***

**The first step is for the Central Jurisdiction to reconstitute their boundaries so that each Annual Conference they have lies within the boundaries of the Regional Jurisdictions. The second step is to ask the Regional Jurisdictions to invite the conferences within their boundaries to join their jurisdiction, to merge. The principle has been used a couple of times today, but if you look at our report, it always says "Merge." That word gives us the two-way dialogue, which we hope happens.**

**After the second step of the Conferences merging into the jurisdiction, than, as rapidly as possible, we hope that the individual conferences within the jurisdiction can merge again so that there are no longer any segregated conferences, but if this thing is going to work, and we might as well say it: In great sections of the country, we have to have the second step of taking in the conferences by conferences first, and after one year, five years, or however long it takes, we hope that they will be able to merge with their brethren in the same jurisdiction.**

******

**As a member of the Commission, I want to point out that though this is an innocent sounding memorial, this would upset the entire voluntary schedule that we have proposed and that we feel will be carried out.**

This would be fine if we could make the jump at once. We don't think you can make it at once. We think you need the intermediate step. We plead that you do not pass this.

I say this has come to a subdivision of a subdivision of the Committee on Conferences. It got there yesterday afternoon and was voted down 15 to nothing, and one abstainer.

Thank you. (*Ibid.*, pp. 310-311.)

Statement Favoring Amendment

KELLY L. JACKSON: *(Washington—C):* Mr. Chairman, I rise in favor of the amendment, because I believe it will help us to eliminate the segregation against which we have fought for many years. We have been accused of many things. We have been accused of dragging our feet, and now we are accused of going too fast....

I rise to support this amendment because I believe that it is definitely directed toward elimination of the Central jurisdiction for which the Church has held its head in shame for lo these many years. I believe this amendment will help Amendment nine to become workable. It is designed to meet the request for speedy dissolution of the Central Jurisdiction. We are called upon to give of ourselves. We are willing as a group to go as far as the next man will go, and I believe that the time has come when no one should be accused of dragging his feet. I believe if this amendment is not passed, the General Conference will go on record as dragging its feet. (*Ibid.*, 311-312.)

Statement Favoring Amendment

WILLIAM T. JANDY, JR.: *(Louisiana—C):* Mr. Chairman and members of the General Conference, I think it needs to be said that we have before us a report that, to me, is not going to bring about the millennium. I approach it with extreme caution. It seems to me that this amendment that is before us is the very meat of what we are trying to do. When we transfer out of Annual Conferences, all we can do as brothers in Christ or as lords of the church, is to proceed.

Reading the *Daily Advocate* of 1956, I read that the Holy Spirit came there.

In 1960, we were told to give Amendment Nine an opportunity.

*Now, we are told to follow along in the spirit of voluntarism.* I would like to say for a matter of information to this conference, that on page 31 of this report, a statement is made that as of the day of this Commission's report, no Central Jurisdictional Annual Conference had voted for merger with the Regional Jurisdiction. I wanted to state for information, that the Louisiana Conference, meeting in session on June 17, 1960, voted 156 to nothing, as found on page 25 of the 1960 *Louisiana Journal*, the words "Be it resolved that the 22nd Session of the Louisiana Conference of the Central Jurisdiction of The Methodist Church registers its disapproval of certain things in the church and requests speedy implementation of Amendment No. Nine, with the abolition not only of the Central Jurisdiction, but all racial discrimination and segregation.

"Two. That the Louisiana Conference of the Central Jurisdiction of the Methodist Church, expressing its sentiments and action, hereby requests under the provisions of Amendment Nine of the Constitution of The Methodist Church, that it be transferred to the jurisdiction to which it is geographically contiguous." (Applause.)

*We volunteered in 1960.* (Laughter and applause.)

I do hope that the members of this General Conference will vote this amendment so that when we in the Central Jurisdiction take the second step, we will do what I believe the world is demanding us to do in the social revolution of which we are a part, to rid ourselves of segregation in all of its insidious forms. I trust that we will pass this amendment. (*Ibid.*, pp. 312-313.)

Statement Favoring Amendment

STANLEY S. MCKEE: *(Southern California-Arizona—W):* I would like to point out that there are two things that this General Conference has constantly had in mind as we have been discussing everything that has to do regarding legislation in reference to the Central Jurisdiction. Part of the time we had in our minds the fact that we are wanting to do away, structurally, with the Central Jurisdiction.

I call your attention to the fact that this [Commission] of Thirty-Six was given primarily this responsibility. This is the thing to which they have directed themselves. This is the thing that they say is the basis on which this report comes to us.

It is my understanding and I think it is the understanding of the General Conference that the Central Jurisdiction is going to meet following the General Conference. They will realign their conferences and their areas so as to align themselves with the boundaries of the conferences and areas within other jurisdictions. Then the action that this report recommends can be taken; that is, that areas and conferences can then be invited by a jurisdiction to come into that given jurisdiction, but this means, then, that the Central Jurisdiction Conference or area will stay in tact.

If this were done throughout the Central Jurisdiction, the Central Jurisdiction would be abolished. That is what the [Commission] is recommending.

**Along with this, from the very first, and it was very difficult for me to understand this a few years ago, our good friend Dr. Brawley, and others, called to our attention that *the real problem is not the doing away with the Central Jurisdiction; the real problem which we face as a church, is the doing away with racial discrimination.***

***All right, now, the attitude here and the things that are proposed in this amendment is that if you vote an area or conference into a jurisdiction, and leave it in tact, you are still practicing discrimination, and I hardly see how anyone could disagree with that idea.***

**It seems to me that the thing represented by this amendment is that the person who has made it, and a great segment of our church, is saying to us that it is more important that when these moves are made, we are doing away with discrimination within the church than it is for us to do away with the Central Jurisdiction.**

**If I understand the people who are back of this memorial, the thing that you are saying is that we should let those jurisdictions that will, vote the Central Jurisdiction into their jurisdictions, and dissolve the conferences and areas so that they are an integral part of the conferences and areas within that jurisdiction. Discrimination will then have been done away with so far as possible structurally.**

**They have said, differently from a few years ago, if there is a jurisdiction within the church that does not want to vote the areas and conferences into that particular jurisdiction on this basis—that is, on the basis that would be present if we pass this amendment, then they are willing to have those conferences and those areas sit in that particular jurisdiction as an indication that we have not yet come to the place where discrimination has been moved out or abolished.**

**I think if we limit this in a matter of depth and see it as the real purpose we are trying to achieve here, we will recognize that this amendment is the most important thing we must [have] before this General Conference and so far as I can see, is the most important issue we will have before us while we are here. I am in favor of it. (*Ibid.* pp.313-314.)**

**Inquiry**

**Question**

**JOHN C. SOLTMAN: *(Pacific Northwest—W)*: This is a question...I would like to ask Mr. Atkinson because it referred back to the point which he brought up, and I think it is germane. We have before us this report, and I am looking at page 5, under reasons, the second paragraph from which Mr. Atkinson quoted, which begins—and this is the key sentence—"Incorporation of this provision into the main body**

of church law would prevent the lawful establishment or maintenance of racially segregated Annual Conferences by regional Jurisdictional Conferences."

In light of the provisions of Amendment Nine, which provides for the transfer of an Annual Conference of the Central Jurisdiction into another jurisdiction, I wonder in what sense this sentence, which I have quoted from the report, is true.

Leonard Slutz replied to Soltman's question in his opposition statement.

Statement Opposing Amendment

LEONARD SLUTZ: Mr. Chairman, I am Leonard Slutz of the Ohio Conference. This is an exceedingly difficult question to answer because we are dealing on the one side with emotion, and what we would like to do, and on the other side we are trying to deal with intellect and what we think we ought to do.

I have complete sympathy with the purpose of this amendment. On the other hand, I think it might throw a roadblock in the path of everything we want to accomplish.

As Mr. Atkinson said. It would be necessary in all instances to take two steps at once, instead of taking one at a time. You could only transfer a conference into a jurisdiction, and immediately dissolve it. You could not transfer it into a jurisdiction and have it remain as a separate conference.

That is what we would prefer to do in every instance if it could be done. Let me be very frank. I am a layman. I can say things that perhaps I shouldn't say.

Let me be specific. In the North Central, we have been working for the last several months on a plan to do just what this amendment would do, to transfer the Lexington Conference into the North Central, and immediately dissolve it. We hope that will be accomplished by July 12th of this year, 1964.

In trying to work out that plan, *we have prepared a written motion that is to be submitted to every Annual Conference of the Central Jurisdiction, and every Annual Conference of the North Central Jurisdiction, between now and July. If this identical motion is adopted by all those conferences and by the two Jurisdictional Conferences, those two steps will take place and all the churches in the states comprising the North Central Jurisdiction will have all the Negro churches in the present regional Annual Conferences. There will be a bishop formerly from the Central Jurisdiction who will be a bishop of the North Central Jurisdiction.*

I am speaking very frankly. We have been told by many people that the same process may not now be possible in the Southeastern Jurisdiction. We have been told it can be done probably very soon in the South Central, but in the Southeastern, there is need for getting acquainted. There is need to work together and plan, doing some of the planning we have been trying to do elsewhere, and so I have heard some very influential people say "We are working hard. We have high hopes that the South Central will invite these conferences into their jurisdiction, but they may have to be separate Annual Conferences for a little while until we get to know them better and can work out the plans." There are plans far more difficult than we have in the North Central. They have many more churches, the pension plan is harder, the minimum salary plan is much harder, and they say we are going to have to work together for a little while before we take the second step.

If this amendment is defeated, nothing is prevented. It would still be possible if the two-step approach could be worked out, it could still be done, just as we intend to do it in the North Central in the next two or three months. If that can't be done, you still have flexibility. You still have the possibility of going the other way. The less preferable way, but it may prove to be the necessary way.

To preserve the flexibility, to make it possible to move it any way that we can get together, I oppose the amendment. (*Ibid.* pp. 314-315.)

### Previous Question Moved

W. Davis Cotton *(Louisiana—SC)* moved the previous question. It was ordered. (DCA, page 163.)

### Summary Statement Opposing Amendment

CHARLES C. PARLIN: *(Newark—NE):* If the Conference will allow me to try to straighten out something, I will try to be helpful to the Conference.

You have two documents distributed, one this morning, called "Proposed Amendment to the Plan." At the bottom, it shows the amendments submitted by Dr. Golden, Dr. King, and Dr. Brawley. These were proposed amendments to the plans which were brought here to Pittsburgh by members of the Central Jurisdiction, and all of which were considered by your Commission, and if the body wishes, we can go through this document proposal by proposal and show you exactly to what extent they are now incorporated in the plan as amended.

You have a second document distributed this afternoon, called "Creative Pursuit of an Inclusive Church," which is a memorial and

**which is going through the machinery of the Legislative Committee as every good memorial should. These were delivered to our commission and were not intended or do not purport to be an attempt to amend our plan. However, we did have this material before us and all the material in this memorial of the General Conference was considered by your commission.**

**This, we are hearing now what is really memorial number two, which is an amendment to number 527 of the *Discipline* and which purports to make mandatory mergers of annual conferences within the jurisdiction. I think that is purely unconstitutional, but it is not my province to say so. This memorial will go through the proper legislative committee and they will decide what to do with it.**

**Our commission felt that it was clearly unconstitutional and therefore did not attempt to adopt it.**

**Again, as those of you who have your *Discipline* can see, look at your constitution on page 14 of the *Discipline* paragraph 15. It says, "The jurisdictional conferences shall have the following powers and duties," and then Number four, under that is, "To determine the boundaries of their annual conferences."** [3]

**The *Discipline* and General Conference cannot give an order that contradicts that part of the constitution. Therefore, it seems to me that the proper procedure, if this is to be properly prepared would be for the Legislative Committee to consider this memorial. If they want to test it out, bring it in as a constitutional amendment, which I think would be necessary. (*Ibid.* p. 316.)**

**Vote on Mayes Amendment**

The vote was taken on the Mayes amendment. The amendment was lost. (DC page 165.)

# Appendix 8

## STATEMENT ON THE PRINCIPLE OF VOLUNTARISM BY W. ASTOR KIRK

It is an historical fact that the "voluntary principle" of the free churches of this country is inherent in the warp and woof of American Methodism. The operation of this principle has meant that the decisive importance of conversion in the evangelical work of the church has been extended to become of decisive importance to the "change of will" in social relationships and in social action. The individual's "free response to God" is seen as the heart of religion, and a voluntary gathering of "converted individuals" is of the essence of the church. The church must extend its influence out into society by voluntary, persuasive means. The assumption is made that one can *alter society* by changing individuals, first from within, and that one can make that change by persuasive appeals to the will and heart only.

The application of the "voluntary principle" to the *structure* of race relations within the institution of The Methodist Church is interesting. Religion deals with the heart and will of individual persons: That is the major premise. The heart and will can only be changed by *voluntary action*: That is the minor premise. *Conclusion:* a voluntary change in the heart and will of individual Methodists must automatically result in a change in the *structure* of race relations within The Methodist Church.

Stated another way, the philosophy of voluntarism assumes that with respect to the *structure* of race relations within The Methodist Church, the important field of action is the individual conscience. This inner, moral, ideal realm is the decisive one, and the details of outward social arrangements or institutional patterns are relatively of secondary importance. As regards the *structure* of race relations, the "voluntary principle" reserves a very high place for persuasion, example, and exhortation, and sees little need for, and much harm in, the exercise of institutional power to change this *structure*.

My views regarding this matter are embodied in the following quotation from the address that I made before the Kansas Conference on June 7, 1962:

> "...We must recognize that there is inherent in the *institution* of The Methodist Church a significant degree of *social power*. Individual members of the church, in both the laity and the clergy, are authorized to exercise that social power as a

**consequence of the *decision-making* positions of leadership within the church to which they have either been elected or appointed. It is my firm conviction that this leadership is morally *obligated* to exercise the institutional power of The Methodist Church in behalf of the implementation of the church's affirmations regarding race relations within its own fellowship**

**"...I am convinced that we must recognize the vital effect of institutional structure on the quality of interracial relationships within The Methodist Church...It is a well established fact that control of individual behavior in our mass society today has shifted from folkways and mores to definitions of appropriate behavior patterns by organizations and institutions and their leaders. In The Methodist Church, as elsewhere in the society at large, institutional and organizational definitions of appropriate (i.e., Christian) behavior patterns regarding race relations may be deliberately formulated and enforced by those persons, in both the laity and in the clergy, who occupy positions of leadership."**

**SOURCE: Memorandum of W. Astor Kirk to A. Dudley Ward, dated June 18, 1962.**

**Appendix 9**

## Cover Letter to Selected Methodists

November 16, 1964

Dear________________:

Attached is a summary statement of fundamental issues, as I conceive them, in a very important case now pending before the Judicial Council. Also enclosed are some materials that give the background of this case. At its request, the Committee of Five of the Central Jurisdiction has been made a party to the proceeding.

I have accepted the responsibility of preparing a brief on behalf of the Committee of Five for submission to the Judicial Council. The purpose of this letter is to solicit your assistance and your counsel and judgment. Specifically, I am writing to request your professional comments and suggestions regarding the basic questions in the case, as outlined in the attached summary statement.

I am mindful of the fact that this is a very busy time of the year for you. However, I do hope you may find it convenient to give me the benefit of your comments and suggestions not later than January 15, 1965. I should point out that in the text of our brief no statements of our professional consultants will be attributed to them without their express consent.

Sincerely yours,

W. Astor Kirk, Chairman,
Committee of Five

Did the 1964 Southeastern Jurisdictional Conference have the constitutional power to *make a recommendation* to its constituent Annual Conferences, with respect to the action it believed said Annual Conferences should take regarding a vote to approve the transfer of certain Central Jurisdiction Annual Conferences to the Southeastern Jurisdiction, in accordance with the transfer procedures of Amendment IX (Division Two, Section VIII, Article V) of the Constitution of The Methodist Church?

**II**

**May the General Conference exercise its applicable legislative powers granted in Division Two, Section I, Article IV (Paragraph 8, 1960 Discipline) of the Constitution of The Methodist Church to *regulate, promote and implement* Annual Conference transfers under Amendment IX of said Constitution, without regard to any expressed or implied constitutional restrictions of Section IV, Article V (Paragraph 15) and Section VIII, Article IV (Paragraph 29) of Division Two of said Constitution, *particularly in view of the express provision of Subparagraph 4 of Amendment IX?***

**III**

**Can the question of whether there shall or shall not be racially segregated Annual Conferences as constituent units of regional Jurisdictions be properly construed as a "distinctively connectional" matter, within the meaning of the *general legislative "empowering"* clause of Division Two, Section I, Article IV (Paragraph 8) of the Constitution of The Methodist Church?**

**What bearing, if any, do the following facts have on this or any related question pertaining to a "distinctively connectional" matter?**

**A. The adoption in 1958 of Amendment IX of the constitution, which provides a method of abolishing the Central Jurisdiction by systematizing procedures for transferring *local churches* and *Annual Conferences* from the Central Jurisdiction to regional Jurisdictions.**

**B. The commitment of The Methodist Church, by action of its 1964 General Conference, "to achieve a racially inclusive fellowship *at all levels of the Church's life.* (Emphasis added.) That commitment is expressed in the specific mandate given to the 1964-1968 Quadrennial Commission on Inter-Jurisdictional Relations.**

**A. The actions of the 1964 General Conference:**

**(1) Prohibiting exclusion of persons on account of race or color from the membership of local churches, or from attending the worship services of local churches.**

**(2) Banning racial segregation and discrimination by general boards and agencies in the recruitment, employment, use, or promotion of their professional and other personnel.**

**(3) Informing educational, health, social welfare, and recreational institutions and agencies related to The Methodist Church that they are expected to cease and desist from any form of racial segregation or discrimination.**

**(4) Advising the Commission for Ecumenical Affairs and the Ad Hoc Committee on EUB Union of its considered judgment that no racially segregated structures should be incorporated in any Plan of Merger of the Evangelical United Brethren Church and The Methodist Church.**

**(5) Directing the Commission for Ecumenical Affairs to continue exploring the possibility of union of the African Episcopal Church, the African Episcopal Zion Church, and the Christian Methodist Episcopal Church with The Methodist Church, the clear implication being that such exploration shall not be conducted on a premise of the future existence of racially segregated units in any possible new structures.**

# REFERENCES


Abingdon Press (1964). *The History of American Methodism, I, II and III.* Nashville, TN: Abingdon Press.

Burns, James M. (1978). *Leadership.* New York: Harper and Row.

Cameron, Richard M. (1961). *Methodism and Society in Historical Perspective. Nashville*, TN: Abingdon Press.

Carter, Paul A. (1952). "The Negro and Methodist Union." *Church History* 21:55-70

Cleveland, Harlan (1972). *The Future Executive: A Guide for Tomorrow's Managers.* New York: Harper & Row, Publishers.

Culver, Dwight W. (1953). *Negro Segregation in The Methodist Church.* New Haven: Yale University Press.

Farish, Hunter D. (1938). *The Circuit Rider Dismounts: A Social History of Southern Methodism, 1865-1900.* Richmond, VA: Dietz Press.

Graham, John H. (1979). *Black United Methodist.* New York: Vantage Press.

Hagood, L. M. (1890). *The Colored Man in the Methodist Episcopal Church.* Cincinnati, OH: Cranston & Stowe.

Hedgeman, Anna Arnold (1964). *The Trumpet Sounds: A Memoir of Negro Leadership.* New York: Holt, Rinehart & Winston.

Kirk, W. Astor (1963). *The Central Jurisdiction Problem:* A Monograph

Prepared for the Second Methodist Conference on Human Relation. Chicago (August 26-30.)

Kluger, Richard (1975) *Simple Justice: The History of* ***Brown v. Board of Education*** *and Black America's Struggle for Equality.* New York: Alfred A. Knopf.

Lincoln, C. Eric (1996). *Coming Through Fire: Surviving Race and Place in America.* Durham, NC: Duke University Press.

Luccock, Halford E. (1949). *The Story of Methodism.* Nashville, TN: Abingdon Press.

Matthews, Donald G. (1965). *Slavery and Methodism: A Chapter in American Morality, 1780-1845.* Princeton: Princeton University Press.

McClain. William B. (1984). *Black People in The Methodist Church.* Cambridge, MA: Schenkman Publishing Company.

Patterson, Orlando (1997). *The Ordeal of Integration: Progress and Resentment in America's "Racial" Crisis.* Washington, DC: Civitas/Counterpoint.

Richardson, Harry V. (1976). *Dark Salvation: The Story of Methodism as it Developed Among Blacks in America* Garden City, NY: Anchor Press.

Singh, Nikhil (2004). *Black Is a Country.* Cambridge: Harvard University Press.

Spong, John S. (2001). *A New Christianity for a New World.* San Francisco: HarperSanFrancisco

Thomas, James S. (1992). *Methodism's Racial Dilemma: The Story of the CentraL Jurisdiction.* Nashville, TN: Abingdon Press.

Walls, William A. (1974). *The African Methodist Episcopal Zion Church: Reality of the Black Church.* Charlotte, NC: A.M.E. Zion Publishing House.

White, Walter (1955). *How Far the Promised Land?* New York: Viking Press.

Wogaman, J. Phillip (1960). *Methodism's Challenge in Race Relations.* Boston: Boston University Press.